AA004297

SENSORDEVICES 2019

The Tenth International Conference on Sensor Device Technologies and Applications

October 27 - 31, 2019

Nice, France

SENSORDEVICES 2019 Editors

Claus-Peter Rückemann, Leibniz Universität Hannover / Westfälische Wilhelms-Universität Münster /North-German Supercomputing Alliance (HLRN), Germany

Paulo E. Cruvinel, Embrapa Instrumentation, Brazil

Arcady Zhukov, University Basque Country (UPV/EHU) - San Sebastian and IKERBASQUE, Basque Foundation for Science, Spain

Irinela Chilibon, National Institute of R&D for Optoelectronics (INOE-2000), Romania

Printed from e-media with permission by:

Curran Associates, Inc.
57 Morehouse Lane
Red Hook, NY 12571

Some format issues inherent in the e-media version may also appear in this print version.

Printed with permission by Curran Associates, Inc. (2020)

International Academy, Research, and Industry Association (IARIA)
412 Derby Way
Wilmington, DE 19810

Phone: (408) 893-6407
Fax: (408) 527-6351

petre@iaria.org

Additional copies of this publication are available from:

Curran Associates, Inc.
57 Morehouse Lane
Red Hook, NY 12571 USA
Phone: 845-758-0400
Fax: 845-758-2633
Email: curran@proceedings.com
Web: www.proceedings.com

Table of Contents

SENSORDEVICES 2019

Forward

The Tenth International Conference on Sensor Device Technologies and Applications (SENSORDEVICES 2019), held between October 27, 2019 and October 31, 2019 in Nice, France, continued a series of events focusing on sensor devices themselves, the technology-capturing style of sensors, special technologies, signal control and interfaces, and particularly sensors-oriented applications. The evolution of the nano-and microtechnologies, nanomaterials, and the new business services make the sensor device industry and research on sensor-themselves very challenging.

Most of the sensor-oriented research and industry initiatives are focusing on sensor networks, data security, exchange protocols, energy optimization, and features related to intermittent connections. Recently, the concept of Internet-of-things gathers attention, especially when integrating IPv4 and IIPv6 networks. We welcomed technical papers presenting research and practical results, position papers addressing the pros and cons of specific proposals, such as those being discussed in the standard fora or in industry consortia, survey papers addressing the key problems and solutions on any of the above topics short papers on work in progress, and panel proposals.

We take here the opportunity to warmly thank all the members of the SENSORDEVICES 2019 technical program committee, as well as all the reviewers. The creation of such a high quality conference program would not have been possible without their involvement. We also kindly thank all the authors who dedicated much of their time and effort to contribute to SENSORDEVICES 2019. We truly believe that, thanks to all these efforts, the final conference program consisted of top quality contributions.

We also thank the members of the SENSORDEVICES 2019 organizing committee for their help in handling the logistics and for their work that made this professional meeting a success.

We hope that SENSORDEVICES 2019 was a successful international forum for the exchange of ideas and results between academia and industry and to promote further progress in the area of sensor devices technologies and applications. We also hope that Nice, France provided a pleasant environment during the conference and everyone saved some time to enjoy the charm of the city.

SENSORDEVICES 2019 Chairs

SENSORDEVICES Steering Committee
Sergey Y. Yurish, International Frequency Sensor Association (IFSA), Spain
Jeong-Woo Choi, Sogang University, Korea
Jerzy P. Lukaszewicz, Nicoulaus Copernicus University, Torun, Poland
Daniele Zonta, University of Strathclyde, UK
Eiji Higurashi, University of Tokyo, Japan
Jean Paul Salvestrini, GeorgiaTech Lorraine, USA
Giovanni Pau, Kore University of Enna, Italy

SENSORDEVICES 2019 Research/Industry Chairs
Winfried Vonau, Kurt-Schwabe-Institut für Mess- und Sensortechnik e.V. Meinsberg, Germany
Paulo E. Cruvinel, Embrapa Instrumentation, Brazil
Dan Wilson, Southern Research Station - Center for Bottomland Hardwoods Research, USA

Yanxia Hou, Institut Nanosciences et Cryogénie | CEA-Grenoble, France
Yoseph Bar-Cohen, Jet Propulsion Laboratory | NASA, USA
Yurong Jiang, Hewlett-Packard Labs, USA
Irinela Chilibon, National Institute of Research and Development for Optoelectronics, Romania

SENSORDEVICES 2019
Committee

SENSORDEVICES Steering Committee

Sergey Y. Yurish, International Frequency Sensor Association (IFSA), Spain
Jeong-Woo Choi, Sogang University, Korea
Jerzy P. Lukaszewicz, Nicoulaus Copernicus University, Torun, Poland
Daniele Zonta, University of Strathclyde, UK
Eiji Higurashi, University of Tokyo, Japan
Jean Paul Salvestrini, GeorgiaTech Lorraine, USA
Giovanni Pau, Kore University of Enna, Italy

SENSORDEVICES 2019 Research/Industry Chairs

Winfried Vonau, Kurt-Schwabe-Institut für Mess- und Sensortechnik e.V. Meinsberg, Germany
Paulo E. Cruvinel, Embrapa Instrumentation, Brazil
Dan Wilson, Southern Research Station - Center for Bottomland Hardwoods Research, USA
Yanxia Hou, Institut Nanosciences et Cryogénie | CEA-Grenoble, France
Yoseph Bar-Cohen, Jet Propulsion Laboratory | NASA, USA
Yurong Jiang, Hewlett-Packard Labs, USA
Irinela Chilibon, National Institute of Research and Development for Optoelectronics, Romania

SENSORDEVICES 2019 Technical Program Committee

Ahmed N Abdalla, FTECK, UMP, Malaysia
Iyad Abuhadrous, Palestine Technical College, Palestine
Jude A. Adeleke, National Space Research and Development Agency, Nigeria
Hani Al Hajjar, Université de technologie de Compiègne (UTC), France
Ahmed Alfadhel, Rochester Institute of Technology, USA / Research Products Development Company (RPDC), Saudi Arabia
Amir R. Ali, German University in Cairo, Egypt
Itziar G. Alonso González, University of Las Palmas de Gran Canaria (ULPGC), Spain
Jesús B. Alonso Hernández, Institute for Technological Development and Innovation in Communications (IDeTIC) | University of Las Palmas de Gran Canaria (ULPGC), Spain
Fabrice Andrieux, Lancaster University, UK
Darius Andriukaitis, Kaunas University of Technology (KTU), Lithuania
Paulo Antunes, Aveiro University, Portugal
Djamila Aouada, University of Luxembourg, Luxembourg
Francisco J. Arcega, University of Zaragoza, Spain
Ammar Aryan, Université de Caen Basse-Normandie, France
Ripendra Awal, Prairie View A&M University, USA
Valerio Baiocchi, "Sapienza" University of Rome, Italy
Yoseph Bar-Cohen, Jet Propulsion Laboratory | NASA, USA
José Barata, Universidade Nova Lisboa, Portugal
Ramón Barber Castaño, University Carlos III of Madrid, Spain
Juan Bautista Talens Felis, Universitat Politècnica de València, Spain

Ali Fares, College of Agriculture & Human Sciences Prairie View A&M University, USA
Attilio Frangi, Politecnico di Milano, Italy
Mounir Gaidi, University of Sharjah, UAE
Filippo Gandino, Politecnico di Torino, Italy
Juan Carlos García García, University of Alcala (UAH), Spain
Nuno Garcia, University of Beira Inteiror, Portugal
Danila Germanese, Institute of Information Science and Technology (ISTI) - National Research Council (CNR), Pisa, Italy
Arfan Ghani, Coventry University, UK
Alfonso Gómez Espinosa, Tecnológico de Monterrey Campus Querétaro, Mexico
Friederike J. Gruhl, Karlsruhe Institute of Technology (KIT) | Institute of Microstructure Technology (IMT), Germany
Banshi D. Gupta, Indian Institute of Technology Delhi, New Delhi, India
Fengshou Gu, University of Huddersfield, UK
Jan Havlík, Czech Technical University in Prague, Czech Republic
Yigang He, Wuhan University, China
Eiji Higurashi, University of Tokyo, Japan
Johan Holmgren, Malmö University, Sweden
Carmen Horrillo Güemes, CSIC, Madrid, Spain
Yanxia Hou, Institut Nanosciences et Cryogénie | CEA-Grenoble, France
Kun Mean Hou, Laboratoire LIMOS UMR 6158 CNRS, France
Wen-Jyi Hwang, National Taiwan Normal University, Taiwan
M. Ichchou, Ecole Centrale de Lyon, France
Raul Igual, EUPT | University of Zaragoza, Teruel, Spain
Emmanuel Iwuoha, University of Western Cape, South Africa
Alberto Izquierdo Fuente, Universidad de Valladolid, Spain
Gotan Jain, K.K.H.A. Arts, S.M.G.L. Commerce and Science College, Chandwad, India
Yurong Jiang, Hewlett-Packard Labs, USA
Yunho Jung, Korea Aerospace University, Korea
Hirokatsu Kataoka, AIST, Japan
Wajahat Ali Khan, Kyung Hee University, South Korea
Jin (Wei) Kocsis, University of Akron, USA
Priscila M. Kosaka, Instituto de Microelectrónica de Madrid (CSIC), Spain
Sapozhnikova Kseniia, D. I. Mendeleyev Institute for Metrology, St.Petersburg, Russia
Anil Kumar, CSIR-CEERI, Pilani, India
Raj Kumar, University of Oslo, Norway
Narito Kurata, Tsukuba University of Technology, Japan
Dong-Weon Lee, Chonnam National University, Korea
Gyu Myoung Lee, Liverpool John Moores University, UK
Kevin Lee, School of Science and Technology - Nottingham Trent University, UK
Martin Lenzhofer, Silicon Austria Labs GmbH, Austria
Dawei Li, Donghua University, Shanghai, China
Tianliang Li, Nanyang Technological University, Singapore
Diego Ettore Liberati, National Research Council of Italy, Italy
Qing Lin, Soongsil University, Korea
Chuan-Ming Liu, National Taipei University of Technology (Taipei Tech), Taiwan
Thurmon Lockhart, Arizona State University, USA
Wen-Shiung Lour, National Taiwan Ocean University, Taiwan

Gilles Lubineau, PSE/KAUST, Saudi Arabia
Jerzy P. Lukaszewicz, Nicoulaus Copernicus University, Torun, Poland
Mai S. Mabrouk, Misr University for Science and Technology, Egypt
Joaquim Miguel Maia, Universidade Tecnológica Federal do Paraná - UTFPR, Brazil
Luca Maiolo, Institute for Microelectronics and Microsystems - National Research Council (IMM-CNR), Roma, Italy
Oleksandr Makeyev, Diné College, USA
Piero Malcovati, University of Pavia, Italy
Reza Malekian, Malmö University, Sweden
Stefano Mariani, Politecnico di Milano, Italy
Vincenzo Marletta, DIEEI - University of Catania, Italy
Moisés Agustín Martínez Hernández,Universidad Autónoma de Querétaro, Mexico
Francisco Martins, University of Lisbon, Portugal
Carlo Massaroni, Università Campus Bio-Medico di Roma, Italy
Vojko Matko, University of Maribor, Slovenia
Demétrio Matos, Design School (ESD-ID +) of the Polytechnic Institute of Cávado and Ave, Barcelos, Portugal
Pier Luigi Mazzeo, National Research Council of Italy (CNR) | Institute of Applied Sciences and Intelligent Systems (ISASI) | DHITECH - University Campus of Lecce, Italy
Lei Mei,California Research Center - Agilent Technologies, USA
Illyas Md Isa, Universiti Pendidikan Sultan Idris, Malaysia
Marek Miskowicz, AGH University of Science and Technology, Poland
Muamer N. Mohammed, University Malaysia Pahang, Malaysia
Carlos Montez, Federal University of Santa Catarina - UFSC, Brazil
Rafael Morales Herrera, University of Castilla-La Mancha, Spain
António J. R. Neves, University of Aveiro, Portugal
Johann F. Osma, Los Andes University / Colombian network on nanoscience and nanotechnology - Red NanoColombia, Colombia
Victor Ovchinnikov, Aalto University, Finland
Claudia Pacholski, Universität Potsdam, Germany
Pujana Paliyawan, Ritsumeikan University Research Organization, Japan
Henryk Palus, Silesian University of Technology, Poland
Vittorio M.N. Passaro, Politecnico di Bari, Italy
Piyush Patel, S. V. National Institute Of Technology, India
Giovanni Pau, Kore University of Enna, Italy
Paolo Perego, Politecnico di Milano, Italy
François Pérès, Toulouse University, France
Manh-Huong Phan, University of South Florida, USA
Ivan Pires, University of Beira Interior, Covilhã / Altran Portugal, Lisbon, Portugal
Fabrizio Pirri, Politecnico di Torino, Italy
Nuno Pombo, Universidade da Beira Interior, Portugal
Shengli Pu, University of Shanghai for Science and Technology, China
Eduardo Quevedo Gutiérrez, Institute for Applied Microelectronics - University of Las Palmas de Gran Canaria, Spain
Mariano Raboso Mateos, Universidad Pontificia de Salamanca, Spain
S. Radhakrishnan, Maharashtra Institute of Technology, India
Vasa Radonic, University of Novi Sad, Serbia
Konandur Rajanna, Indian Institute of Science, India

Copyright Information

Combined Mechanical Stress – the Key Parameter of Fine Tuning of Magnetic Microwires for Sensor Application

Alexander Chizhik
Materials Physics Department
University of the Basque Country
San Sebastian, Spain
email: oleksandr.chyzhyk@ehu.es

Paula Corte-Leon
Materials Physics Department
University of the Basque Country
San Sebastian, Spain
email: paula.corte@ehu.eus

Arkady Zhukov
Materials Physics Department
University of the Basque Country
San Sebastian, Spain
email: arkadi.joukov@ehu.es

Valentina Zhukova
Materials Physics Department
University of the Basque Country
San Sebastian, Spain
email: sckzhzhv@ehu.es

Julian Gonzalez
Materials Physics Department
University of the Basque Country
San Sebastian, Spain
email: julianmaria.gonzalez@ehu.eus

Andrzej Stupakiewicz
University of Bialystok
Bialystok, Poland
email: and@uwb.edu.pl

Przemyslaw Gawroński
AGH University of Science and Technology, Krakow, Poland
email: gawron@newton.ftj.agh.edu.pl

Abstract— **The experimental observation of the spiral domain structure has opened a new possibility of the fine control of the domain structure with different magnetization states in magnetic microwires, which are the base elements of the magnetic sensors. Here, we demonstrate that the tuning of magnetic domain structures in amorphous microwires can be engineered by the combination of tension and torsion mechanical stresses.**

Keywords-soft magnetic materials; amorphous magnetic wires; magneto-optic Kerr effect.

I. INTRODUCTION

Amorphous magnetic wires present a number of properties suitable for technical applications, such as Giant Magneto-Impedance (GMI) effect or magnetic bistability associated with fast domain wall propagation [1]–[4]. Consequently, various types of magnetic wires have been widely investigated during the past years [1]–[7].

While the separate application of different types of mechanical stresses is the usual practice, the combination of two different mechanical stresses could be considered as a new step permitting the fine tuning of the magnetic properties of the microwires.

Our study aimed at performing wide and complex magnetic and magneto-optical investigations of glass covered magnetic microwires under the simultaneous presence of tension and torsion stresses. Also, we have paid special attention to the domain walls motion in the wire being under stress. The essential element of our study is the simulation of the magnetic structure based on the theoretical analysis proposed in [8]. As a result, the spatial distributions of the vector of magnetization and the domain structures have been obtained in the cylindrically shaped magnet. The main idea of our work is the search of new magnetic states, in particular on the surface of microwire, which could be created only by the combination of torsion and tensile stresses.

The paper consists of 4 parts. Section 2 is devoted to the experimental description. Section 3 presents the results of the experiments. In Section 4, the conclusions are presented.

II. EXPERIMENTAL DETAILS

We studied glass-coated microwires (as cast and current annealed) with a $Fe_{3.85}Co_{67.05}Ni_{1.44}B_{11.53}Si_{14.47}Mo_{1.66}$ composition, a metallic nucleus diameter of d = 25.5 μm and a total diameter, including the glass coating, of D = 26.5

μm. The microwires were prepared by the Taylor–Ulitovsky method.

We represent the normalized magnetization, M/M_s as a function of the axial magnetic field, H, where M is the magnetic moment at a given magnetic field and M_s is the magnetic moment of the sample at the maximum magnetic field amplitude.

The study of the magnetization reversal on the surface of microwires has been performed by means of the optical polarizing magnetometer using the longitudinal Magneto-Optical Kerr Effect (MOKE) configuration [9].

Domain wall (DW) propagation is measured by using Sixtus–Tonks-like experiments. The magnetic field, H, is generated by a solenoid applying rectangular shaped voltage. Three pick-up coils are mounted along the length of the wire and propagating DW induces an electromotive force EMF in the coils (see scheme in Figure 1). Each pick-up coil is 2 mm long, the internal diameter is 1 mm, winding thickness is also 1 mm and it has 200 turns.

A pair of Helmholtz coils provided an axial magnetic field H_{ax}. The mechanical torsion stress has been applied. One of the wire ends was mechanically fixed, while the second end was rotary stressed to apply the stress with different angles. Also, tensile stress has been applied during the experiments.

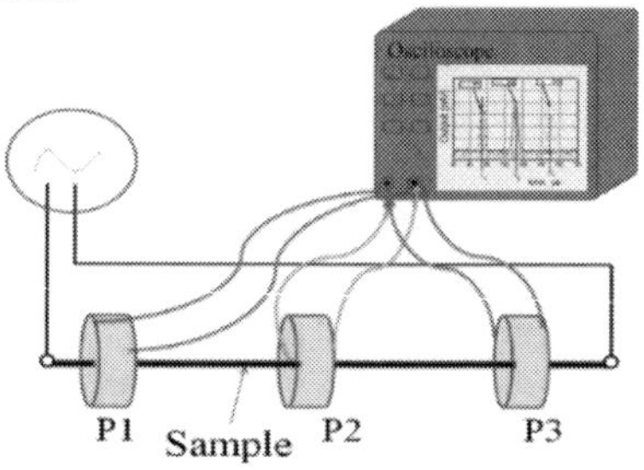

Figure 1. Schematic picture of modified Sixtus–Tonks setup.

III. MAGNETIC MEASUREMENTS

Figures 2 and 3 show the magnetic hysteresis loops obtained in the presence of torsion and tension stresses in as-cast and annealed microwires.

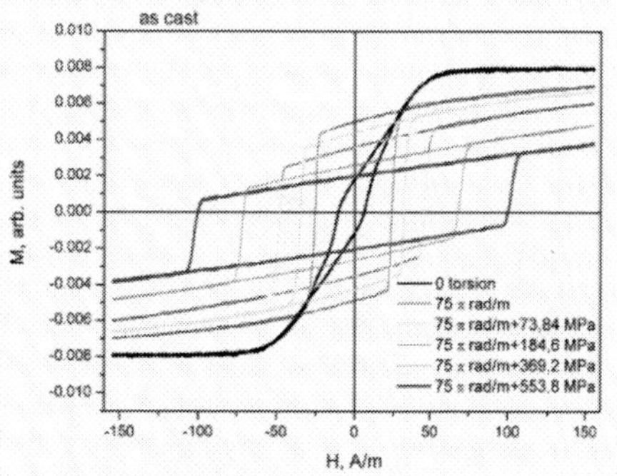

Figure 2. Hysteresis loops of as cast wire in the presence of torsion and tensile stresses.

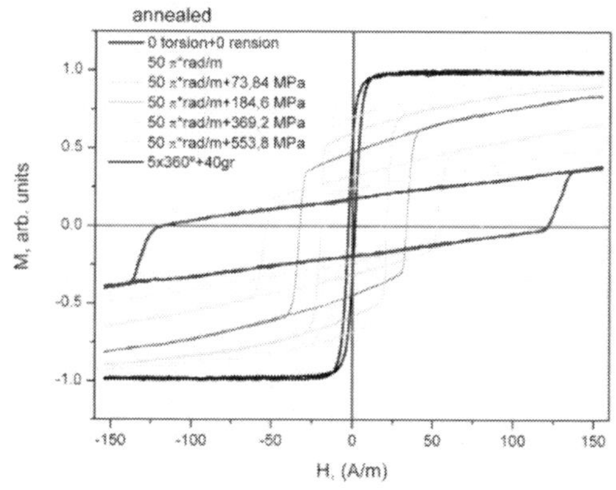

Figure 3. Hysteresis loops of annealed wire in the presence of torsion and tensile stresses.

Without stress, as-cast wire demonstrates a non-rectangular hysteresis loop while the annealed wire demonstrates an almost rectangular curve. In the presence of the stresses, the transformation of hysteresis in the two studied wires looks similar.

First, in the presence of the torsion stress, the hysteresis loop becomes clearly expressed as rectangular curve. Evidently this is related to the bistability effect. At the same time, it is known that the torsion stress induces the formation of the inclined helical structure. So, we could consider that here we observe the so called, helical bistability. Second, the application of tension induces the decrease of the remanent magnetization and the increase of the coercive field.

The observed decrease of the remanent magnetization and the increase of the coercive field must be attributed to the redistribution of internal stresses upon applied external stress and negative magnetostriction coefficient, λ_s, of the studied microwire. Thus, arising of the axial magnetic anisotropy upon torsion can be originated by negative λ_s – values. Such torsion induced axial magnetic anisotropy gives rise to magnetic bistability (rectangular hysteresis loops, see Figure 2). On the other hand, tensile stress, σ, dependence of the switching field, H_s, has been previously observed in microwires with spontaneous and stress-induced magnetic bistability [10][11]. Experimentally, roughly $H_s \sim \sigma^{1/2}$ has been explained considering the H_s relation to the domain wall energy involved in the re-magnetization process of magnetically bistable samples [11]. We can assume a similar mechanism in the present case considering that the magnetic bistability is induced by the torsion stresses and the tensile stress dependence is attributed to the stress dependence of the domain wall energy. On the other hand, considering commonly accepted domain structure of magnetic wires consisting of the axially magnetized inner core and outer domain shell [12], we can deduce that the outer shell volume increases upon tensile stresses. Such modification of the domain structure can be obtained from the relation between the radius of the inner axially magnetized core, R_c, and the wire radius R given by the squire-ness ratio, M_r/M_s as [12]

$$R_c = R(Mr/Ms)^{1/2}, \quad (1)$$

Therefore, the observed tensile M_r/M_s stress dependencies must be associated with rising of the outer shell volume due to negative λ_s values of the studied microwire.

Figures 4 and 5 demonstrate the field dependencies of the DW velocity measured in two studied wires in the presence of the combination of the stresses.

The highest value of the velocity (about 1200 m/s) was obtained in as-cast wire in the presence of only torsion stress. The additional application of the tension increases the start field, shifting in such a way the velocity dependence along the field axis. Also, the decrease of the value of the velocity is observed.

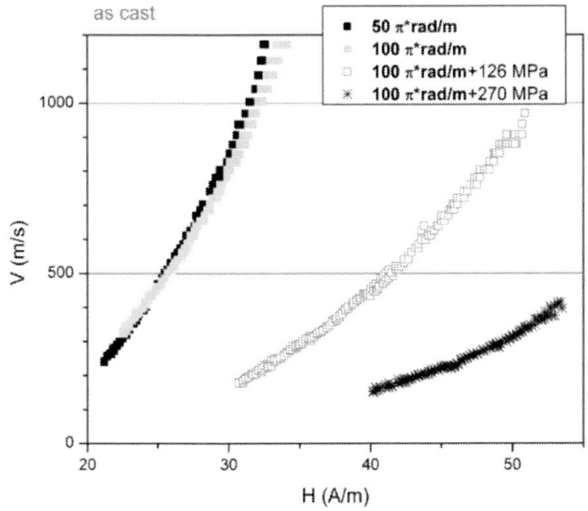

Figure 4. Magnetic field dependence of the DW velocity in the presence of torsion and tensile stresses (as cast wire).

The annealed wire shows a significantly lower value of the velocity (about 400 m/s) when the stresses were not applied. The application of the stresses causes the decrease of the velocity. The lowest value was obtained for the case of the combination of two types of the stresses.

The obtained dependencies of the DW velocity have found the explanation in the frame of the conception of the stress induced transformation of the magnetic structure in as-cast and annealed microwires, demonstrating the clear correlation with the magnetic hysteresis loops.

Measurement uncertainties of Sixtus–Tonks experiments were determined by the thickness of the pick-up coil and do not exceed the size of the experimental points in Figures 4 and 5.

Figure 6 shows the results of the simulation obtained for the different values of parameter ρ ($\rho = R_c/R$) that correspond, according to our approaching, to different values of torsion stress.

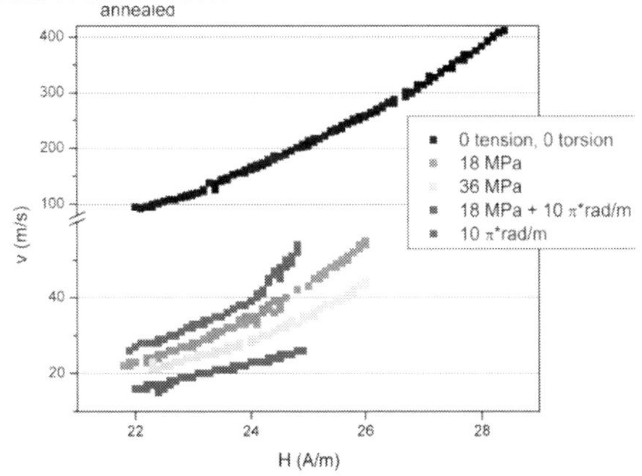

Figure 5. Magnetic field dependence of the DW velocity in the presence of torsion and tensile stresses (annealed wire).

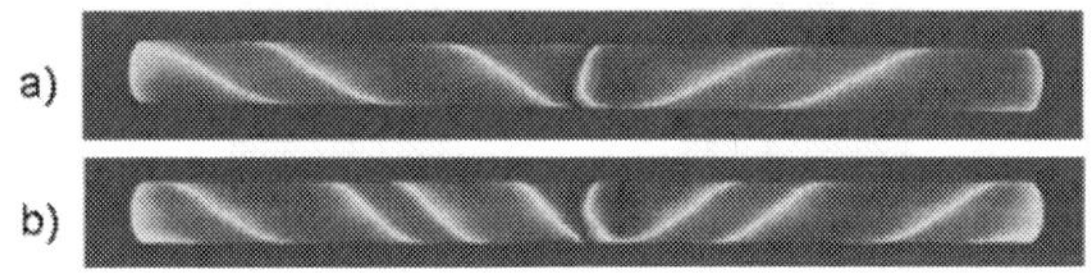

Figure 6. Calculated spiral domain structure obtained for different values of the parameter ρ: a) ρ=0.4, b) ρ=0.8.

The formation of the spiral DW on the wire surface is determined by the competition of different energy contributions: magnetic anisotropy, exchange and the magnetostatic energy. The angle of the DW inclination changes with parameter ρ.

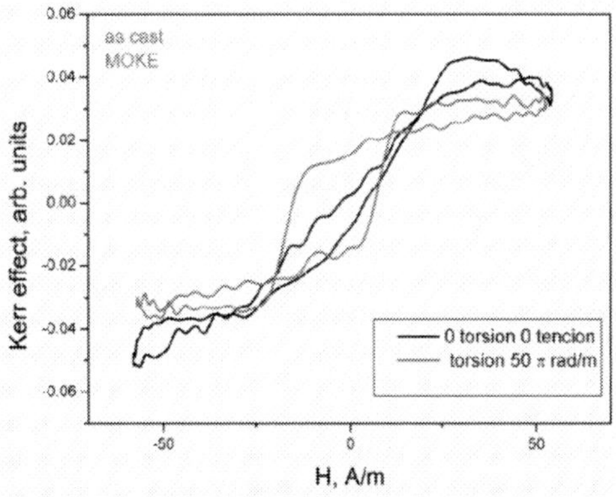

Figure 7. MOKE hysteresis loops of as cast wire in the presence of torsion stress.

Figure 7 demonstrates the independent confirmation of our concept. Here, we can see the torsion stress induced transformation of MOKE hysteresis loop. Torsion stress induces the appearance of a rectangular hysteresis loop. It means the formation of helical structure in the surface of the microwire. Therefore, the torsion stress produces the spiral helical structure in almost the whole thickness of the microwire.

IV. Conclusions

In this work, we propose a new method of control of the magnetic structure in magnetic microwires, which are the base elements of the magnetic sensors. The combination of the torsion and tension stresses gives a new understanding of the transformation of the magnetic structure. The combination of magnetic and magneto-optical techniques with the Sixtus–Tonks experiments permits us to select the predicted magnetic structures. The results of magnetic simulation confirm the validity of our conception.

Acknowledgment

We acknowledge support from the National Science Centre Poland under Grant No. DEC-2016/22/M/ST3/00471. This work was also supported by Spanish MINECO under MAT2013-47231-C2-1-P and Spanish MCIU under PGC2018-099530-B-C31, by the University of Basque Country UPV/EHU (Ref.: PPG17/35) and by the Government of the Basque Country under Elkartek RTM 4.0 project. The research of P.G. was supported in part by PL-Grid Infrastructure.

References

[1] L. V. Panina and K. Mohri, "Magneto-impedance effect in amorphous wires," Appl Phys Lett., vol. 65, pp. 1189-1195, April 1994.

[2] A. Zhukov, Novel Functional Magnetic Materials, Fundamentals and Applications, vol. 231. Springer International Publishing, 2016.

[3] A. Zhukov, M. Ipatov, and V. Zhukova, Advances in Giant Magneto - impedance of Materials, Handbook of Magnetic Materials, ed. K. H. J. Buschow, 24: chapter 2, pp. 139–236, April 2015.

[4] I. Ogasawara and S. Ueno, "Preparation and properties of amorphous wires," IEEE Trans. Magn., vol. 31, pp. 1219-1225, May 1995.

[5] P. Rudkowski, G. Rudkowska, and J. O. Strom-Olsen, "The fabrication of fine metallic fibers by continuous meltextraction and their magnetic and mechanical properties," Mater. Sci. Eng., vol. A 133, pp. 158-162, June 1991.

[6] V. Zhukova, A. Zhukov, V. Kraposhin, A. Prokoshin, and J. Gonzalez, "Magnetic properties and GMI of soft meltextracted magnetic amorphous fibers," Sensors and Actuators (A), vol. 106, pp. 225-230, July 2003.

[7] K. Mohri, T. Uchiyama, L. P. Shen, C. M. Cai, and L. V. Panina, "Amorphous wire and CMOS IC-based sensitive micro-magnetic sensors (MI sensor and SI sensor) for intelligent measurements and controls," J. Magn. Magn. Mater., vol. 249, pp. 351-354, March 2001.

[8] A. Chizhik et al., "Spiral magnetic domain structure in cylindrically-shaped microwires," Scient. Rep., vol. 8, 15090-6, June 2018.

[9] A. Stupakiewicz et al., "Direct imaging of the magnetization reversal in microwires using all-MOKE microscopy," Rev. Sci. Instrum., vol. 85, pp. 103702-5, June 2014.

[10] P. Aragoneses et al., "The Stress dependence of the switching field in glass-coated amorphous microwires," J. Phys. D: Applied Phys., vol. 31, pp. 3040-3045, March 1998.

[11] P. Corte-Leon et al., "Stress dependence of the magnetic properties of glass-coated amorphous microwires", J. Alloys Compound., vol. 789, pp. 201-208, March 2019.

[12] M.Vázquez and D.-X.Chen, "The magnetization reversal process in amorphous wires," IEEE Trans. Magn., vol. 31, no. 2, pp. 1229-1239, June 1995.

Optimization of Giant Magnetoimpedance Effect in Magnetic Microwires

Arcady Zhukov
Dept Materials Physics, Univ. Basque Country, UPV/EHU, 20018 San Sebastian and Ikerbasque, Bilbao Spain
e-mail: arkadi.joukov@ehu.es

Paula Corte-León, Mihail Ipatov, Valentina Zhukova
Department Materials Physics, Univ. Basque Country, UPV/EHU, 20018 San Sebastian, Spain
e-mail: paula.corte@ehu.eus, mihail.ipatov@ehu.eus, valentina.zhukova@ehu.es

Juan Maria Blanco
Department Applied Physics I, Univ. Basque Country, EIG, UPV/EHU, 20018, San Sebastian, Spain
e-mail: juanmaria.blanco@ehu.es

Abstract—**In this work, we present the experimental results of our study of various parameters of the Giant MagnetoImpedance (GMI) effect of magnetic microwires. We observed that the GMI effect and the magnetic softness of microwires can be tailored by controlling the Magnetoelastic anisotropy of as-prepared microwires. On the other hand, the GMI ratio can be optimized selecting appropriate measuring conditions, i.e., the measuring frequency.**

Keywords- giant magnetoimpedance effect; magnetic microwires; magnetic softness.

I. INTRODUCTION

Studies of the Giant MagnetoImpedance (GMI) effect have attracted considerable attention since its rediscovery in 1994 in amorphous wires [1][2]. It is worth noting that the first report on the change of impedance in permalloy wires was published in 1936 [3]. However, GMI studies become one of the most attractive topics of applied magnetism owing to the development of amorphous magnetically soft wires [4]-[8].

The main technological interest in the GMI effect is related to one of the largest sensitivities to a magnetic field (up to 10 %/A/m) among non-cryogenic effects [4]-[8]. Such features of the GMI effect make it quite attractive for development of high performance sensors allowing detection of low magnetic fields and mechanical stresses [9]-[14].

The most common quantity for the characterization of the GMI effect is the GMI ratio, $\Delta Z/Z$, defined as:

$$\Delta Z/Z = [Z(H) - Z(H_{max})] / Z(Hmax) \quad (1)$$

where H is the applied axial Direct Current (DC)-field with a maximum value, H_{max}, up to a few kA/m.

The value of the GMI ratio and its magnetic field dependence are determined by the type of magnetic anisotropy: for achievement of high GMI ratio, the high circumferential magnetic permeability is essentially important [7][8]. Magnetic wires with circumferential easy axis exhibit double-peak magnetic field dependence of the real component of wire impedance (and, consequently, of the GMI ratio). Magnetic wires with longitudinal easy axis present monotonic decay of the GMI ratio with increasing axial magnetic field with GMI ratio maximum at zero magnetic field [7][8]. The highest GMI ratio up to 650% is reported for amorphous microwires [15]-[17]. However, theoretically predicted maximum GMI ratio is about 3000% (i.e., a few times larger than the GMI ratio values reported experimentally) [18]. Additionally, the theoretical minimum of the skin depth is about 0.3 μm [18][19].

The main features of the GMI effect have been successfully explained in terms of classical electrodynamics considering the influence of a magnetic field on the penetration depth of an electrical current flowing through the magnetically soft conductor [1][2]. High circumferential permeability typically observed in Co-rich amorphous wires with nearly-zero magnetostriction coefficient is essential for the observation of a high GMI ratio [1][2][4]-[6]. However, similarly to the magnetic permeability, the GMI effect has a tensor character [4]-[6][20]-[22]. The off-diagonal component of MagnetoImpedance (MI) can present anti-symmetrical magnetic field dependence with a linear region quite suitable for magnetic sensors applications [20]-[22].

One of the tendencies in modern GMI sensors is the size reduction. It must be underlined that the diameter reduction must be associated with the increasing of the optimal GMI frequency range: a tradeoff between dimension and frequency is required in order to obtain a maximum GMI effect [4]-[6][23]. Additionally, the GMI effect at microwave frequencies has been described considering the analogy between the GMI and the ferromagnetic resonance [4]. Consequently, development of thin soft magnetic materials required for miniaturization of the sensors and devices requires an extension of the frequency range for the impedance toward the higher frequencies (GHz range).

Depending on the frequency f of the driving AC current I_{ac} flowing through the sample, different GMI regimes can be considered [4]-[6]:

1. Low frequency (1-10 kHz) range when the skin depth is larger than the sample radius (weak skin effect). The impedance changes in this frequency band are related

to a circular magnetization process exclusively and might not be considered as the GMI effect.

2. At the frequency range from 10-100 kHz to 1-10 MHz (where the GMI effect has been first reported and described), the GMI originates basically with the variation of the skin penetration depth of magnetic conductor due to strong changes of the magnetic permeability caused by a DC magnetic field [1][2][4]-[6]. In this frequency band, both domain walls movement and magnetization rotation are considered as to be responsible for the variation of the circular permeability and, hence, to the skin effect.

3. For the MHz band frequencies (from 1-10 MHz to 100-1000 MHz, depending on the geometry of the sample), the GMI effect is also originated by the skin effect of the soft magnetic conductor, i.e., must be attributed to the GMI. However, at these frequencies, the domain walls are strongly damped. Therefore, the magnetization rotation must be considered as responsible for the magnetic permeability change induced by an external magnetic field [1][2][4]-[8].

4. At GHz frequencies, the magnetization rotation is strongly influenced by the gyromagnetic effect. Increasing the frequency, the GMI peaks are shifted to higher magnetic fields values because the sample is magnetically saturated. At this frequency range, strong changes of the sample's impedance have been attributed to the FerroMagnetic Resonance (FMR) [4]-[6][23].

Recently developed magnetic sensors using the GMI effect allow achieving nT and pT magnetic field sensitivity with low noise [10]-[14][24].

Presently, major attention is focused on high frequency (GHz range) GMI applications owing to the development of thin magnetically soft materials and the recent tendency in miniaturization of magnetic field sensors [4]-[6][10]-[14][24].

The aim of this report is to provide recent results on the optimization of soft magnetic properties and of the GMI effect in magnetic microwires.

The rest of the paper is structured as follows. In Section II, we present the description of the experimental techniques, while in Section III, we describe the results on the effect of post-processing on the GMI ratio of studied microwires. We conclude the paper in Section IV.

II. EXPERIMENTAL DETAILS

As already mentioned in the introduction, the GMI effect usually observed in soft magnetic materials phenomenologically consists of the change of the Alternating Current (AC) impedance, $Z = R + iX$ (where R is the real part, or resistance, and X is the imaginary part, or reactance), when submitted to an external magnetic field, H_0.

The electrical impedance, Z, of a magnetic conductor is given by [1][2]:

$$Z = R_{dc}\, krJ_0(kr)/2J_1(kr) \qquad (2)$$

with $k = (1 + j)/\delta$, where J_0 and J_1 are the Bessel functions, r is the wire's radius and δ the penetration depth given by:

$$\delta = (\pi\sigma\mu_\phi f)^{-1/2} \qquad (3)$$

where σ is the electrical conductivity, f the frequency of the current along the sample, and μ_ϕ the circular magnetic permeability assumed to be scalar. The DC applied magnetic field introduces significant changes in the circular permeability, μ_ϕ. Therefore, the penetration depth also changes through and finally results in a change of Z [1][2].

The GMI ratio, $\Delta Z/Z$, has been evaluated considering (1).

In ferromagnetic materials with high circumferential anisotropy (the case of magnetic wires), the magnetic permeability possesses tensor nature and the classic form of impedance definition is not valid. The relation between the electric field, e, (which determines the voltage) and the magnetic field, h, (which determines the current) is defined through the surface impedance tensor, $\hat{\varsigma}$, [20]-[22][25]:

$$e = \hat{\varsigma}h \quad \text{or} \quad \begin{Bmatrix} e_z = \varsigma_{zz}h_\varphi - \varsigma_{z\varphi}h_z \\ e_\varphi = \varsigma_{\varphi z}h_\varphi - \varsigma_{\varphi\varphi}h_z \end{Bmatrix} \qquad (4)$$

The circular magnetic fields h_φ are produced by the currents i_w running through the wire. At the wire surface $h_z = i/2\pi r$, where r is the wire radius. The longitudinal magnetic fields h_z are produced by the currents i_c running through the exciting coil, $h_z = N_1 i_c$, where N_1 is the exciting coil number of turns. Various excitation and measurement methods are required to reveal the impedance matrix elements. The longitudinal and circumferential electrical field on the wire surface can be measured as voltage drop along the wire, v_w, and voltage induced in the pickup coil, v_c, wound on it [20]-[22][25].

$$v_w \equiv e_z l_w = (\varsigma_{zz}h_\varphi - \varsigma_{z\varphi}h_z)l_w \qquad (5)$$

$$v_c \equiv e_\varphi l_t = (\varsigma_{\varphi z}h_\varphi - \varsigma_{\varphi\varphi}h_z)l_t \qquad (6)$$

where l_w is the wire length, $l_t = 2\pi r N_2$ the total length of the pickup coil turns N_2 wounded directly on the wire.

The methods for revealing the different elements of impedance tensor are shown in Figure 1. The longitudinal diagonal component, ς_{zz}, is defined as the voltage drop along the wire and corresponds to the impedance definition in classical model (Figure 1a)

$$\varsigma_{zz} \equiv \frac{v_w}{h_\varphi l_w} = \left(\frac{2\pi a}{l_w}\right)\left(\frac{v_w}{i_w}\right) \qquad (7)$$

The off-diagonal components $\varsigma_{z\varphi}$ and $\varsigma_{\varphi z}$ and the circumferential diagonal component $\varsigma_{\varphi\varphi}$ arose from cross

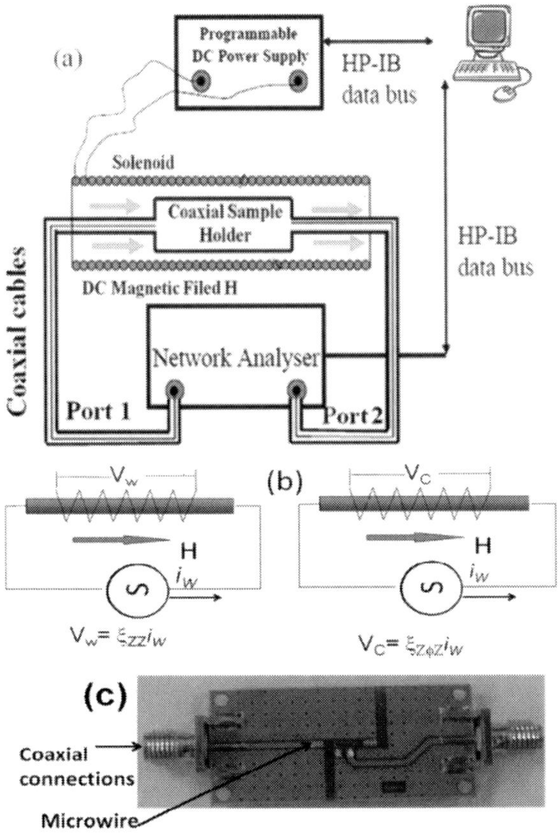

Figure 1. Schematic picture of the experimental set-up for measurements of GMI effect (a), principles for revealing of the diagonal, ς_{zz}, and off-diagonal, $\varsigma_{z\varphi}$, impedance matrix elements (b) and the image of the micro-strip line (c).

sectional magnetization process ($h_\varphi \rightarrow m_z$ and $h_z \rightarrow m_\varphi$) [20]-[22][25].

The use of a specially designed micro-strip sample holder (see Figure 1c) placed inside a sufficiently long solenoid allows measuring of the magnetic field dependence of sample impedance, Z, using a vector network analyzer from the reflection coefficient S_{11} using the expression:

$$Z=Z_0(1+S_{11})/(1-S_{11}) \quad (8)$$

where Z_0=50 Ohm is the characteristic impedance of the coaxial line [26]. The described technique allows measuring of the GMI effect in extended frequency, f, range up to GHz frequencies.

Hysteresis loops have been measured using the fluxmetric method previously described elsewhere [27]. We represent the normalized magnetization, M/M_0 versus the magnetic field, H, where M is the magnetic moment at a given magnetic field and M_0 is the magnetic moment of the sample at the maximum magnetic field amplitude, H_m.

We studied Fe- and Co- rich microwires with metallic nucleus diameters, d, ranging from 10 up to 25 μm prepared using the Taylor-Ulitovsky method described elsewhere [5][8]. The Taylor-Ulitovsky method allows preparation of thinnest metallic wires (with typical diameters of the order of 1 to 30 μm) covered by an insulating glass coating [5][8].

The great advantage of these microwires is that the obtained diameter could be significantly reduced in comparison with the case of amorphous wires produced by the other rapidly quenching methods.

However, in the case of glass-coated microwires, the magnetoelastic anisotropy contribution is even more relevant since the preparation process involves not only the rapid quenching itself, but also simultaneous solidification of the metallic nucleus surrounded by the glass-coating with rather different thermal expansion coefficients [5][8][28]-[30]. The strength of internal stresses, σ_i, is basically affected by three main factors: i) quenching stresses associated to the melt quenching of the metallic alloy; ii) stresses related to the different thermal expansion coefficients of metallic ingot and glass simultaneously solidifying and iii) stresses associated to the drawing of solidifying wire [28]-[30].

In amorphous materials, the magnetocrystalline anisotropy is absent. Therefore, the magnetoelastic anisotropy is the main factor affecting the magnetic properties [5][6].

The magnetoelastic anisotropy, K_{me}, is given as:

$$K_{me} = 3/2\lambda_S\sigma_i \quad (9)$$

where λ_S is the magnetostriction coefficient and σ_i is the internal stresses value [8].

The magnetostriction coefficient, λ_s, value in amorphous alloys can be tailored by the chemical composition [31]-[34]. Generally, Fe-rich compositions present positive λ_s -values (typically $\lambda_s \approx 20 - 40 \times 10^{-6}$), while for the Co-rich alloys, λ_s –values are negative, typically $\lambda_s \approx -5$ to -3×10^{-6}. Vanishing λ_s –values can be achieved in the Co_xFe_{1-x} ($0 \leq x \leq 1$) or Co_xMn_{1-x} ($0 \leq x \leq 1$) systems at x about 0,03 – 0,08 [31]-[34].

However, the internal stresses, σ_i, arise during simultaneous rapid quenching of metallic nucleus surrounding by the glass coating due to the different thermal expansion coefficients. Consequently, the strength of internal stresses can be controlled by glass-coating thickness: the strength of internal stresses increases with the increasing of the glass-coating thickness [28]-[30][35].

III. Experimental Results and Discussion

As mentioned above, the magnitude and the magnetic field dependence of the GMI effect (including off-diagonal components) is intrinsically linked to the magnetic anisotropy [4]-[8]. Magnetoelastic anisotropy is the main source of magnetic anisotropy of amorphous microwires

[4]-[8]. Accordingly, both hysteresis loops, $\Delta Z/Z(H)$ dependence and maximum value of GMI ratio, $\Delta Z/Z_m$, are affected by λ_s sign and value and by the magnitude of internal stresses, σ_i. The magnetostriction coefficient drastically affects the character of the hysteresis loops of magnetic microwires: i) Co-rich microwires (see Figure 2a for $Co_{77.5}Si_{15}B_{7.5}$) with negative magnetostriction constant ($\lambda_s \approx -5x10^{-6}$) have almost unhysteretic loops with extremely low coercivity, H_c. However, the magnetic permeability of $Co_{77.5}Si_{15}B_{7.5}$ microwire is not high enough since they also present high enough magnetic anisotropy field, H_k. ii) Co-Fe-based microwires with vanishing magnetostriction constant ($Co_{67.1}Fe_{3.8}Ni_{1.4}Si_{14.5}B_{11.5}Mo_{1.7}$, $\lambda_s \approx -10^{-7}$) generally present lower H_k –values and, hence, higher magnetic permeability. iii) Finally, Fe-rich microwires ($Fe_{75}B_9Si_{12}C_4$) with positive magnetostriction constant ($\lambda_s \approx 40x10^{-6}$) present rectangular hysteresis loops and, consequently, low magnetic permeability.

As can be appreciated from Figure 3b, $Co_{67.1}Fe_{3.8}Ni_{1.4}Si_{14.5}B_{11.5}Mo_{1.7}$ microwire presents the highest maximum GMI ratio, $\Delta Z/Z_m$ (about 240% at 500 MHz). Quite low $\Delta Z/Z_m$ –values are observed for $Fe_{75}B_9Si_{12}C_4$ microwire ($\Delta Z/Z_m \approx 15\%$, see Figure. 3c). Moderate $\Delta Z/Z_m$ –values ($\Delta Z/Z_m \approx 120\%$) are observed for $Co_{77.5}Si_{15}B_{7.5}$ microwire (see Figure 3a).

The other difference in $\Delta Z/ZH)$ dependencies for microwires with different magnetostriction coefficients is the character of $\Delta Z/Z(H)$ dependencies: for microwire with $\lambda_s>0$ a single maximum $\Delta Z/Z(H)$ dependence with $\Delta Z/Z$ maximum at $H=0$ is observed (Figure 3c). However, for

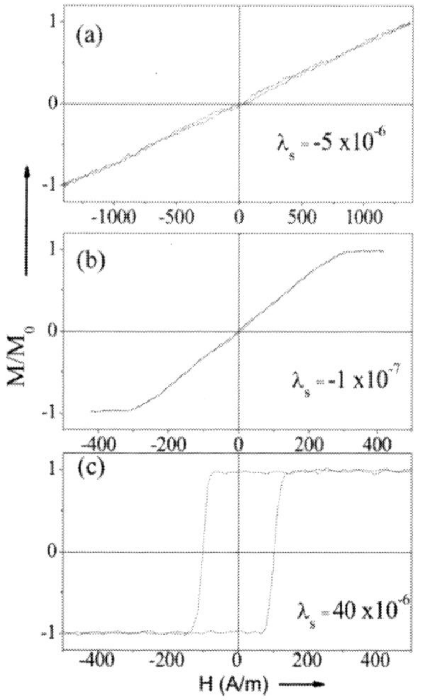

Figure 2. Hysteresis loops of as-prepared $Co_{77.5}Si_{15}B_{7.5}$ (a), $Co_{67.1}Fe_{3.8}Ni_{1.4}Si_{14.5}B_{11.5}Mo_{1.7}$ (b) and $Fe_{75}B_9Si_{12}C_4$ (c) microwires.

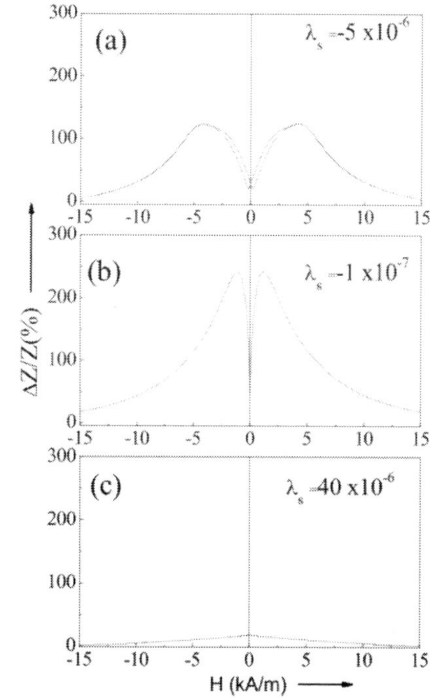

Figure 3. $\Delta Z/Z(H)$ dependencies of as-prepared $Co_{77.5}Si_{15}B_{7.5}$ (a), $Co_{67.1}Fe_{3.8}Ni_{1.4}Si_{14.5}B_{11.5}Mo_{1.7}$ (b) and $Fe_{75}B_9Si_{12}C_4$ (c) microwires measured at 500 MHz.

$\lambda_s<0$ double- maximum $\Delta Z/Z(H)$ dependencies with $\Delta Z/Z$ maximum at $H=H_m$ are observed (Figures 3b,c).

It is commonly assumed that the H_m -value corresponding to the peaks (maximum $\Delta Z/Z$ - value) is linked to the average value of the anisotropy field, H_K, at high frequency values, and to the effective anisotropy distribution in the sample. In this regard, observed $\Delta Z/Z(H)$ dependencies correlate with hysteresis loops: the highest H_m –value is observed for $Co_{77.5}Si_{15}B_{7.5}$ microwire with the highest H_k –value (see Figure 2a). A single maximum $\Delta Z/Z(H)$ dependence with $\Delta Z/Z$ maximum at $H=0$ corresponds to $Fe_{75}B_9Si_{12}C_4$ microwire with axial magnetic anisotropy (Figure 2c).

Such different magnetic anisotropy of microwires with positive and negative magnetostriction is related to the internal stresses distribution, intrinsically related to the fabrication of microwires [4]-[8]. The radial distribution of internal stresses, is calculated considering quenching stresses related to rapid quenching of the metallic alloy from the melt, as well as, complex tensor stresses related with the difference in the thermal expansion coefficients of metal and glass, the axial stresses are the largest ones up to ~ 0.85 R (where R is the metallic nucleus radius) [8]. Thus, the main volume of the microwire nucleus is under the tensile stresses near the axis of the metallic nucleus. However, closer to the surface the compressive stresses are dominant. Additionally, the strength of internal stresses is determined by the thickness of non-magnetic glass-coating:

the strength of internal stresses increases with the increasing of the glass-coating thickness.

Therefore, as reported earlier [5][8], hysteresis loops and the GMI effect are affected by the ratio $\rho=d/D$, where d is the diameter of metallic nucleus and D-total microwire diameter. Some of the examples are shown in Figure 4, where the hysteresis loops and $\Delta Z/Z(H)$ dependencies of as-prepared $Co_{67}Fe_{3.85}Ni_{1.45}B_{11.5}Si_{14.5}Mo_{1.7}$ microwires with different ρ–ratios are shown.

Consequently, the control of internal stresses by tailoring of the ρ–ratio is the effective method for the GMI ratio tuning.

As mentioned above, the other important parameter for the GMI ratio optimization in magnetic microwires is the frequency. Indeed, the frequency must be high enough in order to have the skin depth lower than the sample radius (strong skin effect).

$\Delta Z/Z(H)$ dependencies measured at different frequencies in as-prepared $Co_{67}Fe_{3.9}Ni_{1.4}B_{11.5}Si_{14.5}Mo_{1.6}$ (d=25.6 μm, D= 26.6 μm) microwires are shown in Figure 5a. This composition at given geometry (d=25.6 μm, D= 26.6 μm, ρ=0.96) present high maximum GMI ratio, $\Delta Z/Z_m$: at the optimal frequency of about 300 MHz, $\Delta Z/Z_m$ ≈550% can be achieved (see Figure 5b). However, thinner (d=10.8 μm) microwire of the same chemical composition at this frequency exhibit $\Delta Z/Z_m$ ≈400% (see Figure 5b). From $\Delta Z/Z_m(f)$ dependence for $Co_{67.7}Fe_{4.3}Ni_{1.6}Si_{11.2}B_{12.4}C_{1.5}Mo_{1.3}$ microwires with d=10.8μm and d=25.6 μm we can appreciate that for $Co_{67.7}Fe_{4.3}Ni_{1.6}Si_{11.2}B_{12.4}C_{1.5}Mo_{1.3}$ microwires with

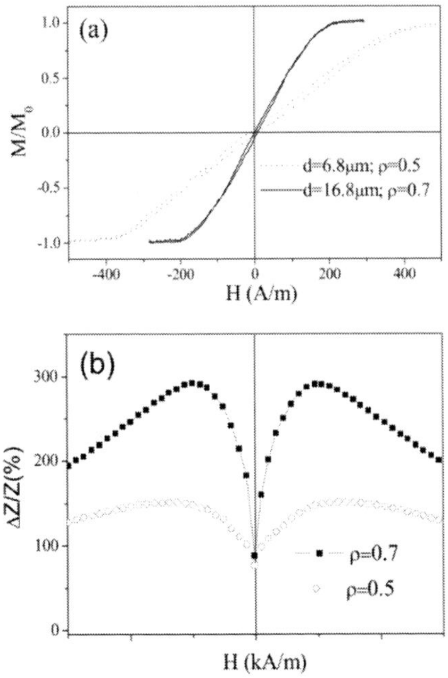

Figure 4. Hysteresis loops (a) and $\Delta Z/Z(H)$ dependencies measured at 500 MHz (b) of as-prepared $Co_{67}Fe_{3.85}Ni_{1.45}B_{11.5}Si_{14.5}Mo_{1.7}$ microwires with different ρ-ratios.

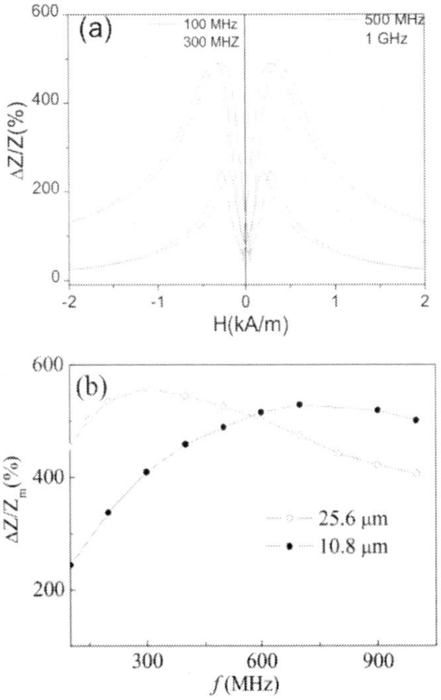

Figure 5. $\Delta Z/Z(H)$ dependencies measured in as-prepared $Co_{67}Fe_{3.9}Ni_{1.4}B_{11.5}Si_{14.5}Mo_{1.6}$ (d=25.6 μm, D= 26.6 μm) microwires (a) and $\Delta Z/Z_m(f)$ dependence for $Co_{67.7}Fe_{4.3}Ni_{1.6}Si_{11.2}B_{12.4}C_{1.5}Mo_{1.3}$ with d=10.8μm, D=13.8μm and d=25.6 μm, D= 26.6 μm microwires.

d=10.8μm the optimal frequency is about 700 MHz, at which $\Delta Z/Z_m$ ≈550% can be achieved.

The aforementioned examples provide the routes for optimization of the GMI effect in Co-rich microwires.

IV. CONCLUSIONS

In this work, we measured the GMI magnetic field, frequency dependencies and hysteresis loops in magnetic microwires produced by the Taylor-Ulitovsky technique.

We observed that the GMI effect and magnetic softness of the microwires are intrinsically related and can be tailored either by controlling the magnetoelastic anisotropy of as-prepared microwires or by controlling their internal stresses and structure by heat treatment. Studies of magnetic properties and the GMI effect of amorphous Co-Fe rich microwires reveal that, by selecting an appropriate chemical composition and geometry, they present GMI effect at GHz frequencies. High GMI effect has been achieved and discussed. The selection of appropriate measuring conditions can be beneficial for optimization of the GMI effect of magnetic microwires.

ACKNOWLEDGMENT

This work was supported by Spanish MCIU under PGC2018-099530-B-C31 (MCIU/AEI/FEDER, UE) and by the Government of the Basque Country under the PIBA 2018-44 project. The authors are grateful for the technical and human support provided by SGIker of UPV/EHU

(Medidas Magnéticas Gipuzkoa) and European funding (ERDF and ESF).

REFERENCES

[1] L. V. Panina and K. Mohri, "Magneto-impedance effect in amorphous wires," Appl. Phys. Lett., vol. 65, pp. 1189-1191, 1994.

[2] R. S. Beach and A. E. Berkowitz, "Giant magnetic-field dependent impedance of amorphous FeCoSiB wire", Appl. Phys. Lett., vol. 64, pp. 3652-3654, 1994.

[3] E. P. Harrison, G. L. Turney, H. Rowe, and H. Gollop, "The electrical properties of high permeability wires carrying alternating current", Proc. R. Soc. Lond. A, vol. 157, pp. 451-479, 1936.

[4] M. H. Phan and H. X. Peng, "Giant magnetoimedance materials: Fundamentals and applications", Prog. Mater. Sci., vol. 53, pp. 323-420, 2008.

[5] A. Zhukov, M. Ipatov, and V. Zhukova, Advances in Giant Magnetoimpedance of Materials, Handbook of Magnetic Materials, ed. K. H. J. Buschow, 24, pp. 139-236 (chapter 2), 2015.

[6] M. Knobel, M. Vazquez, and L. Kraus, Giant magnetoimpedance, Handbook of Magnetic Materials, ed. E. Bruck, 15, pp. 497-563, 2003.

[7] N. A. Usov, A. S. Antonov, and A. N. Lagar`kov, "Theory of giant magneto-impedance effect in amorphous wires with different types of magnetic anisotropy", J. Magn. Magn. Mater., vol. 185, pp. 159-173, 1998.

[8] A. Zhukov et al., "Trends in optimization of giant magnetoimpedance effect in amorphous and nanocrystalline materials", J. Alloys Compd., vol. 727, pp. 887-901, 2017.

[9] K. Mohri, T. Uchiyama, L. P. Shen, C. M. Cai, and L. V. Panina, "Amorphous wire and CMOS IC-based sensitive micro-magnetic sensors (MI sensor and SI sensor) for intelligent measurements and controls", J. Magn. Magn. Mater.,vol. 249, pp. 351-356, 2001.

[10] T. Uchiyama, K. Mohri, and Sh. Nakayama, "Measurement of spontaneous oscillatory magnetic field of Guinea-pig smooth muscle preparation using pico-Tesla resolution amorphous wire magneto-impedance sensor", IEEE Trans. Magn., vol. 47, pp. 3070-3073, 2011.

[11] Y. Honkura, "Development of amorphous wire type MI sensors for automobile use", J. Magn. Magn. Mater., vol. 249, pp. 375-381, 2002.

[12] A. F. Cobeño, A. Zhukov, J. M. Blanco, V. Larin, and J. Gonzalez, "Magnetoelastic sensor based on GMI of amorphous microwire", Sensors Actuat. A-Phys, vol. 91, pp. 95-98, 2001.

[13] S. Gudoshnikov et al., "Highly sensitive magnetometer based on the off-diagonal GMI effect in Co-rich glass-coated microwire", Phys. Stat. Sol. (a), vol. 211 (5) pp. 980–985, 2014.

[14] L. Ding, S. Saez, C. Dolabdjian, L. G. C. Melo, A. Yelon, and D. Ménard, "Development of a high sensitivity giant magneto-impedance magnetometer: comparison with a commercial Flux-Gate", IEEE Sensors, vol. 9 (2), pp. 159-168, 2009.

[15] K. R. Pirota, L. Kraus, H. Chiriac, and M. Knobel, "Magnetic properties and GMI in a CoFeSiB glass-covered microwire", J. Magn. Magn. Mater.,vol. 21, L243-L247, 2000.

[16] A. Zhukov, V. Zhukova, J. M. Blanco, and J. Gonzalez, "Recent research on magnetic properties of glass-coated microwires", J. Magn. Magn. Mater., vol. 294, pp. 182-192, 2005.

[17] P. Corte-León et al., "Engineering of magnetic properties of Co-rich microwires by joule heating", Intermetallics, vol. 105, pp. 92-98, 2019.

[18] L. Kraus, "Theory of giant magneto-impedance in the planar onductor with uniaxial magnetic anisotropy", J. Magn. Magn. Mater., vol. 195, pp. 764-778, 1999.

[19] M. Ipatov, V. Zhukova, A. Zhukov, J. Gonzalez, and A. Zvezdin, "Low-field hysteresis in the magnetoimpedance of amorphous microwires", Phys. Rev. B, vol. 81, p. 134421, 2010.

[20] S. I. Sandacci, D. P. Makhnovskiy, L. V. Panina, K. Mohri, and Y. Honkura, "Off-diagonal impedance in amorphous wires and its application to linear magnetic sensors", IEEE Trans. Magn., vol. 35, pp. 3505-3510, 2004.

[21] P. Aragoneses, A. Zhukov, J. Gonzalez, J. M. Blanco, and L. Dominguez, "Effect of AC driving current on magneto-impedance effect", Sensors Actuat. A-Phys, vol. 81/1-3, pp. 86-90, 2000.

[22] A. S. Antonov, I. T. Iakubov, and A. N. Lagarkov, "Nondiagonal impedance of amorphous wires with circular magnetic anisotropy", J. Magn. Magn. Mater., vol. 187(2) pp. 252–260, 1998.

[23] D. Ménard, M. Britel, P. Ciureanu, and A. Yelon, "Giant magnetoimpedance in a cylindrical conductor", J. Appl. Phys., vol. 84, pp. 2805–2814, 1998.

[24] Y. Honkura and S. Honkura, The Development of a High "Sensitive Micro Size Magnetic Sensor Named as GSR Sensor Excited by GHz Pulse Current", 2018 Progress In Electromagnetics Research Symposium (PIERS — Toyama), Japan, 1–4 August 2018, pp. 324—331.

[25] M. Ipatov, V. Zhukova, J. M. Blanco, J. Gonzalez, and A. Zhukov, "Off-diagonal magneto-impedance in amorphous microwires with diameter 6–10 μm and application to linear magnetic sensors", Phys. Stat. Sol. (a) vol. 205, No. 8, pp. 1779–1782, 2008.

[26] A. Zhukov, A. Talaat, M. Ipatov, and V. Zhukova, "Tailoring the high-frequency giant magnetoimpedance effect of amorphous Co-rich microwires", IEEE Magn. Lett., vol. 6, p. 2500104, 2015.

[27] A. Zhukov, M. Vázquez, J. Velázqez, A. Hernando and V. Larin, "Magnetic properties of Fe-based glass-coated microwires", J. Magn. Magn. Mater. vol. 170, pp. 323-330, 1997.

[28] S. A. Baranov, V. S. Larin, and A. V. Torcunov, Technology, "Preparation and properties of the cast glass-coated magnetic microwires", Crystals, vol. 7 p. 136, 2017.

[29] H. Chiriac and T. A. Óvári, "Amorphous glass-covered magnetic wires: preparation, properties, applications", Progr. Mater. Sci., vol. 40 (5) pp. 333-407, 1996.

[30] A. Zhukov et al., "Ferromagnetic resonance and structure of Fe-based glass-coated microwires", J. Magn. Magn. Mater., vol. 203, pp. 238-240, 1999.

[31] G. Herzer, Amorphous and nanocrystalline soft magnets, in Proceedings of the NATO Advanced Study Institute on Magnetic Hysteresis in Novel Materials, Mykonos, Greece, 1-12 July 1996, ed. George C. Hadjipanayis, NATO ASI Series (Series E: Applied Sciences) vol. 338, pp. 711-730. Kluwer Academic Publishers (Dordrecht/Boston/London) 1997.

[32] A. Zhukov et al., "Magnetostriction of Co-Fe-based amorphous soft magnetic microwires", J. Electr. Mater., vol. 45 (1) pp. 226-234, 2016.

[33] Y. Konno and K. Mohri, "Magnetostriction measurements for amorphous wires", IEEE Trans. Magn., vol. 25, pp. 3623-3625, 1989.

[34] K. Mohri, F.B. Humphrey, K. Kawashima, K. Kimura, and M. Muzutani, "Large Barkhausen and Matteucci effects in FeCoSiB, FeCrSiB, and FeNiSiB amorphous wires", IEEE Trans. Magn., vol. 26, pp. 1789-1781, 1990.

[35] H. Chiriac, T.A. Ovari, and A. Zhukov, "Magnetoelastic anisotropy of amorphous microwires", J. Magn. Magn. Mater. vol. 254-255, pp. 469-471, 2003.

Stress Monitoring of Composites with Fe-based Amorphous Microwires by Non-contact Magnetic Method

Margarita Churyukanova, Sergey Kaloshkin, Andrey Bazlov
Institute of New Materials and Nanotechnologies
National University of Science and Technology "MISIS"
Moscow, Russia
e-mail: mch@misis.ru; kaloshkin@misis.ru; bazlov@misis.ru

Valentina Zhukova, Arcady Zhukov
Dept. Material Physics
UPV/EHU
San Sebastian, Spain
e-mail: arkadi.joukov@ehu.es; valentina.zhukova@ehu.es

Dmitry Louzguine-Luzgin
WPI Advanced Institute for Materials Research
Tohoku University
Sendai, Japan
e-mail: dml@wpi-aimr.tohoku.ac.jp

***Abstract* - The deformation of amorphous materials causes a change in their magnetic properties. If it occurs within the elastic region, such changes are reversible and can be used to control stresses. This applies both to the amorphous alloys themselves and to composites with embedded amorphous microwires. New experimental results on monitoring of the applied tensile stresses in Fe-based amorphous microwires after different regimes of treatment are presented. We investigated the amplitude of the Electro-Motive Force (EMF) signal due to the Barkhausen effect, the saturation magnetostriction and the coercivity. We used a non-contact method for stress monitoring of ferromagnetic microwires. It was found that the dependence of the EMF signal on the axial tensile stress of microwire exhibits a maximum. We observed a significant increase in the maximum of the EMF signal for microwires after annealing and its shift to higher tensile stresses. Using the obtained data, we evaluated the possibility of stress monitoring in a composite material containing such microwires.**

Keywords-amorphous microwires; magnetic properties; stress sensitivity; non-contact method.

I. INTRODUCTION

Amorphous Fe-based microwires are attractive first of all due to their magnetic bistability and Giant MagnetoImpedance (GMI) effect, which is used as a contact method of stress control in various magnetoelastic sensors [1]-[3]. Additionally, their low dimensionality and excellent mechanical properties are appropriate for the development of composites with embedded microwires. In this case, the microwires can be regarded as embedded sensors: their impedance is sensitive to the wire magnetic structure and is responsible for the appearance of a controlled microwave dielectric response [4][5]. The stress-sensitive magnetic properties of the amorphous ferromagnetic microwire have also been used for stress control. This is due to the stress dependence of the switching field that is determined to a great extent by the value of the magnetostriction coefficient of microwires [1]. During the magnetization reversal of the ferromagnetic microwire, jumps in its magnetization (large Barkhausen jumps) occur. They can be registered as the electromotive force peaks depending on the magnetic field [3]. The peak amplitude and the peak position are affected by stress. Consequently, the stress state of the composite material containing such microwires can be controlled by a non-contact method.

The rest of the paper is structured as follows. In Section II, we present the experimental details. Section III contains the results and discussion, and we conclude the work in Section IV.

II. EXPERIMENTAL DETAILS

In this work, we investigated the change in amplitude of the electromotive force signal under tensile stress of Fe-based amorphous microwires with different composition.

Under the influence of the external Alternating Current (AC) magnetic field, generated by the magnetizing coil, the EMF induction is produced in the pick-up coil. Pulses associated with the motion of domain walls appear on the main sinusoidal signal. For given amplitude and frequency of magnetic field, the value of register signal depends on the magnitude of the mechanical stresses in the sample (microwire or the composite). The value of magnetostriction coefficient for as-prepared microwire was measured by a small angle magnetization rotation method.

The tensile stress in the microwire was carried out using a universal Zwick/Roell tensile machine with a high-precision force transducer according to uniaxial stretching. During the experiment, the pick-up coil was placed in the vicinity of the testing sample.

For the stress monitoring of the composite material, a ferromagnetic microwire was introduced into it. The composite samples were made of carbon fiber impregnated with resin and the ferromagnetic microwire was implemented between the layers of prepregs. Afterwards, the composite was compressed and cured under the pressure of 170 MPa at 115°C for 120 min. The composite samples for the tensile tests had an in-plane size of 2x15 cm and a thickness of 1-2 mm.

III. Results and Discussion

In the first step, the amplitude of the EMF signal of the ferromagnetic amorphous microwires with a different composition and geometry was measured. We observed sharp EMF peaks associated with the domain wall propagation under an action of the AC magnetic field on the screen. The amplitude of the EMF signal at a given frequency and amplitude of the external magnetic field was proportional to the magnetic flux of the microwire. For the as-prepared microwire, we measured the value of the magnetostriction coefficient, λs, and found that the amplitude of the EMF signal grows with increasing the magnetostriction coefficient of the investigated microwires: there is a correlation between the amplitude of EMF signal and the magnetostriction coefficient of the investigated microwires. This allowed us to choose the most suitable microwire compositions.

In the second step, we measured the dependence of the EMF voltage of the microwires on the tensile stress. For all investigated microwires, the dependence of the EMF signal on external stress presents a maximum at 60-120 MPa. This peak may be associated with a change of the hysteresis loop of the amorphous microwires under the stress, which must be attributed to the influence of the applied stresses on the velocity of the Domain Wall (DW) propagation and the magnetostriction coefficient. The magnetization of a ferromagnetic material due to strain is known to be proportional to the magnetostriction coefficient and the initial magnetic permeability. The magnetostriction coefficient of ferromagnetic amorphous microwires changes with stresses exhibiting a maximum and their initial magnetic permeability decreases because the domain wall mobility decreases with the applied stresses. Thus, it can be suggested that the observed dependence, which exhibits a maximum, is most likely related to the stress dependences of magnetization and magnetostriction.

After removing the glass coating, i.e., by reducing the internal stresses, there is an increase in the magnitude of the peak by 2 times. We also observed a shift of the EMF peak toward higher values of tensile stresses. For the microwire with removed glass coating, this maximum was observed up to 300 MPa, whereas for the glass-coated microwire - only up to 100 MPa.

In the case of the partially crystalline sample, the internal stresses are smaller due to partial stress relaxation associated with recrystallization of nanocrystalline materials. This sample presents larger stress sensitivity of the EMF signal due to a higher magnetic permeability of this sample. In addition, the maximum EMF amplitude versus stress from partially crystalline microwire is observed at higher stress values. This can be explained by lower values of magnetostriction in a partially crystalline microwire, which leads to higher stress sensitivity for the partially crystalline microwire as compared to the amorphous sample.

Annealing of the Fe-rich microwires leads to improvement of magnetic softness, DW velocity and mobility, and internal stresses relaxation. Owing to this, we observed a significant increase in the maximum of the EMF amplitude for microwires after annealing and its shift to higher tensile stresses.

After the introduction of a microwire in the carbon composite, the overall appearance of the dependence of EMF on stress is maintained. The detected signal from a microwire in the composite is proportional to its deformation. The elastic modulus of the amorphous Fe-based alloy is about 120 GPa [6]. The measured value of elastic modulus for the studied carbon composite is 54 GPa. This means that, for the same strain, the microwire in the composite is exposed to twice higher stress value than the composite matrix. This, at first, reduces the range of possible stresses measured from microwire embedded in the composite, and, secondly, leads to the appearance of strong stresses at the interface between the microwire and the composite matrix. The main cause of the breakdown of the connection between the microwire and the composite is the destruction of the glass coating. Low limit of glass coating deformation becomes, therefore, an obstacle to expanding the measuring range of mechanical stresses in the composite.

IV. Conclusion

The magnetic properties of a ferromagnetic microwire, embedded in the composite matrix, depend on its stress-strain state. This allows stress monitoring in composites by non-contact induction method. Using a microwire without glass coating as a stress-sensitive element, we can expand the range of stress control in the composite material by this method.

Acknowledgment

The authors acknowledge the Russian Foundation for Basic Research (Grant 16-53-48012) and the Ministry of Education and Science of the Russian Federation in the framework of Increase Competitiveness Program of NUST «MISIS» (K2-2014-013 and K2-2017-089).

References

[1] P. Aragoneses et al., "The Stress dependence of the switching field in glass-coated amorphous microwires," J. Phys. D: Applied Phys. V.31, pp. 3040-3045,1998.

[2] A. F. Cobeño, A. Zhukov, J. M. Blanco, V. Larin, and J. Gonzalez, "Magnetoelastic sensor based on GMI of amorphous microwire," Sensors and Actuators A, v.91, pp.95-98, 2001.

[3] J. Olivera et al., "An Embedded Stress Sensor for Concrete SHM Based on Amorphous Ferromagnetic Microwires," Sensors, v.14, pp. 19963-19978, 2014.

[4] M. Ipatov, V. Zhukova, A. Zhukov, and L.V. Panina, "Microwave Metamaterials Containing Magnetically Soft Microwires," Advances in Science and Technology, v.75, pp. 224-229, 2010.

[5] F.X. Qin et al., "Effects of wire properties on the field-tunable behaviour of continuous-microwire composites," Sensors and Actuators A, v. 178, pp.118- 125, 2012.

[6] H. Chiriac, T.A. Ovari, and Gh. Pop, "Internal stress distribution in glass-covered amorphous magnetic wires," Phys. Rev. B., v.42, 101- 105, 1995.

Phase Transitions in Metastable Fe-Ga Alloys

Igor S. Golovin, Valeria Palacheva, AbdElKariem Mohamed
Department of Physical Metallurgy of non-Ferrous Metals
National University of Science and Technology "MISIS"
Moscow, Russia
e-mail: i.golovin@misis.ru, lera.palacheva@mail.ru, abdelkarim.abdelkarim@feng.bu.edu.eg

Anatoliy Balagurov, Ivan Bobrikov, Natalia Samoylova, Sergei Sumnikov
Frank Laboratory of Neutron Physics
Joint Institute for Nuclear Research
Dubna, Russia
e-mail: bala@nf.jinr.ru, bobrikov@nf.jinr.ru, rny03@nf.jinr.ru, sumnikovsv@gmail.com

Abstract — **In the present study, we have investigated the time and temperature dependence of the transition of as-cast metastable Fe-(9-33at.%)Ga 'Galfenol' alloys to the equilibrium state along with corresponding changes in their functional properties and anelastic effects that accompany these transitions. To characterize such a Time-Temperature Transformation (TTT) diagram, we used both long-time isochronal annealing (up to 300hrs) and instant heating treatments with different temperature protocols. In-situ neutron diffraction, X-Ray Diffraction (XRD), Differential Scanning Calorimetry (DSC), Vibrating-Sample magnetometer (VSM), Vickers Hardness (HV), Scanning Electron Microscope-Electron Backscatter Diffraction (SEM-EBSD), Mössbauer and mechanical spectroscopy techniques were used.**

Keywords-Fe-Ga; neutron diffraction; phase transitions; equilibrium.

I. INTRODUCTION

Fe-Ga bulk poly- and single crystals, foils and nanowires found various applications with the main emphasis on their enhanced magnetostriction properties. Several important questions about the structure and properties of Fe-Ga alloys remain open: e.g., Joulian *vs.* non-Joulian magnetostriction [1], the origin of different short range ordered clusters and their contribution to properties [2], pseudoelasticity [3], anomalous temperature dependence of Young's modulus [4], damping capacity and anelasticity of phase transitions [5], etc.

The equilibrium phase diagram does not reflect the real structure of Fe-Ga alloys neither in the as-cast state nor after annealing followed by air or furnace cooling [6]. The metastable phase diagram, proposed by Ikeda et al. in 2002 [7], is too general and it corresponds only to the chosen regimes of cooling of Fe-Ga alloys. Functional properties of the Fe-Ga alloys are extremely sensitive to particular details of the phase transition from the metastable (as-cast, as-quenched, air-cooled) state with A2 or short and long range $D0_3$ ordered structures with positive magnetostriction to the equilibrium state with $L1_2$ structure and negative magnetostriction [8][9].

The aim of this paper is twofold: it is not only to study both the structure and sequence of phase transitions in metastable Fe-Ga alloys, but also to examine the rates of the transitions using different techniques, including both *in situ* tests with different heating rates and long-term isothermal annealing treatments. Those characteristics are of high interest and importance in order to design specific microstructures with desired properties.

The rest of the paper is structured as follows: In Section II, we describe the experimental procedure; the results are presented in Section III. Finally, we conclude in Section IV.

II. EXPERIMENTS

The Fe-Ga alloys were produced by induction melting followed by casting in an Indutherm MC-20 V mini furnace under protective high-purity argon gas. The chemical composition of the produced ingots was analysed by Energy Dispersive X-ray Spectroscopy (EDX). The tolerance (±0.1) comes from the calibration by measuring standard samples with a purity of 99.9999% of element. The standard error of measurement of the chemical composition is 0.1-0.2% wt. In this paper, we use only atomic %.

Neutron Diffraction (ND) patterns were measured with a High-Resolution Fourier Diffractometer (HRFD) operating at the fast pulsed reactor IBR-2 which, is a powerful neutron source at Joint Institute for Nuclear Research Dubna, Russia (JINR). The HRFD can be switched between high-resolution ($\Delta d/d \approx 0.0015$) and high-intensity ($\Delta d/d \approx 0.015$) diffraction modes, both of which are needed for a joint analysis of the changes in the atomic structure and microstructure of the material upon heating or cooling. A detailed description of the method is given in [10], where a comparative analysis of the results obtained on as-cast and powder samples of the Fe-27Ga alloy was carried out. Most of the *in situ* experiments were carried out with heating and cooling rates of 2 °C/min. Some tests were also carried out with cooling rates of 1, 4, 8 °C/min, respectively.

XRD analysis of the crystallographic structure of the samples was performed with a Bruker D8 Advanced diffractometer with Cu K_α radiation. The room temperature XRD tests and selected SEM-EBSD tests we used after 300 hrs annealing in vacuum at different temperatures, namely: 300, 350, 400, 450, 500, 575°C, respectively.

Internal Friction (IF), or the loss factor Q^{-1}, were obtained from forced vibrations by measuring the phase lag tanφ between the applied cyclic stress and the resulting strain: $\sigma = \sigma_0 \cos(\omega t)$ and $\varepsilon = \varepsilon_0 \cos(\omega t+\varphi)$, correspondingly. $\omega = 2\pi f$ and φ is the phase lag or the loss angle. The temperature-dependent measurements were conducted as a function of temperature between 0 and 600 °C using forced bending single cantilever vibrations with $\varepsilon_0 = 7\times10^{-5}$ with heating and cooling rates of 2 °C/min.

DSC experiments using a Labsys Setaram system with heating rates of 5, 10 and 20 °C/min in air atmosphere allowed us to carry out the sample's thermal analysis.

The dilatometry tests were recorded at temperatures ranging from 20 °C to 800 °C at the heating rate of 5 °C/min using a Dilatometer Linseis L75.

Magnetization (VSM) curves were obtained using a VSM-130 vibrating sample magnetometer with a heating rate of 6 °C/min under a magnetic field of ≈400 kA/m.

SEM-EBSD microstructures of the alloys were identified by SEM operating at 20kV using a TESCAN VEGA LMH microscope with a LaB6 cathode and an energy dispersive X-ray microanalysis system (Oxford Instruments, Software Advanced AZtecEnergy). Both backscattered electron and secondary electron imaging were used in the analysis. EBSD analysis of the alloys was investigated using the NordlysMax2 detector (Oxford Instruments, Software Advanced AZtecEnergy) with a Crystal Structure Database supplied by Oxford Instruments. The Mean Angular Deviation (MAD) of 0.25 was used in the analysis.

III. Results

To characterize a TTT diagram, which is isothermal transformation diagram we used long-time isochronal annealing (up to 300 hrs), instant heating and instant cooling treatments with different cooling rates from 1 to 2500 °C/min.

A. *As-cast alloy structures at room temperature*

According to their structure, the as-cast samples can be divided into four groups:

1. **$x < 20$**, A2 structure,
2. **$20 < x < 27$**, A2 as a matrix with $D0_3$ clusters embedded into the matrix (existence of small amount of B2 clusters is also not excluded),
3. **$27 < x < 31$**, $D0_3$ and B2 structures.
4. **$x > 31$**, B2 or $D0_3$ plus a phase with unresolved structure.

Within the second group, there are two subgroups:

2a. **$21 < x < 23$**, lattice parameter and width of fundamental peaks decrease,

2b. **$23 < x \leq 27$**, lattice parameter increases linearly while the intensity of superstructure peak (111) increases, reaches maximum, and decreases.

The lattice parameter is more sensitive to the beginning of the ordering process than the peak intensities. Up to $x \approx 27$, the ordered clusters occupy a relatively small volume as compared to the volume of a disordered matrix.

B. *Phase transitions at heating of as-cast alloys*

Second order phase transition in Fe-19Ga type alloys

Ordering in Fe-19Ga type alloys is studied and confirmed for different regimes of heat treatment of the samples [11]. Transmission electron microscopy study suggests that ordering results in formation of small $D0_3$ type ordered clusters.

In situ neutron diffraction study confirms disordering of Fe-19Ga structure at heating above 400°C and ordering at slow cooling. By means of internal friction and vibrating sample magnetometry measurements, which have high sensitivity to atomic disordering and change in magnetization, ordering temperature (T_O) was determined to be 500-550°C at heating and 525-485°C at cooling. It looks like that doping with Tb enhances this effect, but more careful study is needed in future, as both Tb and Ga concentrations influence on the temperature ordering-disordering reaction and degree of ordering.

First order phase transition in Fe-27Ga type alloys

Using the *in situ* neutron scattering technique (Fig. 1), we have defined ranges of phase transitions in the bulk samples of Fe-Ga alloys with 25 to 28 %Ga under constant heating with the rate 1 and 2 K/min [12][13]. We underline different rates of lattice parameters $a(D0_3)$ and $a(L1_2)$ increases in the temperature range of their co-existing, which lead to an anelastic behaviour of the alloy in this temperature range. Using a combination of neutron scattering technique with heat flow, magnetization, and internal friction tests analyses, we proved that a transient internal friction P_{Tr} peak accompanies the $D0_3$ to $L1_2$ phase transition during heating in a wide range of Ga concentrations [14].

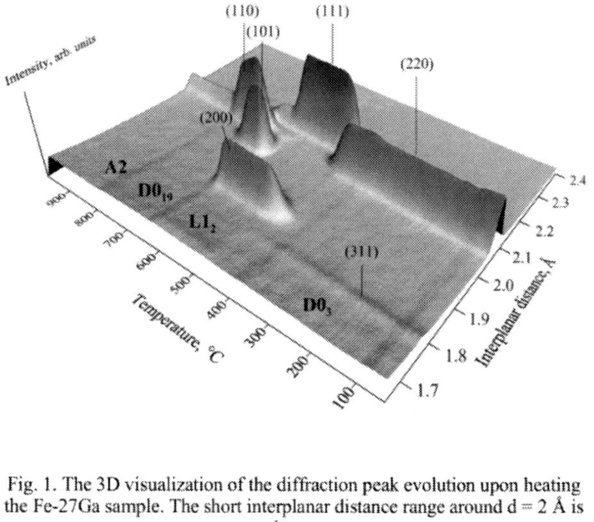

Fig. 1. The 3D visualization of the diffraction peak evolution upon heating the Fe-27Ga sample. The short interplanar distance range around d = 2 Å is shown.

C. Phase transitions at isothermal annealing

Isothermal annealing of Fe–(27-28)Ga alloys at 400 to 470 °C leads to the $D0_3 \rightarrow L1_2$ phase transition. The analysis of the intensities of the fundamental and superstructure diffraction peaks over time in *in situ* regime reveals that the transition between the ordered structures $D0_3$ and $L1_2$ occurs through the formation of the disordered state [15]. In other words, the sequence $D0_3 \rightarrow A2 \rightarrow A1 \rightarrow L1_2$ is realized, where A1 and A2 are disordered fcc and bcc structures (Fig. 2). The transition process begins with a rather abrupt disappearance of the ordering in the $D0_3$ phase, i.e. the formation of the A2 bcc structure. Then, the bcc → fcc transformation, apparently via a mechanism like the $\alpha \rightarrow \gamma$ transition in pure iron, occurs, followed by the formation of the ordered $L1_2$ phase. An important difference in the bcc → fcc transition in Fe–xGa alloys at $x \sim (27\text{–}28)$ is significantly lower temperature than in pure iron ($T_c \approx 911$ °C). As in pure iron, the diffraction patterns for these alloys show no evidence of tetragonal distortion, i.e. the A2 → A1 transition occurs in small local sample volumes in time intervals too short to allow observation of changes in the diffraction pattern.

During disordering ($D0_3 \rightarrow A2$) and ordering ($A1 \rightarrow L1_2$) transitions, the lattice deformation is homogeneous and very small ($\varepsilon \leq 0.001$), whereas during the first-order A2 → A1 transition, the linear deformations are heterogeneous and large: $\varepsilon_c \approx 0.266$, $\varepsilon_{ab} \approx -0.105$.

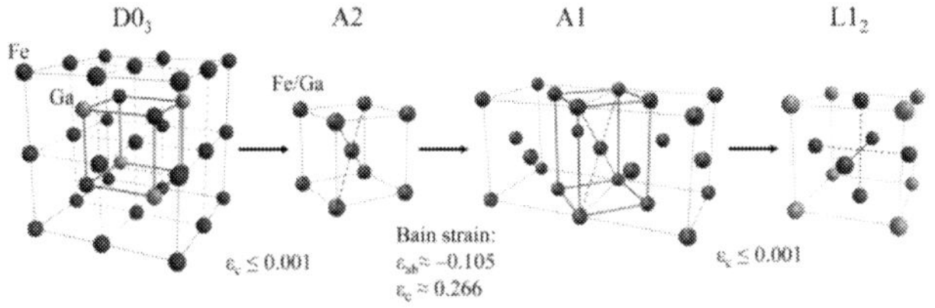

Fig. 2. Schematic diagram of the $D0_3 \rightarrow A2 \rightarrow A1 \rightarrow L1_2$ structural transitions in the Fe-27Ga type alloys during isothermal annealing. $D0_3$ and A2 are bcc-based ordered and disordered structures. A1 and $L1_2$ are fcc-based disordered and ordered structures. The lattice deformation is small for the $D0_3 \rightarrow A2$ and $A1 \rightarrow L1_2$ transitions and relatively large for the A2 → A1 transition.

The kinetics of the whole transition process cannot be described within the Avrami model [16], since the value of the Avrami parameter n does not remain constant with the annealing time. However, it is possible to find out intervals with $n(t) \approx$ const. For the initial stage of the transition in Fe-27Ga, the Avrami parameter is close to $n = 2$ for all annealing temperatures between 400 and 470°C, which corresponds to the model with a constant growth rate of new-phase grains and a decreasing nucleation rate.

D. Long-term (300°C) annealing at 300-575°C

300 hrs annealing in vacuum of as-cast Fe-Ga samples was applied in order to achieve equilibrium state. Our experimental points are added to equilibrium phase diagram [17] based on Gödecke and Köster [18] studies. Each point illustrates the ratio between bcc phase (here we do not distinguish between A2 and $D0_3$ structures), fcc-derived $L1_2$ phase, and R (Fe_6Ga_5) phase. These phases are shown by green, red and blue colours, correspondingly. Our results demonstrate significant deviation from the generally accepted diagram [17]: obviously, the boundary between the A2 and (A2+$L1_2$) ranges is located at lower Ga content. This observation is in favour of the less known phase diagram suggested by Bras et al. [19]. Nevertheless, both diagrams fail to explain experimental points close to the (A2+$L1_2$) and $L1_2$ boundary. We suggest that the range of single A2 phase is more narrow as compared with existing phase diagrams. Also, the results presented in Fig. 3 support a typical C-type of TTT diagram (Fig. 4). 300 hrs annealing at 575, 400, 350 and 300°C is not enough to complete transition to equilibrium phase, in contrast with annealing at 500 and 450°C, which are close to the 'nose' of the C curve.

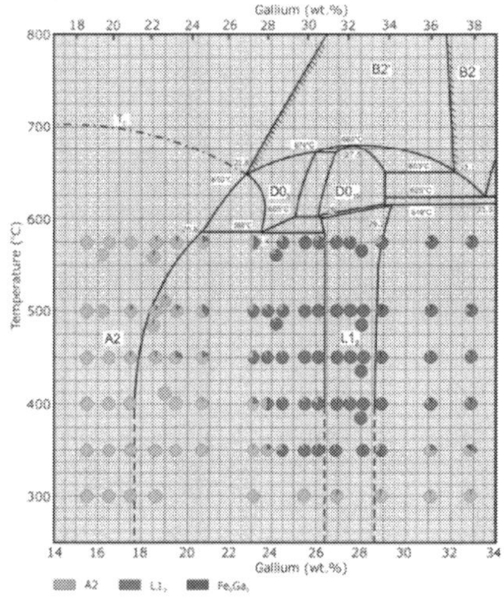

(a)

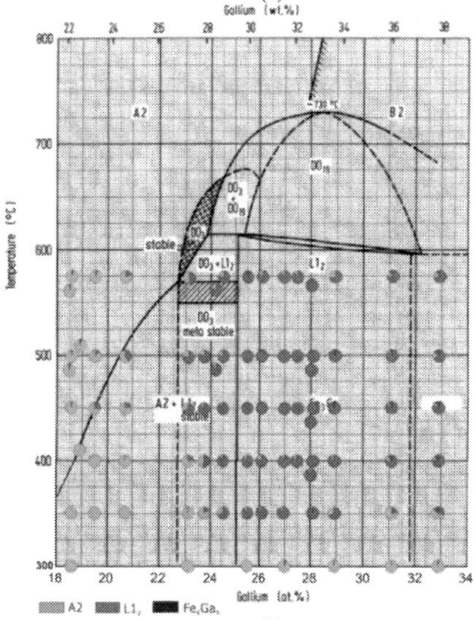

(b)

Fig. 3. Fe-Ga equilibrium phase diagrams [16] (a) and [18] (b) with experimental points illustrating the ratio between bcc (A2/$D0_3$), $L1_2$ and R (Fe_6Ga_5) phases after 300hrs annealing.

E. Phase transitions at cooling and critical cooling rates

The Fe-27%Ga sample was cooled down from 900°C with well-controlled cooling rates from 1 to 2000 °C/min. Sample structures were examined to identify the first and second critical cooling rates. The scheme of the TTT diagram is shown in Fig. 4. The first critical cooling rate, V_{Cr1}, is defined in this paper as the cooling rate of beginning of the appearance of the equilibrium $L1_2$ phase out from the metastable $D0_3$ phase, and the second critical cooling rate, V_{Cr2}, is the cooling rate at which no metastable phase (A2, B2 or $D0_3$) is fixed in the sample structure at cooling.

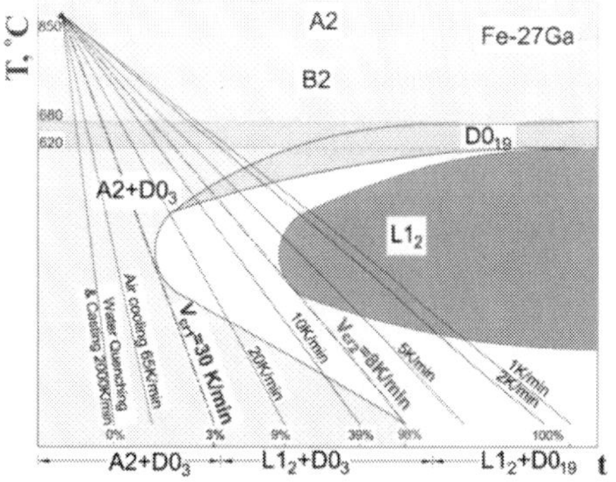

Fig. 4. Scheme of temperature - time transformation (TTT) diagram for Fe-27Ga alloy with two critical cooling rates of 30 and 8 K/min and indication of final structures at room temperature for given cooling rates according to our results.

IV. CONCLUSIONS

In this paper, we have analysed structure in the Fe-(9-33)Ga as-cast alloys and their phase transitions in them at instant heating, short-term *in situ* isothermal and long-term annealing, and phase transitions after annealing in A2 range of phase diagram and subsequent cooling with different rates. Results reveal that the boundary between the A2 and ($A2+L1_2$) ranges is located at lower Ga content and the appearance of $L1_2$ depends on the cooling rate.

ACKNOWLEDGMENT

This work is supported by the Russian Science Foundation (project No. 19-72-20080).

REFERENCES

[1] H. D. Chopra and M. Wuttig, "Non-Joulian magnetostriction." Nature, vol. 521, May 2015, pp. 340-343, doi:10.1038/nature14459.

[2] C. Mudivarthi, M. Laver, J. Cullen, A. B. Flatau, and M. Wuttig, "Origin of magnetostriction in Fe-Ga." Journal of Applied Physics, vol. 107, May 2010, pp. 09A957, doi:10.1063/1.3359814.

[3] H. Y. Yasuda, M. Aoki, A. Takaoka, and Y. Umakoshi, "Pseudoelasticity in Fe_3Ga single crystals." Scripta Materialia, vol. 53, April 2005, pp. 253–257, doi:10.1016/j.scriptamat.2005.03.032.

[4] M. Li et al., "Anomalous temperature dependence of Young's modulus in $Fe_{73}Ga_{27}$ alloys." Journal of Alloys and Compounds, vol. 701, April 2017, pp. 768-773, https://doi.org/10.1016/j.jallcom.2017.01.175.

[5] I. S. Golovin and J. Cifre, "Structural mechanisms of anelasticity in Fe–Ga-based alloys." Journal of Alloys and Compounds, vol. 584, September 2014, pp. 322–326, http://dx.doi.org/10.1016/j.jallcom.2013.09.077.

[6] I. S. Golovin et al., "Comparative study of structure and phase transitions in Fe-(25–27)%Ga alloys." Journal of Alloys and Compounds, vol. 811, November 2019, pp. 152030, https://doi.org/10.1016/j.jallcom.2019.152030.

[7] O. Ikeda, R. Kainuma , I. Ohnuma, K. Fukamichi, and K. Ishida, "Phase equilibria and stability of ordered b.c.c. phases in the Fe-rich portion of the Fe–Ga system." Journal of Alloys and Compounds, vol. 347, December 2002, pp. 198-205, https://doi.org/10.1016/S0925-8388(02)00791-0.

[8] I. S. Golovin et al., "From metastable to stable structure: the way to construct functionality in Fe-27Ga alloy." Journal of Alloys and Compounds, vol. 751, June 2018, pp. 364-369, https://doi.org/10.1016/j.jallcom.2018.04.127.

[9] I. S. Golovin et al., "Phase transitions in Fe-27Ga alloys: guidance to develop functionality." Intermetallics, vol. 100, September 2018, pp. 20-26, https://doi.org/10.1016/j.intermet.2018.05.016.

[10] A. M. Balagurov, I. S. Golovin, I. A. Bobrikov, V. V. Palacheva, S. V. Sumnikov, and V. B. Zlokazov, "Comparative study of structural phase transitions in bulk and powdered Fe-27Ga alloy by real-time neutron thermodiffractometry." J. Appl. Crystallogr, vol. 50, February 2017, pp. 198-210, https://doi.org/10.1107/S1600576716020045.

[11] I. S. Golovin et al., "In situ studies of atomic ordering in Fe-19Ga type alloys." Intermetallics, vol. 105, February 2019, pp. 6-12, https://doi.org/10.1016/j.intermet.2018.10.029.

[12] I. S. Golovin, A. M. Balagurov, V. V. Palacheva, I. A. Bobrikov, and V. B. Zlokazov, "In situ neutron diffraction study of bulk phase transitions in Fe-27Ga alloys." Materials and Design, vol. 98, May 2016, pp. 113-119, https://doi.org/10.1016/j.matdes.2016.03.016.

[13] I. S. Golovin and A. M. Balagurov, Structure induced anelasticity in iron intermetallic compounds and alloys, Materials Research Forum LLC, USA, 2018.

[14] I. S. Golovin, V. V. Palacheva, J. Cifre, and C. Jiang, "Internal friction in Fe-Ga alloys at elevated temperatures." Journal of Alloys and Compounds, vol. 785, May 2019, pp. 1257-1263, https://doi.org/10.1016/j.jallcom.2019.01.265.

[15] A. M. Balagurov, N. Y. Samoylova, I. A. Bobrikov, S. V. Sumnikov, and I. S. Golovin, "The first and second-order isothermal phase transitions in Fe_3Ga-type functional intermetallic compounds." Acta Crystallographica Section B: Structural Science, Crystal Engineering and Materials, vol. 75, 2019, RA5070, in press.

[16] M. Avrami, "Kinetics of phase change. I General theory." Journal of Chemical Physics, vol. 7, 1939, pp. 1103-1112, doi:10.1063/1.1750380.

[17] O. Kubaschewski, Iron-binary phase diagrams, Springer-Verlag, Berlin, 1982.

[18] T. Gödecke and W. Köster, "Über den aufbau des systems Eisen-Gallium zwichen 10 und 50 at.% Ga und dessen abhängigkeit von der wärmebehandlung." Z. Metallkde, vol. 68, 1977, pp. 758-764.

[19] J. Bras, J.J. Couderc, M. Fagot, J. Ferre, "Transformation ordre-desordre dans la solution solide de fer-gallium." Acta Metallurgica, vol. 25, Sept. 1977, pp. 1077-1084, https://doi.org/10.1016/0001-6160(77)90137-7.

Temperature Instability of the Off-Diagonal Magnetoimpedance Sensors Based on Co-Rich Amorphous Microwires

Sergei Gudoshnikov, Vadim Tarasov, Vadim Mashera
National University of Science and Technology «MISiS»
Moscow, Russia
Email: gudosh@izmiran.ru, vptar@misis.ru, masherovvadim@mail.ru

Vladimir Odintsov, Boris Liubimov
Pushkov Institute of Terrestrial Magnetism, Ionosphere and Radio Wave Propagation, (IZMIRAN)
Troitsk, Moscow, Russia
Email: vodin@izmiran.ru, b.lubimoff@gmail.com

Yury Grebenshchikov
Financial University under the Government of the Russian Federation, (FU)
Moscow, Russia
Email: yugreb@izmiran.ru

Abstract **— Temperature instability of the off-diagonal magnetoimpedance sensor is discussed based on experiments accomplished with Co-rich amorphous ferromagnetic microwire. The glass-coated microwire produced by the Tailor-Ulitovsky method of $Co_{69}Fe_4Cr_4Si_{11}B_{12}$ composition with an internal core of 6.8 μm and a glass shell of 14.7 μm radius was tested. The magnetoimpedance sensor was a 5 mm long piece microwire with a small pick-up coil of 80 turns wounded around the microwire. The saturation magnetization, anisotropy field of the microwire and off-diagonal component of impedance at 4 MHz frequency were investigated in the temperature range of −20 to +80 °C. The measured data were used to determine the influence of these parameters on the temperature dependence of the pick-up coil elecro-motive force amplitude. It was found that the change of the offset drift near the zero magnetic field is ~ 0.125 (A/m)/°C and the coefficient of sensitivity is about +2.6%/ °C.**

Keywords — amorphous ferromagnetic microwires; magnetoimpedance; temperature stability.

I. INTRODUCTION

Recently, much attention has been paid to the study of the Giant Magneto-Impedance (GMI) effect in soft magnetic materials, which involves changes in the complex resistance of the ferromagnetic conductor *Z(H)*, when exposed to an external magnetic field *H*. The increased interest in the GMI effect is associated primarily with the possibility of creating on its basis inexpensive, miniature and highly sensitive magnetometers for various technical applications. Among the materials with the GMI effect, the best results were achieved in amorphous ferromagnetic microwires in a glass-coated microwire produced by the Tailor-Ulitovsky [1] method.

The best microwires are characterized by an ideal cylindrical shape, a small number of defects per unit length, a uniform distribution of magnetization and very small values of the magnetic anisotropy field (~ 100 A/m and less). In cobalt-rich microwires with a total radius of 5-15 micrometers, high values of the GMI ratio ($\Delta Z/Z$ ~ 600% [2]) have been obtained. Laboratory models of GMI magnetometers with an equivalent magnetic field noise level less than 10 $pT/Hz^{1/2}$ in the low frequency range from 0 to 1 kHz have been developed on the basis of such microwires [3][4]. One of the problems of such magnetometers is their strong temperature instability. Studies conducted by [5] have shown that the temperature instability of such magnetometers can be up to 100 nT per °C or more. To explain such a high temperature instability, a simplified model of the off-diagonal GMI effect is proposed in this work, and the results of the temperature studies of the GMI-sensor are presented.

The rest of the paper is structured as follows. Section II presents the description of the GMI sensor, research equipment and measurement methods. Section III describes the behavior of the GMI sensor in a temperature range of 20 °C to +80 °C, and a simplified model of the microwire's off-diagonal GMI effect. The results of modeling are compared with experimental data. Conclusions are given in Section IV.

II. MATERIALS AND METHODS

Measurements were carried out on a GMI sensor, in which 5 mm segment of the glass-coated microwire, radius of a ferromagnetic core r_0 of about 6.8 μm, total radius 14.7 μm and the composition of $Co_{69}Fe_4Cr_4Si_{11}B_{12}$ was used as a sensitive element [6]. To register the signals proportional to the off-diagonal impedance component $Z_{\varphi z}(f,H)$, a pick-up coil with radius 0.25 mm, containing N = 80 turns of copper wire with a diameter of 40 μm was wounded onto the microwire.

For the off-diagonal operation, the microwire was excited by sinusoidal current I_{ac} with a frequency of f = 4 MHz and amplitude of 1.0 mA. In addition, a small direct bias current I_{dc}. = 2.0 mA was applied to the microwire. The scheme of excitation and registration of the GMI sensor signal is shown in Figure 1. The Electro-Motive Force (EMF) pick-up coil signal was amplified and then detected by a lock-in detector with 4 MHz reference signal. During GMI measurements, the GMI-sensor was placed within a solenoid powered by a linearly varying low-frequency current. The solenoid could generate the axial magnetic field of amplitude ± 1000 A/m. The temperature dependences of the off-diagonal GMI response versus the applied magnetic field and the offset drift were measured.

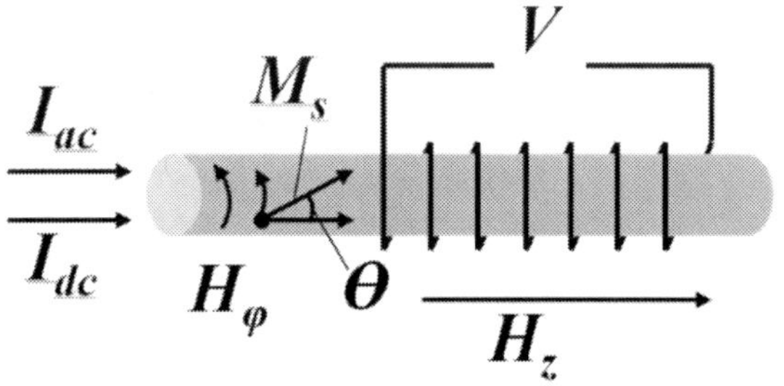

Figure 1. The scheme of excitation and registration of the GMI sensor signal.

At temperature measurements, the GMI sensor was placed inside the temperature chamber providing temperature in the range of -20 °C to +80 °C. To protect against external magnetic field, a magnetic shield with a shielding coefficient K ~ 1000 was used. The residual magnetic field in the magnetic shield did not exceed 50 nT.

Magnetic hysteresis loops of the microwires were measured using a conventional Quantum Design Physical Property Measurement System (PPMS) at the temperature range of -20 °C to +80 °C.

III. Results and Discussions

A. *The temperature off-diagonal response of the GMI sensor*

Figure 2 shows the amplitude of 4 MHz EMF signals, induced in the pick-up coil, versus the longitudinally applied magnetic field H_z at different temperatures -20 °C, 20 °C and 80 °C. These curves correspond to the off-diagonal responses of the GMI sensor.

The inset in Figure 2 shows the behavior of the output voltage (in arbitrary units – a.u.) of the GMI sensor for two values of applied magnetic fields (0 A/m - circles, 13 A/m - squares) depending on the heating temperature. The output voltage grew monotonically with increasing temperature. The sensitivity $\Delta U/\Delta H$ for the low magnetic field region at -20 °C is 0.012 a.u./A/m and 0.032 a.u./A/m at 80 °C. This represents an increase of 260 % and corresponds to a temperature coefficient of sensitivity of +2.6%/ °C. The EMF offset (the top curve on the inset in Figure 2) varies from 0.06 a.u. at -20 °C to 0.156 a.u. at +80 °C. The difference corresponds to a change of 12.5 % of the full voltage scale at -20 °C. This change corresponds to a temperature coefficient of the offset drift of 0.125 A/m / °C (157 nT/°C).

B. *Low frequency model of the off-diagonal sensor*

To interpret the temperature behavior of the GMI sensor, we used a simplified model for the case of microwire excitation by Alternating Current (AC) I_{ac} with a relatively low frequency, when the skin depth is more than the microwire radius. In addition, it is assumed that at each point of the microwire, a magnetization reaches its limit value M_s and can change only in direction.

Under the above conditions, in the external longitudinal field H_z and circumferential field H_φ, the direction of the magnetization vector M_s at each microwire's point corresponds to the minimum energy and is determined by the equality:

$$h_1(\alpha,h)=\pm\frac{h-\alpha}{\alpha}\sqrt{1-\alpha^2}, \qquad (1)$$

where: $h_1=H_\varphi/H_a$; $h=H_z/H_a$ are dimensionless circumferential and longitudinal applied magnetic fields normalized on the anisotropy field of H_a, and $\alpha = M_z/M_s$ is a dimensionless component of the longitudinal microwire magnetization of M_z normalized to the saturation magnetization of M_s ($\alpha=\cos\theta$, Figure 1). The two signs in (1) correspond to different directions of azimuthal magnetization ($\sin\theta$). The equilibrium curves $h_1(\alpha)$ of equality (1) for three fixed values of h (04, 1.0, 1.6) are shown in Figure 3. A complete set of curves, similar to those shown in Figure 3, allows to determine the evolution of the microwire magnetization average value under the influence of circular and longitudinal magnetic fields.

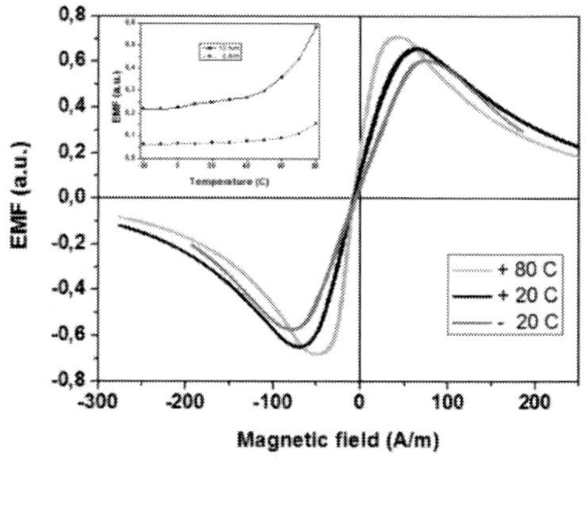

Figure 2. Experimental dependences of the off-diagonal EMF signals versus magnetic field at different temperatures. Inset shows the EMF signals for zero (circles) and applied magnetic fields 13 A/m (squares).

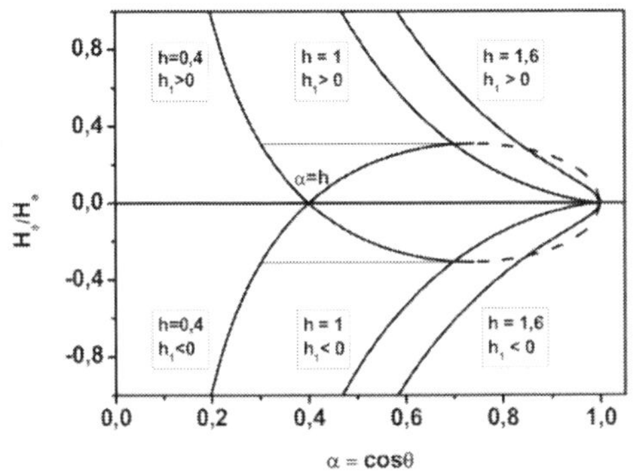

Figure 3. The equilibrium curves $h_1(\alpha)$ of equality (1) for three fixed values of h (0.4, 1.0, 1.6)

If AC current I_{ac} flows through the microwire, the azimuthal field H_φ generated by it will cause a periodic change in the average longitudinal magnetization M_z and create an alternating magnetic flux in the pick-up coil [7]: $\Phi = \pi r_0 \mu_0 M_s \bar{\alpha}$. Here, $\bar{\alpha}$ is the average magnetization across the microwire section, which is associated with external fields and its value on the microwire surface α_s by the expression:

$$\bar{\alpha} = \begin{cases} \frac{2}{h_1^2}\left(-h - \frac{h^3}{6} + \frac{h}{2}\alpha_s^{\ 2} - \frac{\alpha_s^{\ 3}}{3} - h\ln\left(\frac{h}{\alpha_s}\right) + \frac{h^2}{\alpha_s}\right), & h \le 1 \\ \frac{2}{h_1^2}\left(-h^2 - \frac{h}{2} + \frac{1}{3} + \frac{h}{2}\alpha_s^{\ 2} - \frac{\alpha_s^{\ 3}}{3} - h\ln\left(\frac{h}{\alpha_s}\right) + \frac{h^2}{\alpha_s}\right), & h > 1 \end{cases} \quad (2)$$

The magnitude of the EMF pick-up coil is proportional to the time derivative of the magnetic flux Φ and is determined by the expression:

$$EMF(t) = -\pi\mu_0 M_s r_o^2 N \frac{\partial(\bar{\alpha})}{\partial t} \quad (3)$$

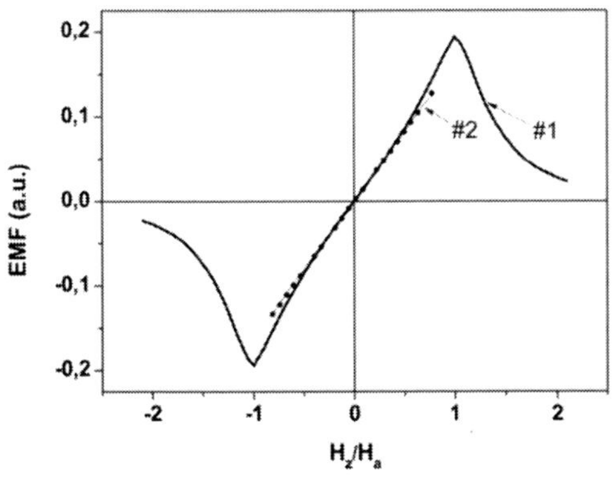

Figure 4. Calculated dependences of the EMF pick-up coil from the dimensionless longitudinal field using expressions (3) - #1 and (4) - #2.

The EMF response can be expanded in Fourier series in multiple frequencies f, $2f$, $3f$, … As an example, the EMF calculation result at the frequency f is shown in Figure 4, black line #1.

On the basis of the proposed model, it can be shown that the dependence of the EMF pick-up coil amplitude in the field region of $-H_a < H_z < +H_a$ (Figure 4) is approximately described by the following expression:

$$EMF \approx -\frac{M_s}{H_a}\frac{H_z}{H_a} N r_0 \frac{dI_{ac}}{dt} \quad (4)$$

This dependence is shown in Figure 4 as a short dotted line #2. The expression in (4) contains only two parameters that depend on temperature. These are the saturation magnetization M_s and the anisotropy field H_a.

C. *Temperature effect estimation*

To simulate the temperature behavior of the GMI sensor, we measured the temperature dependences of relative saturation magnetization, $M_s/M_{s40}(T)$, and anisotropy field, $H_a(T)$. The results of these measurements are shown in Figure 5.

The temperature dependence of relative magnetization with an applied magnetic field of 10^4 A/m is presented in Figure 5 by square symbols (left axis). The data were normalized on the saturation magnetization measured at temperature -40 °C. Under heating treatment, the relative magnetization decreases slowly with increasing temperature from -20 °C to 100 °C. It varies between 0.96 at -20 °C and 0.82 at +100 °C, which is a decrease of 14%. This percentage corresponds to a temperature coefficient of 0.12%/°C.

The temperature dependence of the anisotropy field is presented in Figure 5 by circle symbols (right axis). The value of the anisotropy field for each temperature was determined as the value of the field corresponding to the maximum of the off-diagonal response (Figure 2). Under heating treatment, the anisotropy field decreases with increasing temperature from -20 °C to 80 °C. It varies between 75 A/m at -20 °C and 40 A/m at +80 °C., which is a decrease of 53%. This percentage corresponds to a temperature coefficient of 0.53%/°C.

Using the experimental data in Figure 5, we estimated the ratio of the coefficient M_s/H_a^2 from expression (4) for temperature values -20 °C and +80 °C. This ratio is of order of 5.3/1.7 ~ 3.1. The same ratio for the sensitivity $\Delta U/\Delta H$, obtained from the experiment (part III.A.), gives value 0.156/0.06 = 2.6. The obtained agreement between the experimental and model data indicates the possibility of using the proposed approach for the analysis of the temperature properties of microwires.

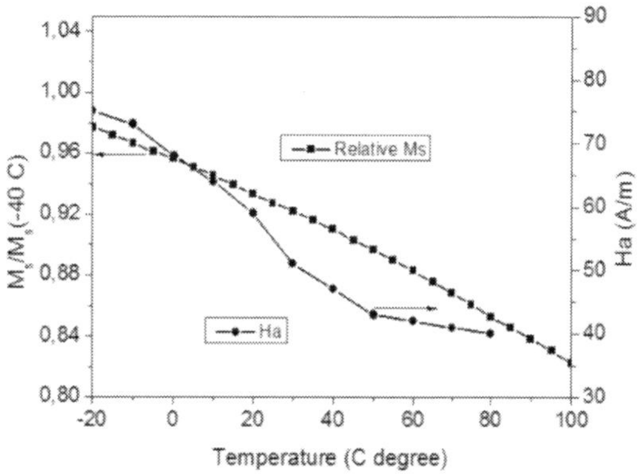

Figure 5. Temperature dependences of the relative saturation magnetization (squares) and anisotrpy field (circles).

IV. CONCLUSION

In conclusion, we have studied the problem of temperature stability of off-diagonal GMI sensors based on $Co_{69}Fe_4Cr_4Si_{11}B_{12}$ glass coated microwires. In the temperature range of −20 to +80 °C, the investigated microwires were characterized by high offset drift 0.125 (A/m)/°C and large temperature sensitivity +2.6%/ °C. The obtained temperature dependences off-diagonal response are satisfactorily explained in the framework of a simple model. The proposed model shows that the main sources of temperature instability of the GMI sensor are the temperature dependences of the saturation magnetization and anisotropy field of the microwire. The improvement of these parameters will increase the temperature stability of the GMI sensor. It is known that thermal treatment of microwires significantly affect the temperature behavior of GMI [8][9]. The data obtained show that the heat treatment should be carefully selected, according to the effect on the anisotropy field, to ensure the thermal stability of the microwires.

ACKNOWLEDGMENT

This work was supported in the frame of the program of the Ministry of Education and Science of the Russian Federation "Organization of scientific research" (Assignment # 3.7477.2017/BY).

REFERENCES

[1] V. Larin et al, "Preparation and properties of glass coated microwires," J. Magn. Magn. Mater., vol 249, N1-2, pp. 39-45, 2002.

[2] V. Zhukova et al, "Optimization of giant magnetoimpedance in Co-rich amorphous microwires," IEEE trans. magn., vol. 38, N5, pp. 3090-3094, 2002.

[3] T. Uchiyama, S. Nakayama, K. Mohri, and K. Bushida, "Biomagnetic field detection using very high sensitivity magnetoimpedance sensors for medical applications," Phys. Status Solidi A, vol. 206, N4, pp. 639-643, 2009.

[4] S. Gudoshnikov et al, "Highly sensitive magnetometer based on the off-diagonal GMI effect in Co-rich glass-coated microwire," Phys. Status Solidi, vol. 211, N5, pp. 980-985, 2014.

[5] J. Nabias, A. Asfour, and J-P. Yonne, "Temperature Dependence of Giant Magnetoimpedance in Amorphous Microwires for Sensor Application," IEEE trans. magn., vol. 53, N4, pp. 4001005-4001005 (5), 2017.

[6] A. Popova et al, "Influence of technological parameters on magnetic properties of Co-rich amorphous ferromagnetic microwires," KnE Materials Science, vol. 2018, pp. 323–331, 2018.

[7] S. Gudoshnikov et al, "The model of the off-diagonal magnetoimpedance sensor with a moderate frequency of an excitation signal," J. Magn. Magn. Mater., in press.

[8] M. Malatek, P.Ripka, and L. Kraus, "Temperature offset drift of GMI sensors," Sens. Actuators A, Phys., vol. 147, pp. 415-418, 2008.

[9] A. Dzhumazoda et al, "Temperature stable magnetoimpedance (MI) of current annealed Co-based amorphous microwires," J. Magn. Magn. Mater., vol 474, pp. 374-380, 2019.

Novel Sensing Technique for Non-destructive Composites Monitoring

Paula Corte-León, Valentina Zhukova, Mihail Ipatov,
Department Materials Physics, Univ. Basque Country, UPV/EHU, 20018 San Sebastian, Spain
e-mail: paula.corte@ehu.eus, valentina.zhukova@ehu.es, mihail.ipatov@ehu.eus

Juan Maria Blanco,
Department Applied Physics I, Univ. Basque Country, EIG, UPV/EHU, 20018, San Sebastian, Spain
e-mail: juanmaria.blanco@ehu.es

Alexandra Allue, Koldo Gondra
Gaiker Technological Centre, 48170, Zamudio, Spain
e-mail: allue@gaiker.es, gondra@gaiker.es

Arcady Zhukov
Dept Materials Physics, Univ. Basque Country, UPV/EHU, 20018 San Sebastian and Ikerbasque, Bilbao Spain
e-mail: arkadi.joukov@ehu.es

Abstract— **In this paper, we observed the evolution of the transmission and reflection parameters of composites containing magnetic microwire inclusions during the composites matrix polymerization. A remarkable change of the reflection and transmission in the range of 4-7 GHz upon the matrix polymerization is observed. The observed dependencies are discussed considering variation of temperature and stresses during the thermoset matrix polymerization and their influence on magnetic properties of glass-coated microwires. The obtained results are considered as a base for a novel sensing technique allowing non-destructive and non-contact monitoring of the composites utilizing ferromagnetic glass-coated microwire inclusions with magnetic properties sensitive to tensile stress and temperature.**

Keywords- giant magnetoimpedance effect; magnetic microwires; magnetic softness; polymerization; composites.

I. INTRODUCTION

Amorphous magnetic materials can present an unusual combination of excellent magnetic properties (e.g., high magnetic permeability, Giant MagnetoImpedance (GMI), effect, magnetic bistability, Matteucci and Widemann effects) and superior mechanical properties (plasticity, flexibility) making them suitable for numerous industrial applications [1]-[6]. The aforementioned soft magnetic properties are originated by the absence of the magnetocrystalline anisotropy and defects (dislocations, grain boundaries, etc.), typical for crystalline magnets [1]-[3][6]-[8]. Furthermore, the preparation method involving rapid melt quenching is quite fast and inexpensive and the above mentioned magnetic softness can be realized without any complex post-processing treatments [3]-[5].

The development of novel applications of amorphous materials requires new functionalities, i.e., reduced dimensions, enhanced corrosion resistance or biocompatibility [8]. Therefore, great attention has been paid to the development of alternative fabrication methods allowing the preparation of amorphous materials at micro-nano scale involving melt quenching [6]-[8].

Glass-coated microwires prepared using the Taylor-Ulitovsky method fit to most of aforementioned expectation: such magnetic microwires have micro-nanometric diameters (typically 0.5-50 μm) covered by thin, insulating, biocompatible and flexible glass-coating [7]-[11] and can present excellent magnetic softness or magnetic bistability [7][9][11]. These features of the glass-coated microwires allow development of new exciting applications in various magnetic sensors [12]-[16], as well as in smart composites with tunable magnetic permittivity [17]-[19]. One more advantage of the glass-coated microwires is excellent mechanical properties [5].

Recently, the stress dependence of hysteresis loops and GMI effect are proposed for the mechanical stresses monitoring in Fiber Reinforced Composites (FRC) containing microwires inclusions or using magnetoelastic sensors based on stress dependence of various magnetic properties [18][20][21]. One of the common problems in the composite materials is the monitoring of the matrix polymerization as well as stresses monitoring. Usually, the polymerization process monitoring is performed by different sensors, like the pressure transducers and dielectric sensors [22]. However, employed sensors require direct contact with the resin and of its electronic associated [22]. One of the proposed solutions for non-destructive FRC monitoring is the use of piezoelectric fibers with diameters of 10 to 100 μm [23]. However, this solution requires electrical field supply plates occupying a significant area.

One of the promising solutions addressing the problem of non-destructive FRC monitoring is a novel sensing technique involving free space microwave spectroscopy utilizing ferromagnetic microwire inclusions presenting the high frequency impedance quite sensitive to tensile stress and magnetic field [17][18][24]. Mentioned above glass-coated microwires, with metallic nucleus diameters of 0.5 - 50 μm, presenting excellent mechanical and corrosive properties fit perfectly the requirements of this technique making it suitable for remote stresses and temperature monitoring in FRCs [17][18][24].

In this work, we provide our recent results on the study of stresses arising during the polymerization of the matrix in

FRCs on permittivity of the FRC with embedded microwire inclusions.

Consequently, in this paper, we present new experimental results on direct monitoring of the polymerization process in the FRC preparation using embedded Co-based glass-coated microwires.

In Section II, we present the description of the experimental techniques, while in Section III we describe the results on in-situ observation of the effect of matrix polymerization on the transmission, T, reflection, R, parameters of microwire arrays measured using the free-space system and compare them with the effect of applied tensile stresses on hysteresis loops of the studied microwires. We conclude in Section IV.

II. Experimental Details

Glass-coated $Fe_{3.8}Co_{65.4}Ni_1B_{13.8}Si_{13}Mo_{1.35}C_{1.65}$ (metallic nucleus diameter, d=18.8 μm, total diameter, D=22.2 μm, ρ =d/D= 0.88) microwires with low negative magnetostriction coefficients, λ_s, have been prepared by Taylor-Ulitovsky technique described elsewhere [7][8][11][12]. As previously reported by us, as-prepared $Fe_{3.8}Co_{65.4}Ni_1B_{13.8}Si_{13}Mo_{1.35}C_{1.65}$ microwires present good magnetic softness, high GMI effect and low negative magnetostriction coefficients, λ_s, of about -$0.1x10^{-6}$ [25][26].

The temperature during the polymerization process has been measured by a standard thermocouple.

For the composite matrix, we used a vinylester resin (DERAKANE 8084 resin), accelerated with Cobalt Octoate (0,3 pph) and catalyzed with Methyl Ethyl Ketona (MEK 60%, 1,5 pph). DERAKANE 8084 epoxy vinyl ester resin is an elastomer modified resin designed to offer increased adhesive strength, superior resistance to abrasion and severe mechanical stress, while providing greater toughness and elongation. The liquid resin exhibit the following properties: the density at 25°C is of 1.02 g/mL, the dynamic viscosity at 25°C is of 360 MPa and the styrene content is of 40%. All technical resin information appears in its technical data sheet (Document 1820 V5 F2, Language ES "draft", © 2017 Ashland Inc.).

Consequently, we used the free space measurement system, previously described in details in [18][24]. In this method, the microwire inclusions embedded in the polymeric matrix play the role of "the elementary scatterers", when the electromagnetic microwave irradiates the composite. At sufficiently high frequencies (GHz range), both the microwire magnetic and conductive properties will contribute to the microwave dielectric properties of the composite materials filled with short conductive microwire inclusions which now depends not only on the matrix and the embedded wires conductivity, but also on an effective ac permeability [18]. Consequently, the external stimuli (magnetic field, applied stresses, etc.) will significantly modulate the initial dielectric properties of the composite matrix [18].

In our free-space measurement system we followed the near field measurement scheme [18] which includes broadband horn antennas and the Through Reflection Line (TRL) free-space calibration. The reflection (R) and transmission (T) coefficients were measured in free-space. The experimental set-up consists of a pair of broadband horn antennas (1-17 GHz) and a vector network analyzer. The composite was placed in a 20 x 20 cm^2 window to avoid the edge effects. This window limits the applicable frequency range in 4-17 GHz. More detailed description of the free space systems is given in our previous publications [18] [24].

The composites with ordered glass coated amorphous wires embedded in the thermoset matrix polymerization were prepared (see Figure 1).

The polymerizing matrix provides external stimuli for the microwire inclusions (see Figure 1), which affects the magnetic properties and the GMI effect of microwires.

Hysteresis loops of single microwires have been measured using the fluxmetric method previously described

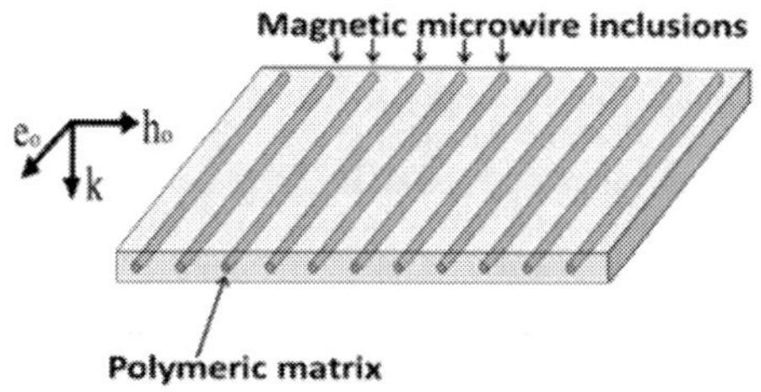

Figure 1. Sketch of a FRC with embedded microwires.

in details elsewhere [27]. In order to evaluate the influence of the external parameters (i.e., applied stress), similarly to that we recently described [22][28][29], we represent the hysteresis loops and normalized magnetization, M/M_0, versus magnetic field, H, where M is the magnetic moment at a given magnetic field and M_0 is the magnetic moment of the sample at the maximum magnetic field amplitude, H_m.

The stress has been applied during the annealing as well as during the sample cooling with the furnace.

Furthermore, the effect of applied stresses on hysteresis loops of individual microwires has been measured in order to compare with the effect of the matrix polymerization.

The value of applied stresses within the metallic nucleus has been evaluated as previously described [25]:

$$\sigma_m = \frac{K \cdot P}{K\,S_m + S_{gl}}, \quad (1)$$

where $k = E_2/E_1$, E_1 and E_2 are the Young's moduli at room temperature for the metallic alloy and the glass respectively, P is the applied mechanical load (up to 20 g), and S_m and S_{gl} are the cross sections of the metallic nucleus and the glass coating respectively. The value of the applied stresses evaluated using (1) was up to 472 MPa.

The Differential Scanning Calorimetry (DSC) measurements were performed using DSC 204 F1 Netzsch calorimeter in Ar atmosphere at a heating rate of 10 K/min up to temperature, T, of 900 °C.

However, the internal stresses, σ_i, arise during simultaneous rapid quenching of metallic nucleus surrounding by the glass coating due to the different thermal expansion coefficients. Consequently, the internal stresses magnitude can be controlled by the glass-coating thickness: the strength of internal stresses increases with the increasing of the glass-coating thickness [28]-[30][35].

III. EXPERIMENTAL RESULTS AND DISCUSSION

During the polymerization process of the resin, volume shrinkage of about 8.2 % occurs and solid cured resin is obtained. The mechanical properties of the cured resin are the following: tensile strength of 76 MPa, tensile modulus of 2,9 GPa, and tensile elongation of 8-10%. However, additionally to the matrix shrinkage a considerable heating takes place.

Therefore, in order to understand the processes during the polymerization of the composite that can affect the microwires, we have measured the evolution of temperature using a thermocouple. The obtained temperature changes during the polymerization represented at temperature, T, versus time, t, are shown in Figure 2. As can be observed from the Figure 2, the matrix polymerization produces a heating of the composite up to 80 °C.

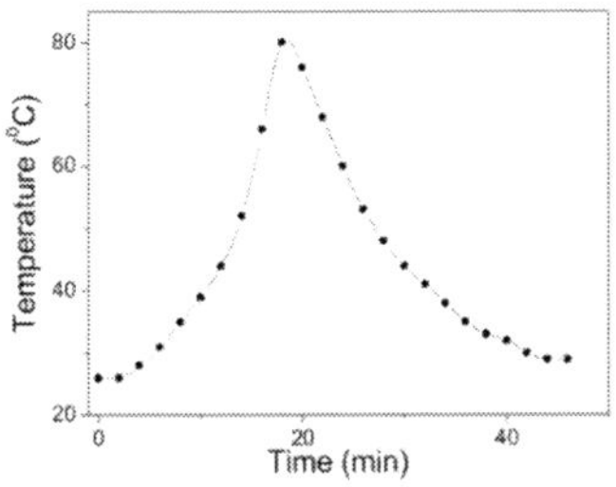

Figure 2. Evolution of temperature upon the polymerization.

In order to ensure that the employed microwires maintain their amorphous structure we performed the DSC studies of the crystallization temperature in order to evaluate the crystallization temperature. As can be observed from Figure 3 the crystallization temperature, T_{cr}, (determined as the beginning of the first crystallization peak) is about 554 °C (see Figure 3). Therefore, all the changes observed in the experiments must be attributed to the magnetoelastic behavior of the employed microwires only.

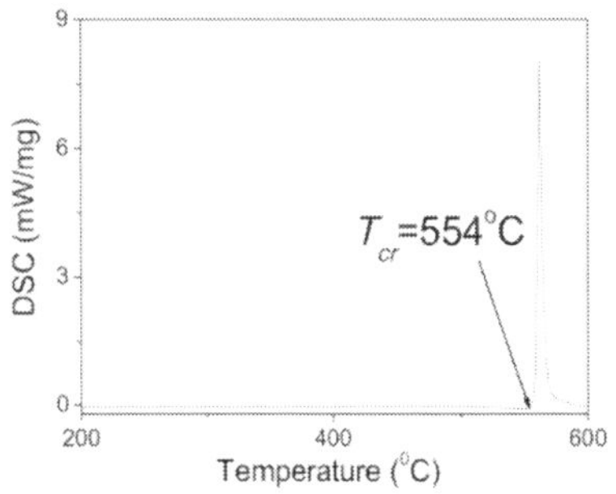

Figure 3. DSC curves of as-prepared $Fe_{3.8}Co_{65.4}Ni_1B_{13.8}Si_{13}Mo_{1.35}C_{1.65}$ microwires.

As described above, we performed in-situ experiments of composites placed inside the anechoic chamber with the glass-coated microwires embedded in a polymerized composite. We measured the transmission, T, and reflection, R, parameters of the composite containing Co-rich microwires ($Fe_{3.8}Co_{65.4}Ni_1B_{13.8}Si_{13}Mo_{1.35}C_{1.65}$) using the free space system.

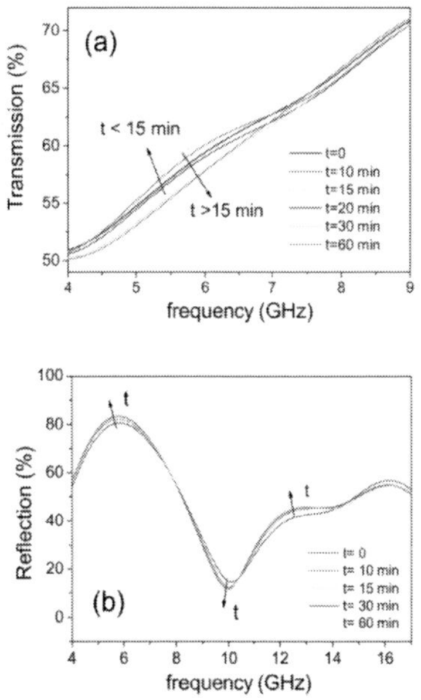

Figure 4. The Transmission, T (a) and reflection, R (a) parameters measured using the free-space system during the composite polymerization.

As can be appreciated from Figure 4, considerable variation of the T-parameter is observed in the range of frequency, f, of 4-7 GHz upon thermoset matrix polymerization (Figure 4). A non-monotonic variation of T-parameter upon polymerization is observed (Figure 4a). Additionally, some changes of R-parameter are also observed in a wide f- range (Figure 4b).

From experimentally measured T and R parameters, the absorption, A, parameter can be evaluated. Similarly to T

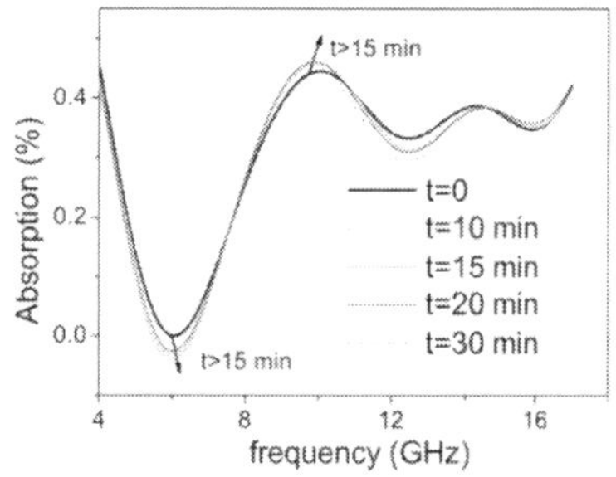

Figure 5. The Absorption, A, evaluated from data on T and R during the composite polymerization.

and *R* parameters, some changes in *A(f)* dependence during the polymerization are observed (see Figure 5).

The observed changes of the electromagnetic properties can be related to two main phenomena arising during the composite matrix polymerization: heating and mechanical stresses.

As we mentioned above, the polymerization is accompanied by a change of density, matrix shrinkage heating. Although generally, the distribution of the internal stresses arising at polymerization is non-homogeneous [30], an important fact is that the matrix shrinks as it cools. Therefore, we can assume that the matrix shrinkage produces compressive stresses in the magnetic nucleus of the glass-coated microwires.

The observed *T(f)* dependencies are non-monotonic: some increase of *T* observed up to *t*=15 min (at $f \approx 4$-7 GPa)

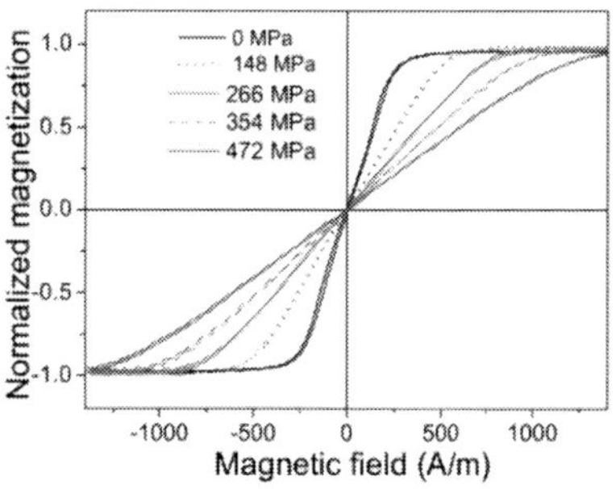

Figure 6. Effect of applied stress on hysteresis loops of as-prepared $Fe_{3.8}Co_{65.4}Ni_{1}B_{13.8}Si_{13}Mo_{1.35}C_{1.65}$ microwires.

followed by *T* decrease at *t*>15 min. Such evolution of *T*-parameter can therefore be associated with the heating and consequent cooling of the FRC.

However, the hysteresis loops of the studied samples are considerably affected by the applied tensile stresses, as shown in Figure 6.

To understand the effect of heating on the magnetic properties, we must consider the character of the internal mechanical stresses in the magnetic microwires. In fact, the main part of the mechanical stresses is originated by the difference in the thermal expansion coefficients of the metallic alloy and the glass-coating [31]-[34]. As shown elsewhere [35], the main part of the metallic nucleus of the microwire (up to $r \sim 0.85\ R$, where R is the metallic nucleus radius, r- metallic nucleus radius), has tensile stresses. Therefore, the difference in the thermal expansion coefficients of the metallic alloy and the glass-coating upon heating becomes smaller, allowing the reduction of the internal stresses. This assumption has recently been confirmed by direct observation of the heating effect on hysteresis loop of Co-rich microwires with vanishing magnetostriction coefficient [35]. The transformation of the hysteresis loop from linear to rectangular upon heating was explained by the easy anisotropy direction change from circumferential to axial upon heating.

In contrast to the temperature that non-monotonously changes during the polymerization, we assume that the compressive stresses, due to the matrix shrinkage, change monotonously. Therefore, we assume that the changes observed in Figures 5 and 6 are originated by both heating and matrix shrinkage during the polymerization.

Eventually, the same technique can be used for the remote monitoring of stress or temperature, not only during the polymerization, but also for real time non-destructive monitoring of local stresses and temperature during the exploitation of the composites.

IV. CONCLUSIONS

In this work, we propose a novel sensing technique for non-destructive and non-contact monitoring of the composites utilizing ferromagnetic glass-coated microwire inclusions with magnetic properties sensitive to tensile stress and temperature. To demonstrate it, we have studied in-situ the impact of the matrix polymerization on the evolution of the transmission and reflection parameters of the composites with microwire inclusions.

We observed a considerable variation of the *T*-parameter (in the range of 4-7 GHz) and *R*-parameter upon the composite polymerization using the free space technique. The observed dependencies are discussed considering the matrix shrinkage during the polymerization and heating during the matrix polymerization and their influence on the magnetic properties of the glass-coated microwires.

The obtained experimental results yield new and important insights suitable for the development of a novel sensing technique for non-destructive and non-contact monitoring of the FRCs utilizing ferromagnetic glass-coated microwire inclusions.

Consequently, a novel sensing technique for non-destructive and non-contact monitoring of the composites utilizing ferromagnetic glass-coated microwire inclusions with quite soft magnetic properties and tunable magnetic permittivity sensitive to tensile stress and temperature is proposed.

ACKNOWLEDGMENT

This work was supported by Spanish MCIU under PGC2018-099530-B-C31 (MCIU/AEI/FEDER, UE) and by the Government of the Basque Country under PIBA 2018-44 and Elkartek (RTM 4.0) projects. The authors thank for technical and human support provided by SGIker of UPV/EHU (Medidas Magnéticas Gipuzkoa) and European funding (ERDF and ESF).

REFERENCES

[1] J. Durand, "Magnetic Properties of Metallic Glasses" in Topics in Applied Physics, vol. 53, 1983, Glassy Metals II. Atomic Structure and Dynamics, Electronic Structure, Magnetic Properties, Editors: H. Beck and H. -J. Güntherodt, Springer-Verlag, Berlin, Heidelberg, New York, Tokyo.

[2] G. Herzer, "Amorphous and Nanocrystalline Materials", in: Encyclopedia of Materials: Science and Technology, pp. 149–157, Elsevier Science Ltd., 2001, ISBN: 0-08-0431526.

[3] A. P. Zhukov, "The remagnetization process of bistable amorphous alloys", Mater. Des., vol. 5, pp. 299-305, 1993.

[4] M. Hagiwara, A. Inoue, and T. Masumoto, "Mechanical properties of Fe–Si–B amorphous wires produced by in-rotating-water spinning method", Metall. Trans. A, vol. 13, pp. 373-382, 1982.

[5] T. Goto, M. Nagano, and N. Wehara, "Mechanical properties of amorphous $Fe_{80}P_{16}C_3B_1$ filament produced by glass-coated melt spinning", Trans. JIM, vol. 18, pp. 759-764, 1997.

[6] D. C. Jiles, "Recent advances and future directions in magnetic materials", *Acta Mater.*, vol. 51, pp. 5907-5939, 2003.

[7] A. Zhukov, M. Ipatov and V. Zhukova, "Advances in Giant Magnetoimpedance of Materials", in Handbook of Magnetic Materials, ed. K. H. J. Buschow, vol. 24, ch. 2, 2015, pp. 139-236.

[8] High Performance Soft Magnetic Materials (ed. A. Zhukov), Springer Series in Materials Science, vol. 252, Springer International Publishing, 2017, p. 216, ISBN: 0933-033X, DOI: 10.1007/978-3-319-49707-5.

[9] H. Chiriac, S. Corodeanu, M. Lostun, G. Ababei, and T. A. Óvári, "Rapidly solidified amorphous nanowires", J. Appl. Phys., vol. 107, 09A301, 2010.

[10] D. Kozejova et al., "Biomedical applications of glass-coated microwires", J. Magn. Magn. Mater., vol. 470, pp. 2-5, 2019.

[11] A. Talaat et al., "Ferromagnetic glass-coated microwires with good heating properties for magnetic hyperthermia", Sci. Rep., vol. 6, p. 39300, 2016.

[12] A. Zhukov et al., "Trends in optimization of giant magnetoimpedance effect in amorphous and nanocrystalline materials", J. Alloys Compd., vol. 727, pp. 887-901, 2017.

[13] A. F. Cobeño, A. Zhukov, J. M. Blanco, V. Larin, and J. Gonzalez, "Magnetoelastic sensor based on GMI of amorphous microwire", Sens. Actuat. A-Phys., vol. 91, pp. 95-98, 2001.

[14] A. Zhukov et al., "Magnetoelastic sensor of level of the liquid based on magnetoelastic properties of Co-rich microwires", Sens. Actuat. A-Phys., vol. 81/1-3, pp. 129-133, 2000.

[15] D. Makhnovskiy, N. Fry, and A. Zhukov, "On different tag reader architectures for bistable microwires", Sens. Actuat. A-Phys., vol. 166, pp. 133-140, 2011.

[16] D. Praslička et al., "Possibilities of measuring stress and health monitoring in materials using contact-less sensor based on magnetic microwires", IEEE Trans. Magn., vol. 49(1), pp. 128-131, 2013.

[17] F. X. Qin et al., "Effects of wire properties on the field-tunable behaviour of continuous-microwire composites", Sens. Actuat. A-Phys., vol. 178, pp. 118– 125, 2012.

[18] D. Makhnovskiy, A. Zhukov, V. Zhukova, and J. Gonzalez, "Tunable and self-sensing microwave composite materials incorporating ferromagnetic microwires", Adv. Sci. Tech., vol. 54, pp. 201-210, 2008.

[19]. F Qin and H. X. Peng, Ferromagnetic microwires enabled multifunctional composite materials, Prog. Mater. Sci., vol. 58 (2), pp. 183-259, 2013.

[20] M. Churyukanova et al., "Non-contact method for stress monitoring based on stress dependence of magnetic properties of Fe-based microwires", J. Alloys Compd., vol. 748(5), pp. 199-205, 2018.

[21] J. Olivera et al., "An embedded stress sensor for concrete SHM based on amorphous ferromagnetic microwires", Sensors, vol. 14, pp. 19963-19978, 2014.

[22] A. Allue et al., "Smart composites with embedded magnetic microwire inclusions allowing non-contact stresses and temperature monitoring", Compos. Pt. A: Appl. Sci. Manuf., vol. 120, pp. 12-20, 2019.

[23] L. J. Nelson, "Smart piezoelectric fibre composites", Mat. Sci. and Tech., vol. 18, pp. 1245-1256, 2002.

[24] L. Panina, M. Ipatov, V. Zhukova, J. Gonzalez, and A. Zhukov, "Tuneable composites containing magnetic microwires", ch. 22, pp. 431-460, DOI: 10.5772/21423 in Book: Metal, ceramic and polymeric composites for various uses, Ed. J. Cuppoletti, 2011, DOI: 10.5772/1428, ISBN: 978-953-307-353-8, (ISBN 978-953-307-1098-3) InTech - Open Access Publisher (www.intechweb.org), Janeza Trdine, 9, 51000 Rijeka, Croatia.

[25] V. Zhukova et al.,"Tailoring of magnetoimpedance effect and magnetic softness of Fe-rich glass-coated microwires by stress-annealing", Sci. Rep., vol. 8, p. 3202, 2018.

[26] A. Zhukov et al., "Magnetostriction of Co-Fe-based amorphous soft magnetic microwires", J. Electr. Mater., vol. 45(1), pp. 226-234, 2016.

[27] A. Zhukov, M. Vázquez, J. Velázqez, A. Hernando, and V. Larin, "Magnetic properties of Fe-based glass-coated microwires", J. Magn. Magn. Mater., vol. 170, pp. 323-330, 1997.

[28] A. Zhukov, A. Talaat, M. Ipatov, J. M. Blanco, and V. Zhukova, "Tailoring of magnetic properties and GMI effect of Co-rich amorphous microwires by heat treatment", J. Alloys Compd., vol. 615, pp. 610–615, 2014.

[29]. A. Zhukov et al., "Manipulation of magnetic properties of glass-coated microwires by annealing", J. Magn. Magn. Mater., vol. 383, pp. 232–236, 2015.

[30] J. A. Nairn and P. Zoller, "Matrix solidification and the resulting residual thermal stresses in composites", J. Mater. Sci., vol. 20(1), pp. 355–367, 1985.

[31] A. S. Antonov, V. T. Borisov, O. V. Borisov, A. F. Prokoshin, and N. A. Usov, "Residual quenching stresses in glass-coated amorphous ferromagnetic microwires", J. Phys. D: Appl. Phys., vol. 33, pp. 1161-1168, 2000.

[32] H. Chiriac, T. A. Ovari, and Gh. Pop, "Internal stress distribution in glass-covered amorphous magnetic wires", Phys. Rev. B, vol. 42, p. 10105, 1995.

[33] A. Zhukov et al., "Ferromagnetic resonance and structure of Fe-based glass-coated microwires", J. Magn. Magn. Mater., vol. 203, pp. 238-240, 1999.

[34] S. A. Baranov, V. S. Larin, and A. V. Torcunov, "Technology, preparation and properties of the cast glass-coated magnetic microwires", Crystals, vol. 7, p. 136, 2017.

[35] H. Chiriac, T. A. Ovari and A. Zhukov, "Magnetoelastic anisotropy of amorphous microwires", J. Magn. Magn. Mater., vol. 254-255, pp. 469-471, 2003.

Cooperative Communication between Vehicles and Road Infrastructures through Visible Light

Manuela Vieira, Manuel Augusto Vieira, Paula Louro,
ADETC/ISEL/IPL,
R. Conselheiro Emídio Navarro, 1959-007
Lisboa, Portugal
CTS-UNINOVA
Quinta da Torre, Monte da Caparica, 2829-516,
Caparica, Portugal

e-mail: mv@isel.ipl.pt, mv@isel.pt, plouro@deetc.isel.pt

Pedro Vieira
ADETC/ISEL/IPL,
R. Conselheiro Emídio Navarro, 1959-007
Lisboa, Portugal
Instituto das Telecomunicações
Instituto Superior Técnico, 1049-001,
Lisboa, Portugal
e-mail: pvieira@isel.pt

***Abstract*—A vehicular communication system that combines illumination, signaling, communications, and positioning functions is presented. The bidirectional communication between the infrastructures (I) and the vehicles (V) is performed through Visible Light Communication using the street lamps, the traffic signals and the headlights to broadcast the information. Wavelength Division Multiplex photodetectors receive and decode the information. White polychromatic-LEDs (Light Emitting Diodes) are used for lighting and also to implement the decoding operation. This allows modulating separate data streams into four wavelengths which together multiplex to white light. A traffic scenario is proposed, along with the transmitter to receiver setup. The performance of a cooperative driving system (I2V2V2I2V) is evaluated. Streams of messages containing the physical address ID of the emitters are used, transmitting a codeword that is received and decoded by the receivers. As a proof of concept, a cooperative vehicular traffic scenario is presented and bidirectional communication established and tested. A traffic signal phasing in a light controlled crossroad is presented. The experimental results confirm that the cooperative vehicular architecture is a promising approach concerning communications between road infrastructures and cars, fulfilling data privacy.**

Keywords- Vehicular Communication; Light Fidelity; Visible Light Communication; white LEDs; SiC photodetectors; OOK modulation scheme; Traffic control.

I. INTRODUCTION

Visible Light Communication (VLC) holds special importance when compared to existing forms of wireless communications [1]. Only Light-Emitting Diodes (LED) lamps can be used for the transmission of visible light [2]. VLC seems to be appropriate for providing wireless data exchange for automotive applications in the context in which the LED lighting began to be widespread in transportation, being integrated in traffic infrastructures (street lighting and traffic signals) and in the vehicle lighting systems. Compared to Radio Frequency based communications, VLC offers robustness against jamming attacks, a smaller interference domain, and a large license-free spectrum [3].

Vehicular Communication Systems are a type of network in which vehicles and roadside units are the communicating nodes, providing each other with information, such as safety warnings and traffic information [4][5]. Communication between fixed locations and vehicles (infrastructure-to-vehicle, I2V) between vehicles (vehicle-to-vehicle, V2V), and between vehicles and fixed locations (vehicle-to-infrastructure, V2I) is essential to transfer information in real time. The I2V applications focus on utilizing the traffic related infrastructure, such as traffic lights or streetlights, to communicate useful information. Hence, VLC can be realized as a secondary application in LED arrays that are placed for lighting [6].

A problematic in vehicular VLC is the design of a proper sensor. In the past, we have developed a receiver based on amorphous SiC technology that enhances the transmission capacity of the optical communications in the visible range and allows reaching outdoor high speed communication. The core of the device is a tandem a-SiC:H/a-Si:H pin/pin light controlled filter. When different visible signals are encoded in the same transmission path [7], the device multiplexes the different optical channels, performs different filtering processes (amplification, switching, and wavelength conversion) and decodes the encoded signals, recovering the transmitted information [8].

In this paper, a traffic scenario for a light controlled crossroad is proposed, along with the transmitter to receiver setup. The paper is organized as follows. After the introduction (Section I), in Section II, the performance of a cooperative driving system is analyzed. To achieve cooperative vehicular communications (I2V2V2I2V), in

Section III, streams of messages containing the physical address ID of the emitters are used, transmitting a codeword that is received and decoded by the SiC pin/pin devices. As a Proof of Concept (PoC), a traffic scenario with bidirectional cooperative communication between the infrastructures and the vehicles is presented and tested in Section IV. Finally, in Section V, conclusions are addressed.

The proposed vehicular communication system involves wireless communication, smart sensoring and optical sources network, building up a transdisciplinary approach framed in cyber-physical systems.

II. Vehicular Communication

A. Traffic Scenario

A I2V2V2I2V communication link in a light traffic controlled crossroad was simulated. The illustration of the proposed scenario is displayed in Figure 1a. Using the I2V communication, each street lamp (transmitter) sends a message, which is received and processed by a SiC receiver, located at the vehicle's rooftop. Using the headlights as transmitters, the information is resent to a leader vehicle (V2V) or a "request" message to go forward is sent directly to a crossroad receiver (V2I), at the traffic light, interconnected to a local manager that feeds one or more signal heads. For crossroad coordination, a local controller emitter, sends a "response" message to the vehicles approaching the intersection.

To build the vehicular I2V communication system, it is proposed a simplified cluster of unit square cells in an orthogonal topology that fill all the service area. We have assumed that the crossroad is located in the interception of line 2 with column 3 of the network, and the emitters at the nodes along the roadside. Two traffic flows are considered, one in the horizontal direction (W: West) with two vehicles approaching the crossroad (Vehicle 1) and the other (Vehicle 3) with a third vehicle (Vehicle 2) oncoming on the vertical direction (S: South). The lighting plan and generated joint footprints are illustrated in Figure 1b. The luminaries, placed at the nodes of the network, are based on commercially available white polychromatic LEDs made of Violet (V: 400 nm) and polychromatic Red, Green and Blue (RGB) LEDs. while the others provide constant current Only one chip of each LED is modulated for data transmission, the Red (R: 626 nm), the Green (G: 530 nm) or the Blue (B: 470 nm) while the others provided constant current for white illumination. Each transmitter, $X_{i,j}$, carries its own colour, X, (RGBV), as well as its horizontal and vertical ID position in the surrounding network (i,j) and sends a message that includes the synchronism, its physical ID and the traffic information. The geometric scenario used for calculation uses a smaller size square grid (2 cm), to improve its practicality. To receive the information from several transmitters, the receiver has to be positioned where the circles from each transmitter overlap, producing, at the receiver, a Multiplex (MUX) signal that, after demultiplexing, acts twofold as a positioning system and a data transmitter. The nine possible allowed overlaps (footprint regions) are pointed out in Figure 1b.

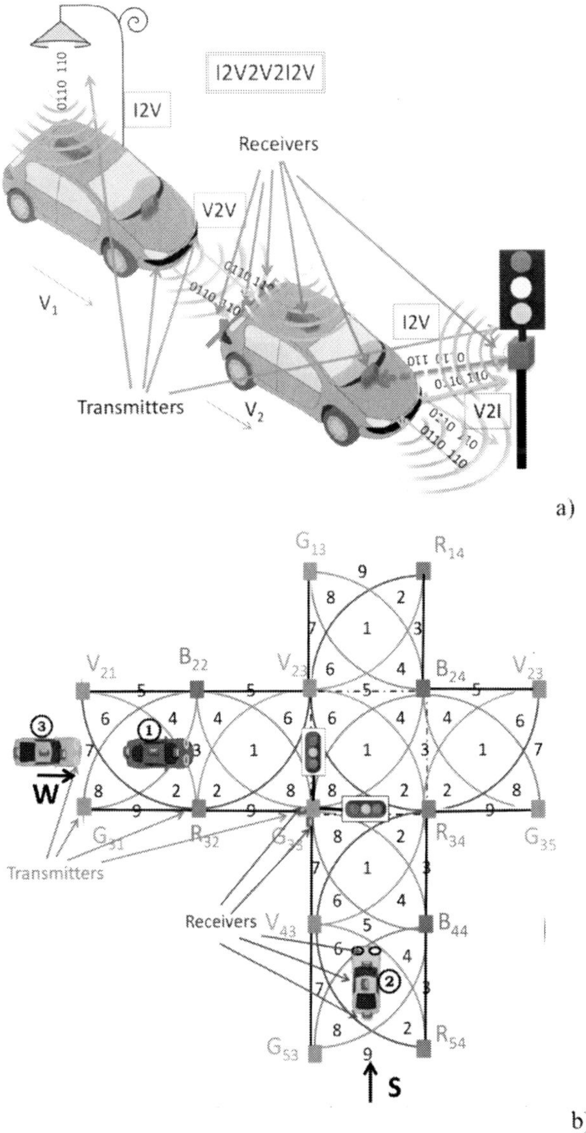

Figure 1. a) Traffic scenario. Illustration of the proposed vehicular I2V2V2I2V communication link. b) Lighting plan and generated joint footprints in a crossroad. Footprints: #1 (R+G+B+V); #2 (R+G+B); #3(R+B); #4 (R+ B+V), #5 (B+V) ; #6 (G+B+V); #7(G+V), #8 (R+G+V), #9 (R+G),

Each LED transmits its own data depending on the area it locates. The device receives different signals, identifies the footprint, finds its centroid and stores it as the reference point [9]. To build the V2V system between a leader vehicle and a follower, the follower sends the message that is received by the leader and can be retransmitted to the next car [10][11] or to the infrastructure. The leader vehicle infers the driving distance and the relative speed between both [12]. Therefore, each vehicle receives two different messages: one transmitted by the streetlight (I2V) and one coming from the follower vehicle (V2V), and a comparison can be performed.

For the manager's intersection crossing coordination, the connected vehicle and the intersection manager exchange information through two specific types of messages, "request" (V2I) and "response" (I2V). Two receivers are located at the same traffic light, facing the crossroads. When one head vehicle enters in the infrastructure´s capture range of one of the receivers, a request message is received and decoded by the corresponding receiver interconnected to the intersection manager (local controller of the traffic light). Each driver approaching the intersection area from S, W (or both) sends an approach "request". Those messages contain the assigned ID positions, speeds, and flow (W, S) direction of the vehicles. So, the "request" contains all the information that is necessary for a vehicle's space-time reservation for its intersection crossing. The intersection manager uses the "request" information to convert a it in a sequence of timed rectangular spaces that each vehicle needs to occupy in the intersection. Using a white LED, the intersection manager's acknowledgment is sent to an in-car application of the head vehicle. The response includes both the infrastructure and the vehicle identifications and the "confirmed vehicle" message. Once the response is received, the vehicle is required to follow the occupancy trajectories (footprint regions, see Figure 1b) provided by the intersection manager. If a "request" has any potential risk of collision, the control manager only sends back to the vehicle (V2I) the "response" after the risk of conflict disappears.

B. *Coding Techniques*

To encode the messages, an On-Off keying (OOK) modulation scheme was used. The OOK is considered suitable for applications in which the communication distance is more important than data rate. The advantages of OOK include its simplicity and ease of implementation. The codification of the optical signals is synchronized and includes the information related to the position ID of the transmitters and the message to broadcast. We have considered a 32 bits codification. Each frame is divided into three or four blocks, depending on the kind of transmitter: street lamps (Figure 2a) or traffic light (Figure 2b). We assigned the first block the synchronization (SYNC) in a [10101] pattern and the last one to the message to transmit (Payload Data). A stop bit is used at the end of each frame. In Figure 2a, an example of the codification used to drive the street lamps LEDs in the crossroad is illustrated. Here, the second block (6 bits) is assigned to ID-BIT [rrr;ccc] of the emitter, the first three bits give the ID binary code of the line and the next three the ID binary code of the column.

$R_{3,4}$, $G_{3,3}$, $B_{2,4}$ and V_{23} are the transmitted node packets, in a time slot, inside the crossroad. In Figure 2b, a response message of the traffic controller emitter located at the traffic light is displayed. The second block (INFO) in a pattern [000000] means that a response message is being sent by the controller manager. The third block (6 bits) identifies the vehicle position (ID) for which the message is intended. Here, the signal controller [000000] responds to a request of a vehicle located in the crossroad at position # 1 ($R_{3,4}$, $G_{3,3}$, $B_{2,4}$ and V_{23}).

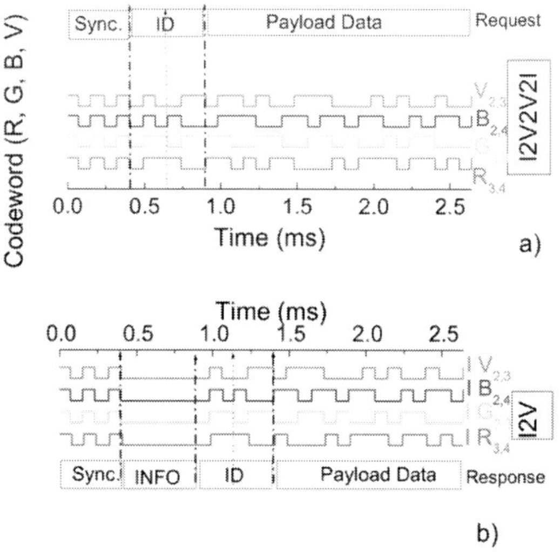

Figure 2. Frame structure representation. a) Codification used to drive the street lamps LEDs in the crossroad. $R_{3,4}$, $G_{3,3}$, $B_{2,4}$ and $V_{2,3}$ are the transmitted node packet, in a time slot, from the crossroad in the network. b) Encoded message response of the controller to a vehicle located in the crossroad (#1, $R_{3,4}$, $G_{3,3}$, $B_{2,4}$ and $V_{2,3}$).

C. *Signal Decoding, Positioning and Driving Distance*

In a stamp time, Figure 3a displays a MUX signal acquired by the a-SiC:H/a-Si:H pin/pin light controlled filter [8]. On top, the signals used to drive LEDs are shown to track the *on/off* states of each input. The bit sequence was chosen to allow all the *on/off* sixteen possible combinations of the four input channels. Results show that the MUX signal presents as many off separated levels as the *on/off* possible combinations of the input channels, allowing decoding the transmitted information [13]. All the sixteen ordered levels (d_0-d_{15}) are pointed out at the correspondent levels, and displayed as horizontal dotted lines. On the right-hand side of Figure 3, the match between MUX levels and the 4 bits binary code ascribed to each level is shown. Hence, the signal can be decoded by assigning each output level to a 4- digit binary code [X_R, X_G, X_B, X_V], with X=1 if the channel is *on* and X=0 if it is *off*.

In Figure 3b, the normalized MUX signals acquired by a receiver at the crossroad, in positions #1, #3 and #5 (see Figure 1b), are displayed. The MUX signal presented in Figure 3a was used for calibration purposes. On the right-hand side of the figure, the match between MUX levels and the 4 bits binary code ascribed to each level is shown. The decoded packet of transmitted information when all the four transmitters are received simultaneously (#1) is presented in the top of the figure. Comparing the calibrated levels (dotted lines in Figure 3a) with the different generation levels (dotted lines in Figure 3b), in the same time frame, a straightforward algorithm [10] was used to build a 1-to-32 demultiplexer function.

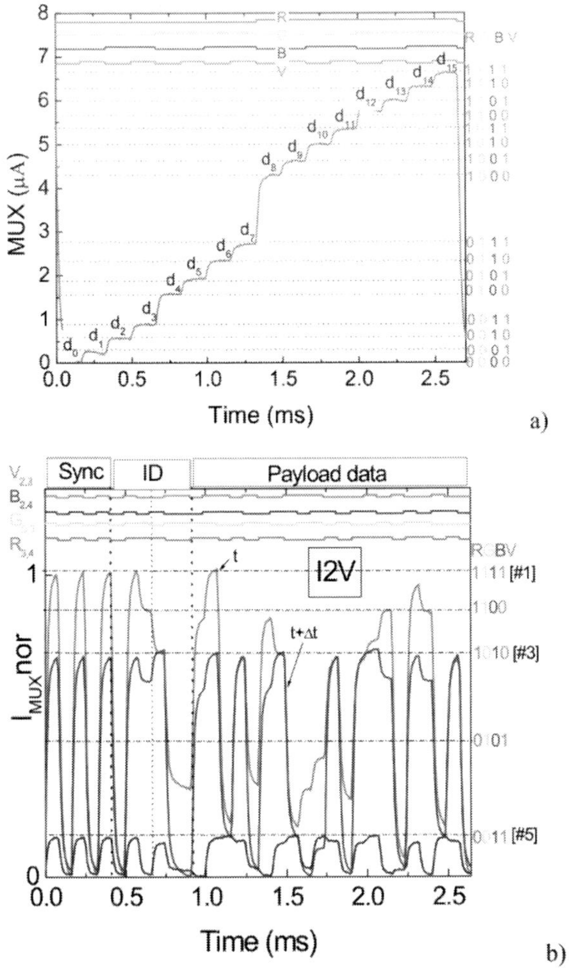

Figure 3. a) MUX signal of the calibrated cell. On the top the transmitted channels packets [R, G, B, V] are depicted. b) MUX/DEMUX signal inside the crossroad for a vehicle in positions #1, #3, #5, #7 and #9. On the top the transmitted channels packets [$R_{2,3}$, $G_{3,3}$, $B_{2,4}$, $V_{2,3}$] are decoded.

After decoding the MUX signals, the localization of the mobile target is direct. Taking into account the frame structure (Figure 2), the position of the receiver inside the navigation cell and its ID in the network is revealed. The position comes directly from the synchronism block, where all the received channels are, simultaneously, *on* or *off*. The 4-bit binary code ascribed to the higher level identifies the receiver position and is displayed in the right side of the Figure 3a. For instance, the level [1010] corresponds to the level d_{10} where the red and the blue channels are simultaneously *on*, so, position #3 is assigned to the receiver. Each decoded message carries, also, the transmitter's node address. So, the next block of six bits gives the ID of the received node. In #3, the location of the transmitters are $R_{3,4}$ and $B_{2,4}$ while in #1 the assigned transmitters are $R_{3,4}$, $G_{3,3}$ $B_{2,4}$ and $V_{2,3}$. The last block is a 20 bit word and is reserved for the transmission of the traffic message (payload data). The vehicle speed can be calculated by measuring the traveled distance overtime, using the ID's transmitters tracking. In order to obtain the receiver's speed, two measures are required: distance and elapsed time (assuming uniform motion). The distance is fixed while the elapsed time, Δt, will be obtained through the instants where the number of received channels changes. At the initial instant, t, the receiver moves West from #1 to #3 (Figure 3b). The decoded MUX message changes from four ($R_{3,4}$ $G_{3,3}$ $B_{24}V_{2,3}$) to two ($R_{3,4}$ $B_{2,4}$) transmitted channels at $t+\Delta t$. The spacing between reference points is fixed (Figure 1b) while the correspondent time integrated by the receiver varies and depends on the vehicle's speed crossing the crossroad. The receivers compute the geographical position in the successive instants (path) and infer the vehicle speed. In the following, this data will be transmitted to another leader vehicle through the V2V communication or to the control manager at the traffic light through V2I [14].

III. Bidirectional Communication

A. *Cooperative Communication*

In the proposed scenario, when a vehicle coming from W reaches position # 3 or one from S position #5 it sends a message to the controller requesting permission to cross the intersection (Figure 1b). If there is permission, it goes forward; otherwise, it stops at the respective stop lines (W # 7; S # 9). Three instants are considered, t_1, t_2 and t_3. At t_1 and t_2, Vehicle 1 and Vehicle 2 approach, respectively, the intersection and contact optically the intersection manager (controller) by sending a request message to the receiver (V2I) at the traffic light that faces the road. All the requests must contain the vehicle positions and the approach velocities. As a follower exists (Vehicle 3), the request message from Vehicle 1 includes its position and speed received previously by V2V. This information alerts the controller to a later request message (V2I), at t_3, confirmed later by the following vehicle. Therefore, three subsequent instants have to be predictable, t'_1, t'_2 and t'_3, as the correspondent access times of the Vehicles 1, 2 and 3 to the crossroad.

An example of messages exchange executed by the control manager is shown in Figure 4. Here, the MUX signal at each receiver and the assigned decoded messages (at the top of the figures) are displayed at the request times, t_1 and t_2 (Figure 4a) and at the response times, t'_1 and t'_2 (Figure 4b) for Vehicles 1 and 2, respectively.

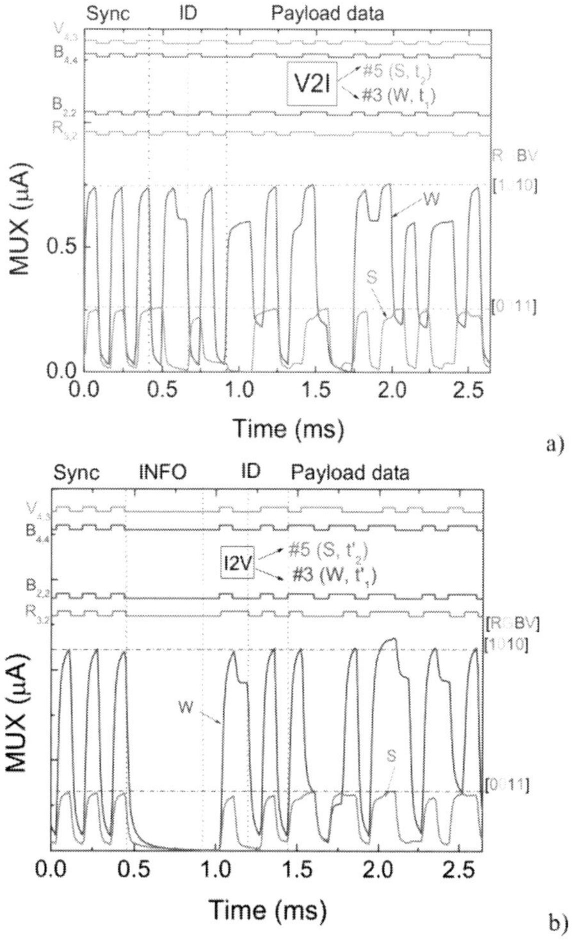

Figure 4. V2I2V MUX/DEMUX signals. On the top the transmitted channels packets [R, G, B, V] are decoded. a) Request message: V2I communication from Vehicles 1 and 2 and the infrastructure at t_1 and t_2. b) Response message: I2V communication between the control manager and the Vehicle 1 and Vehicle 2 at t'_1 and t'_2.

At the request times, the positions of both vehicles are identified: W #3 ($R_{3,2}$ and $B_{2,2}$) for Vehicle 1 and S #5 ($B_{4,4}$ and $V_{4,3}$) for Vehicle 2. At the access times, t'_1 and t'_2 (Figure 4b), the connected vehicles receive their own responses (ID: W #3 or S #5) from the control manager (INFO: 000000). At these times, each connected vehicle is required to follow the occupancy trajectories (footprint regions) provided by the intersection manager (payload data).

B. Traffic Signal Phasing

Signal phasing is the sequence of individual signal phases within a cycle that define the order in which pedestrians and vehicular movements are assigned the right-of-way. Safety requirements dictate that two vehicles consecutively accessing the intersection and belonging to the same flow must be separated by tailgate distance. If the two consecutive vehicles belong to different flows, they must be separated by vehicle stopping distance, which is larger than tailgate distance for practical values of the system parameters.

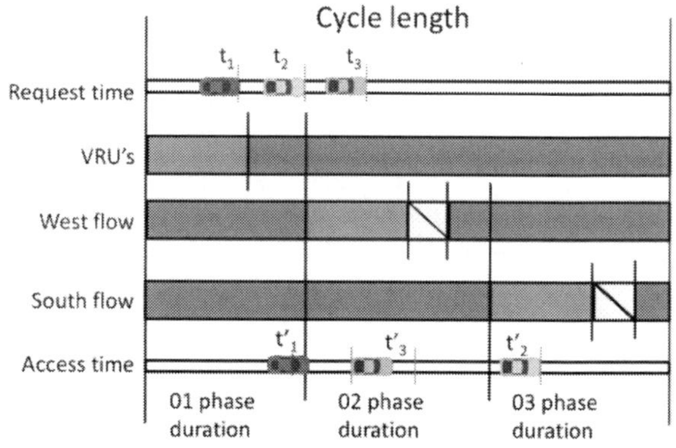

Figure 5. Phasing of traffic flows: phase number 01(pedestrian phase), phase number 02 (W flow), phase number 03(S flow).

A traffic scenario was simulated (Figure 1). A brief look into the basic anatomy and the process of timing traffic signals is given in Figure 5. The sequential diagram describes the phasing of the traffic flows composed of two single-lane road phases crossing at the square intersection area: the W flow stage (02 phase) and the S flow stage (03 phase). Green splits are calculated by dividing the cycle length in proportion to the critical lane volumes. Each driving vehicle is then assigned an individualised time to request ($t_{1,2,3}$) and access ($t'_{1,2,3}$) the intersection. During the course of phases 02 and 03 the pedestrians, through a pushbutton, request to pass the crossroad and are acknowledged. The phase 01 stage, "Walk" interval begins at the end of phase 03 and the controller sends a response message to nomadic road user's devices (e.g., smartphone, tablets). Sufficient time must be provided to cross the entire travelled width of the street. In phase 01 the "don't walk" interval is calculated based on the length of the crosswalk.

A first-come-first-served approach could be realized by accelerating or decelerating the vehicles such that they arrive at the intersection when gaps in the conflicting traffic flows and pedestrians have been created for them. However, a one-by-one service policy is not efficient at high vehicle arrival rates. From a capacity point of view, it is more efficient if Vehicle 3 is given access at t'_3 before Vehicle 2, t'_2 to the intersection, then, forming a west platoon of vehicles before (t'_2) giving way to the south conflicting flow, as stated in Figure 5.

IV. Conclusions and Future Trends

This paper presents a distributed mechanism for the performance management of a traffic light controlled crossroad network, where connected vehicles receive information from the network (I2V), interact with each other

(V2V) and with the infrastructure (V2I). A control manager coordinates the crossroad and interacts with the vehicles (I2V). VLC is the transmission technology. A simulated traffic scenario was presented and a generic model of cooperative transmissions for vehicular communications services was established. The experimental results confirmed that the proposed cooperative VLC architecture is suitable for the intended applications. The introduction of VLC between connected vehicles and the infrastructures, I2V2V2I2V communication allows the direct monitoring of relative speed thresholds and inter-vehicle spacing. The distance between conflicting vehicles and the trajectories of other opposing vehicles should also be monitored and optimized.

In order to move towards real implementation, the performance of such systems still needs improvement. As further work, the research team plans to finalize the embedded application, for experimenting in several road configurations with either static or moving vehicles.

ACKNOWLEDGEMENTS

This work was sponsored by FCT – Fundação para a Ciência e a Tecnologia, within the Research Unit CTS – Center of Technology and systems, reference UID/EEA/00066/2019 and projects reference IPL/2018/II&D_CTS/UNINOVA_ISEL and by: IPL/IDI&CA/2018/LAN4CC/ISEL.

REFEEENCES

[1] S. Schmid, G. Corbellini, S. Mangold, and T. R. Gross, "An LED-to-LED Visible Light Communication system with software-based synchronization," in 2012 IEEE Globecom Workshops, pp.1264–1268, 2012.

[2] I. L. Azevedo, M. G. Morgan, and F. Morgan, "The Transition to Solid-State of the IEEE , vol.97, no.3, pp. 481-510, March 2009.

[3] H. Parth Pathak, F. Xiaotao, H. Pengfei, and M. Prasant, "Visible Light Communication, Networking and Sensing: Potential and Challenges," September 2015, IEEE Communications Surveys & Tutorials 17(4): Fourthquarter 2015, pp. 2047 – 2077, 2015.

[4] N. Kumar, N. Lourenço, D. Terra, L. N. Alves, and R. L. Aguiar, "Visible Light Communications in Intelligent Transportation Systems," IEEE Intelligent Vehicules Symposium, 748-753. 2012.

[5] S. Yousefi, E. Altman, R. El-Azouzi, and M. Fathy, "Analytical Model for Connectivity in Vehicular Ad Hoc Networks," IEEE Transactions on Vehicular Technology, 57, pp. 3341-3356, 2008.

[6] C. Liu, B. Sadeghi, and E. W. Knightly, "Enabling vehicular visible light communication (V2LC) networks," Proceedings of the Eighth ACM international workshop on Vehicular inter-networking (VANET '11), ACM, New York, NY, USA, pp. 41-50, 2011.

[7] M. A. Vieira, P. Louro, M. Vieira, A. Fantoni, and A. Steiger-Garção, "Light-activated amplification in Si-C tandem devices: A capacitive active filter model," IEEE sensor journal, 12(6), pp. 1755-1762, 2012.

[8] M. A. Vieira, M. Vieira, P. Vieira, and P. Louro, "Optical signal processing for a smart vehicle lighting system using a-SiCH technology," Proc. SPIE 10231, Optical Sensors, 102311L, 2017.

[9] M. A. Vieira, M. Vieira, P. Vieira, and P. Louro, "Vehicle-to-Vehicle and Infrastructure-to-Vehicle Communication in the Visible Range," Sensors & Transducers, 218 (12), pp. 40-48, 2017.

[10] M. A. Vieira, M. Vieira, P. Louro, and P. Vieira, "Smart Vehicle Lighting System in the Visible Range: Vehicle-to-Vehicle Communication," The Eighth International Conference on Sensor Device Technologies and Applications. SENSORDEVICES 2017. - Rome, Italy. Copyright (c) IARIA ISBN: 978-1-61208-581-4, pp. 57-62, 2017.

[11] M. A. Vieira; M. Vieira; P Vieira; and P. Louro,. "Optical signal processing for a smart vehicle lighting system using a-SiCH technology," Proc. SPIE. 10231 Optical Sensors 2017, 102311L., 2017.

[12] M. A. Vieira, M. Vieira, P. Vieira, and P. Louro, "Cooperative vehicular communication systems based on visible light communication," Opt. Eng. 57(7), 076101, 2018.

[13] M. A. Vieira, M Vieira, J. Costa, P. Louro, M Fernandes, and A. Fantoni, "Double pin Photodiodes with two Optical Gate Connections for Light Triggering: A capacitive two-phototransistor model," in Sensors & Transducers Journal, 10 Special Issue, pp. 96-120, 2011.

[14] M. A. Vieira, M. Vieira, P. Louro, and P. Vieira, "Vehicular Visible Light Communication I2V2V2I Connected Cars," The Ninth International Conference on Sensor Device Technologies and Applications, SENSORDEVICES 2018. Copyright (c) IARIA, 2018. ISBN: 978-1-61208-660-6, pp. 175-180, 2018.

Visible LED-Assisted Navigation System for Large Indoor Environments

Manuela Vieira, Manuel Augusto Vieira, Paula Louro, Alessandro Fantoni
ADETC/ISEL/IPL,
R. Conselheiro Emídio Navarro, 1959-007
Lisboa, Portugal
CTS-UNINOVA
Quinta da Torre, Monte da Caparica, 2829-516,
Caparica, Portugal

e-mail: mv@isel.ipl.pt, mv@isel.pt, plouro@deetc.isel.pt, afantoni@deetc.isel.ipl.pt

Pedro Vieira
ADETC/ISEL/IPL,
R. Conselheiro Emídio Navarro, 1959-007
Lisboa, Portugal
Instituto das Telecomunicações
Instituto Superior Técnico, 1049-001,
Lisboa, Portugal
e-mail: pvieira@isel.pt

***Abstract*— This paper investigates the applicability of an intuitive advertising system for large indoor environments using Visible Light Communication (VLC). This VLC based positioning system includes the use of the visible light signal to light the space and to transmit the information for positioning of travelers and of advertising campaigns in the surroundings. An LED-assisted positioning and navigation VLC system is proposed. A VLC scenario for large environments is analyzed, the emitters and receivers are characterized and the communication protocol presented. Different layouts are investigated. Square and hexagonal meshes are tested and a 2D localization design, demonstrated by a prototype implementation, is presented. The key differences between both topologies are discussed. For both, the transmitted information, indoor position, path direction, as well as bidirectional communication are determined. The results showed that the LED-aided VLC navigation system makes possible to determine the position of a mobile target inside the network, to infer the travel direction as a function of time and to interact with the information received.**

Keywords- Visible Light Communication; Indoor positioning; Advertising, Optical sensors; Large indoor environments; SiC technology; Transmitter/receiver; Multiplexing/de-multiplexing techniques.

I. Introduction

Advertising is used to stimulate market demand. The purpose is to transmit the right message to the right receiver at the right time, as well as the collection, understanding and decoding of the message in a proper manner. Usually, advertisement signs are used to communicate, and they are placed in geographically identified areas in order to capture customers' attention. The most obvious method of using signs is through billboards located in high traffic areas. Indoor billboards are designed in order to attract the attention of those moving past the sign. Handheld devices make up the growing mobile device market. Such devices allow customers to stay informed, gather information and communicate with others without being tied to a physical location and offer significant opportunity for marketers to reach customers at anytime and anyplace. Also, with geographic positioning features included in newer mobile devices, the medium has the potential to provide marketers with the ability to target customers based on their geographic location.

Airports are among the largest shopping centres. They must satisfy high service requirements. Business travellers have all the information concerning their flight on their boarding pass. With a clearly arranged Web interface, they can see the most frequented areas inside an airport and can take action if certain areas become overcrowded, meaning that those places can be highlighted on an interactive map. Additionally, it is also an advantage if the shopping function is complemented by other features, for example, if the customer could be informed about the current waiting times or be given recommendations.

Nowadays, indoor positioning methods are mainly based on Wi-Fi [1], Bluetooth, Radio-Frequency Identification (RFID) [2] and Visible Light Communications (VLC) [3]. VLC is a data transmission technology [4] that can easily be employed in indoor environments since it can use the existing LED lighting infrastructure with simple modifications [5][6]. In this paper, we propose the use of modulated visible light, carried out by white polychromatic low cost LEDs. This means that the LEDs are useful twofold by providing illumination as well as communication. The use of white polychromatic LEDs offers the possibility of Wavelength Division Multiplexing (WDM), which enhances the transmission data rate. A WDM receiver based on tandem a-SiC:H/a-Si:H pin/pin light controlled filter can be used [7][8] to decode the received information. Here, when different visible signals are encoded in the same optical transmission path, the device multiplexes the different optical channels, performs different filtering processes (amplification, switching, and wavelength conversion) and finally decodes the encoded signals recovering the transmitted information.

Research is still necessary to design LED arrangements that can optimize communication performance while meeting the illumination constraints for a variety of large indoor layouts. The main idea is to divide the space into spatial beams originating from the different light sources, and identify each beam with a unique timed sequence of light signals. Fine-grained indoor localization can enable several applications in airports, supermarkets and shopping malls. Information on the exact location of products can greatly improve the customer's shopping experience and enable customer analytics and marketing [9].

In this paper, an LED-assisted positioning and navigation VLC system is proposed. The paper is organized as follows. After the introduction (Section I), in Section II, a VLC scenario for large environments is established, the emitters and receivers are characterized and the communication protocol is presented. In Section III, different layouts are analyzed. Square and hexagonal meshes are tested and a 2D localization design' demonstrated by a prototype implementation, is presented. The key differences between the two topologies are discussed. For both, the transmitted information, indoor position, path direction as well as bidirectional communication are determined. Finally, in Section IV, conclusions and future trends are addressed.

The proposed LED aided system involves wireless communication, smart sensors and optical sources network, building up a transdisciplinary approach framed in cyber-physical systems.

II. SYSTEM DESIGN

A. VLC Scenario

The indoor environment chosen is an airport and two topologies were considered: the square for the main hall and the hexagonal for the marketing zones. The reported plan and the proposed scenario are presented in Figure 1. Here, a user navigates from outdoor to indoor. The user sends a request message to find out what gate he/she is boarding at, and in the available time until boarding, he/she adds customized points of interest, routes from restaurants, shops, and halls within the airport. The requested information is sent by the emitters from the ceiling to the receiver. The traveler is equipped with a receiver. After the check-in at the main airport entrance, the user passes through airport security and, depending on the available time until boarding, he/she can go directly to the gate or shop, eat or rest. After registration, he/she sends to the central controller a message request in order to add, in the available time, customized points of interest, routes from restaurants, shops, gates, halls to boarding or the right track. On his path, the passenger is advised how to reach its destination and the possibility to use location based advertising (available selection of goods advice and restaurants).

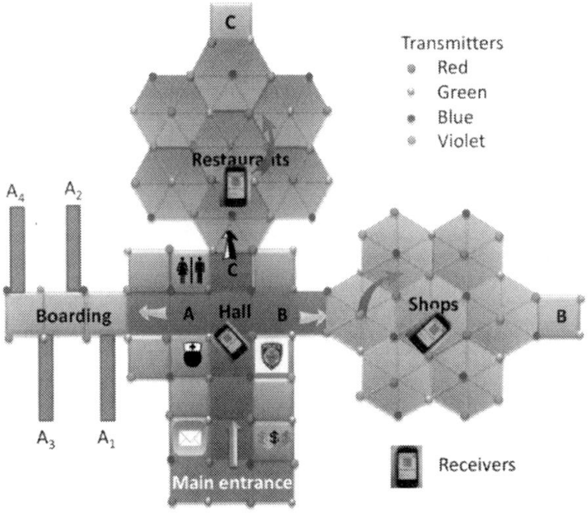

Figure 1. Optical infrastructure and indoor layout.

B. The Emitters for Large Environments

LED bulbs, at the nodes of the network, act as transmitters, broadcasting the information. An optical receiver extracts its location to perform positioning and, concomitantly, the transmitted data from each transmitter. To synchronize the signals from multiple LEDs, the transmitters use different IDs, allowing the signal to be reconstructed at the receiver.

Ceiling plans for the LED array layout are shown in Figure 2. Two topologies were set for the unit cell: the square, (Figure 2a) and the hexagonal (Figure 2b). Red (R; 626 nm), Green (G; 530 nm), Blue (B; 470 nm) and violet (V; 390 nm) LEDs, at the nodes of the network, are used [10][11]. In both topologies, each node, $X_{i,j}$, carries its own color, X, (RGBV) as well as its ID position in the network (i,j). In both, the grid sizes were chosen to avoid overlap in the receiver from adjacent grid points. To improve its practicality, the tested geometric scenario in the experimental results uses a grid in smaller size (with 2 cm between adjacent nodes).

For data transmission, commercially available polychromatic white LEDs were used. On each node, only one chip is modulated for data transmission. To receive the information from several transmitters, the receiver must be positioned where the irradiated circles from each transmitter overlap, producing at the receiver, a multiplexed (MUX) signal that, after demultiplexing, acts twofold as a positioning system and a data transmitter. The generated regions, defined onwards as footprints, are pointed out in Figure 2 and reported in Table I.

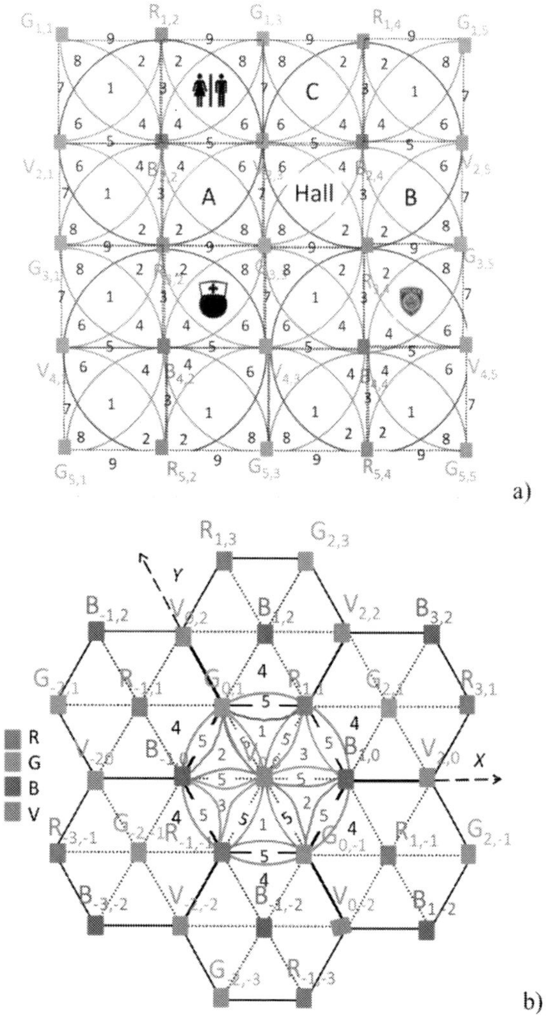

Figure 2. Optical infrastructure and storage model (LED array = RGBV color spots): a) Clusters of cells in orthogonal topology (square). b) Clusters of cell in hexagonal topology.

TABLE I. FINE-GRAINED TOPOLOGIES: FOOTPRINT REGIONS.

Footprint regions	Square topology	Hexagonal topology
#1	RGBV	RGV
#2	RGB	GBV
#3	RB	RBV
#4	RBV	RGB
#5	BV	RGBV
#6	GBV	-
#7	GV	-
#8	RGV	-
#9	RG	-

The device receives multiple signals (footprints), finds the centroid of the received coordinates and stores it as the reference point position.

C. *The receiver*

The VLC photosensitive receiver is a pinpin photodetector based on a multilayer hetero-structure, p-i'(a - SiC:H)-n/p-i(a-Si:H)-n sandwiched between two transparent contacts [8]. The device offers high sensitivity and linear response, generating a proportional electrical current. Its quick response enables the possibility of high speed communications. The device operates within the visible range using, for data transmission, the modulated light supplied by the RGBV LEDs transmitters. The generated photocurrent is processed using a trans-impedance circuit obtaining a proportional voltage. The voltage is then processed, by using signal conditioning techniques (adaptive bandpass filtering and amplification, triggering and demultiplexing), until the data signal is reconstructed at the data processing unit (digital conversion, decoding and decision) [12].

D. *The OOK Modulation Scheme*

An on-off keying modulation scheme was used. To create a communication protocol to ensure the required system performance and overcome the technology constraints, a 32 bits data frame was designed.

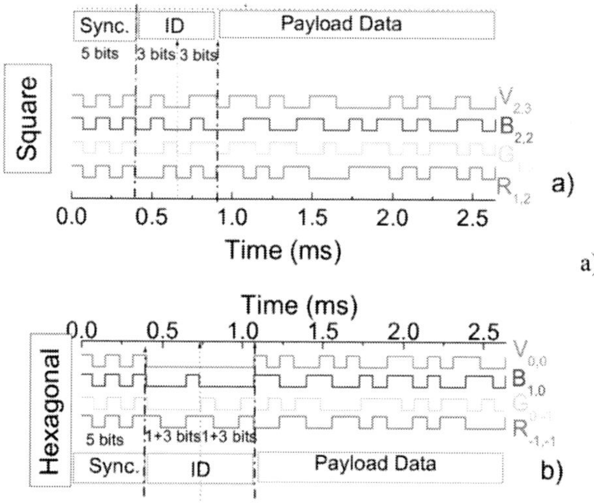

Figure 3. Data frame structure. Representation of one original encoded message, in a time slot: a) Square topology. b) Hexagonal topology.

Three control fields, one for synchronism (Sync.) and two for the identification of the cell (ID) begin each frame. This sequence is followed by a fourth block that is for the payload, as shown in Figure 3, for both topologies: a) Square topology; R_{12}; $G_{1,3}$; $B_{2,2}$ and $V_{2,3}$ are the transmitted node packet from the array in the network. b) Hexagonal topology; $R_{-1,-1}$; $G_{0,-1}$; $B_{1,0}$ and $V_{0,0}$ are the transmitted node packet from the array in the network. A stop bit is used at the end of each frame. The first five bits are used for time synchronization. The same synchronization header [10101], in an *on-off* pattern, is imposed simultaneously to all emitters. Each colour signal (RGBV) carries its own ID-BIT, so, the next bits give the coordinates of the emitter inside the array ($X_{i,j}$). The cell's IDs are encoded using a binary representation for the decimal number. In the square topology (Figure 3a), six bits are used: the first three for the binary code of the line and the other three for the column. In the hexagonal topology, 60° Cartesian coordinates were applied (Figure 2b). An extra bit was added at the beginning of the binary code to represent the number's sign: setting that bit to *0* is for a positive number, and setting it to *1* is for a negative number. The remaining bits in the number indicate the absolute value. So, the next eight bits (ID) are assigned, respectively, to the *x* and *y* coordinates (*i,j*) of the emitter in the array (Figure 3b). For both, the last bits in the frame are reserved for the message sent by the X_{ij} node (payload data). With this information, the method will give an exact, unique answer, *i.e.*, the location of the receiver in the array ($X_{i,j}$).

Results show that, in the square network, $R_{1,2}$, $G_{1,3}$, $B_{2,2}$ and $V_{2,3}$ are the transmitted node packets, in a time slot, from the unit cell where the restrooms are located (Figure 2a). In the hexagonal network, the nodes $R_{-1,-1}$, $G_{0,-1}$, $B_{1,0}$ and $V_{0,0}$, located in the first ring of the restaurant zone (Figure 2b), are the transmitters.

III. SYSTEM EVALUATION

A. Positioning

In Figure 4, a MUX signal due to the joint transmission of four R, G, B and V optical signals, in a data frame, is displayed.

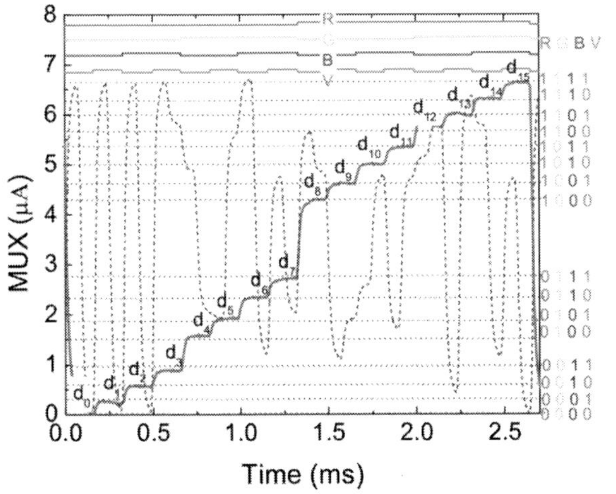

Figure 4. MUX signal of the calibrated cell. On the top the transmitted channels packets [R, G, B, V] are depicted. A received MUX signal is also superimposed to exemplify the decoding algorithm.

The data acquisition was obtained with the presence of environment light. The bit sequence (on the top of the figure) was chosen to allow all the sixteen possible *on/off* combinations of the four input channels (2^4).

Results show that the code signal presents as many separated levels as the *on/off* possible combinations of the input channels, allowing decoding the transmitted information [12]. All the ordered levels (d_0-d_{15}) are pointed out at the correspondent levels and are displayed as horizontal dotted lines. On the right hand side, the match between MUX levels and the 4 bits binary code assigned to each level is shown. For demonstration of the decoding technique, a signal received in the same time frame in #1, is also added (dotted curve). Comparing the calibrated levels (d_1-d_{15}) with the different assigned 4-digit binary code, the decoding is straightforward. Each decoded message also carries the transmitter's node address. So, the next block of six bits, in the square topology (or eight in the hexagonal one), gives de ID of the received node.

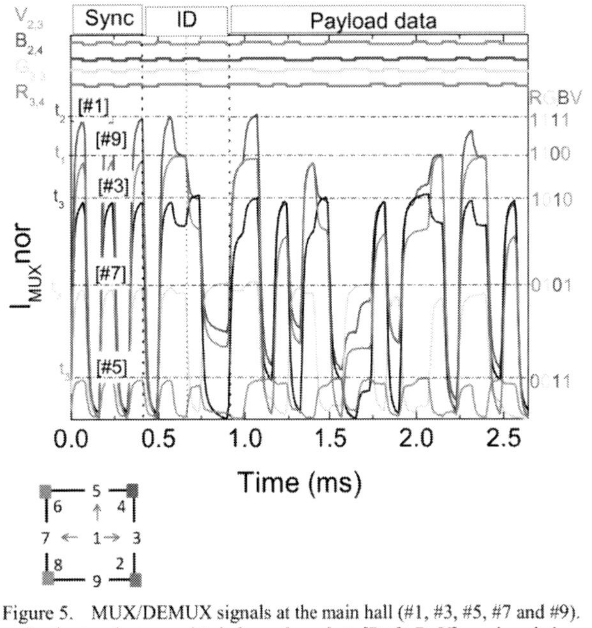

Figure 5. MUX/DEMUX signals at the main hall (#1, #3, #5, #7 and #9). On the top the transmitted channels packets [R, G, B, V] are decoded.

In Figure 5, the MUX signals acquired at the main hall in different positions (#1, #3, #5, #7 and #9) are displayed. On the top, the transmitted channels packets [R, G, B, V] are decoded. Here, in position #9 the network locations of the transmitters are $R_{3,4}$ [011;100] and $G_{3,3}$ [011;011] while in #1 the assigned transmitters are $R_{3,4}$, $G_{3,3}$, $B_{2,4}$ and $V_{2,3}$. The last block is reserved for the transmission of the advertising (payload data). The stop bit (0) is always used at the end of each frame.

B. Travel direction

To compute the point-to-point along a path, we need the data along the path. The input of the aided navigation system is the coded MUX signal, and the output is the system state decoded at each time step (Δt). As a proof of concept, in the lab, a navigation data bit transition was tested by moving the receiver along a known pattern path. In this example (Figure 5), at t_1, the user enters the hall by line #9, goes to position #1 at t_2 and chooses the boarding terminal or the marketing zones at t_3, being directed into one of the three indicated directions (A # 7; B # 3 or C # 5).

The results show that, as the receiver moves between generated point regions, the received information pattern changes. Between two consecutive data sets, there is a navigation data bit transition (channel is missing or added). We observe that, when the receiver moves from #9 to # 1 (Figure 5), two different ID channels are added ($B_{2,4}$ and $V_{2,3}$). Here, the 4-binary bit code has changed from [1100] to [1111].

In Figure 6, a path crossing the hexagonal topology is also tested. Here, the receiver enters the restaurants area (#4> #5> #3).

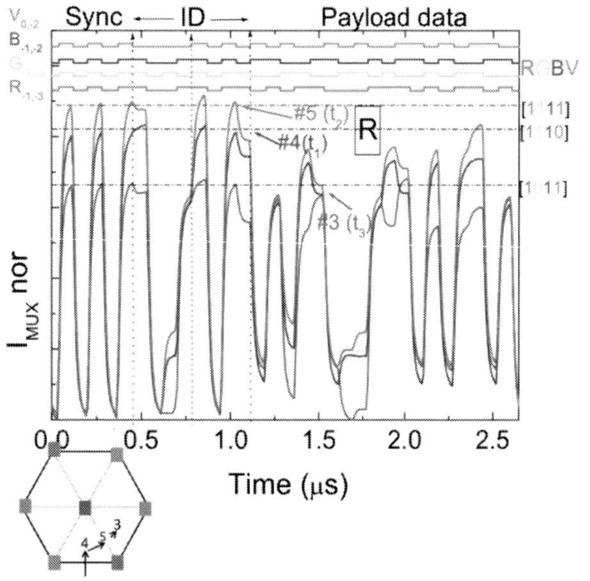

Figure 6. Fine-grained indoor localization and navigation in successive instants. Signal acquisition through the restaurants area (R). On the top the transmitted channels packets are decoded [R, G, B, V].

Taking into account Figure 2b and the frame structure (Figure 3b), results show that, at t_1, the receiver was located at #4 [1110]/ $R_{-1,-3}$ $G_{-2,-3}$ $B_{-1,-2}$. At t_2, it arrives at #5 [1111]/ $R_{-1,-3}$ $G_{-2,-3}$ $B_{-1,-2}$. $V_{0,-2}$, and then, at t_3, it moves towards #3, [1011]/ $G_{-2,-3}$ $B_{-1,-2}$. $V_{0,-2}$.

The main results from both topologies show that fine grained localization is achieved by detecting the wavelengths of the received channels in each region. The location and path of a mobile receiver was obtained based on the LED-based navigation system. In an orthogonal layout (hall), the square topology is the best. It allows crossroads and the client can walk easily in the horizontal, vertical, or both directions. In concentric layouts, to fill all the space with hexagons presents advantages (restaurants, and shops areas). Here, the client can move around and walk between the different rings toward the outside region.

C. Bidirectional communication

Bidirectional communication between VLC emitters and receivers in a handheld device can be established through a control manager linked to an indoor billboard. Each ceiling lamp broadcasts a message with its ID and advertising, which is received and processed by the receiver. Using a white polychromatic LED as transmitter, the receptor sends to the local controller a "request" message with its location (ID) and adds its needs for the available time (payload data). For route coordination, the local controller emitter sends the "response" message.

In Figure 7, the MUX signal assigned to a "request" and a "response" message are displayed. At the top, the decoded information is presented. On the right side, the match between the MUX signal and the 4-binary code is pointed out. Here, in a time slot, the traveler, in position #3 ($R_{3,2}$, $B_{2,2}$), sends to the central controller the message "request" in order to add the points of interest (boarding or the right track). After that, it is advised through a "response" message, that the request was received, how to reach the destination in time and how to use location based advertising.

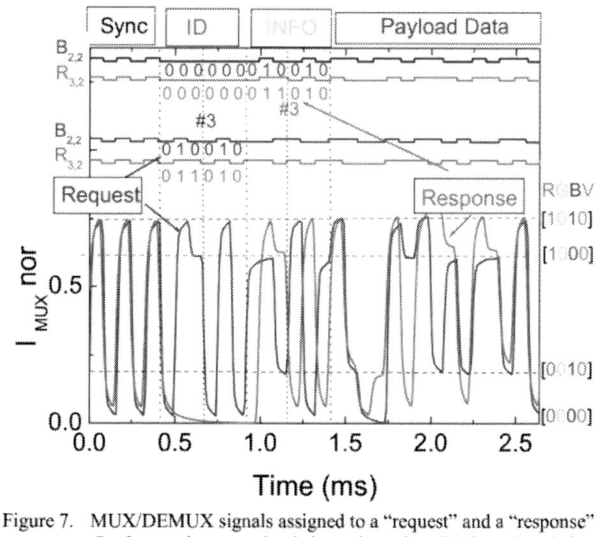

Figure 7. MUX/DEMUX signals assigned to a "request" and a "response" message. On the top the transmitted channels packets [$X_{i,j}$] are decoded.

Taking into account the frame structure (Figure 3), results show that the codification of both signals is synchronized (Sync). The "request" message includes the complete address of the traveler (Sync+ID) and the help need (payload data). In the "response" message, the block

(ID), in a pattern [000000], means that a response message, from the local manager, is being sent. The next block (6 bits) identifies the address (INFO) for which the message is intended and finally in the last block appears the requested information (payload data). Here, the emitter controller [000000] responds to a request of a passenger located in position # 3 ($R_{3,2}$, $B_{2,2}$) and sends back the requested information.

IV. CONCLUSIONS

An LED-assisted navigation system for large indoor environments was proposed. For lighting, data transmission and positioning, white LEDs were used. A SiC optical MUX/DEMUX mobile receiver decodes the data and based on the synchronism and ID of the joint transmitters it infers its path location, timing and user flows.

A VLC scenario for an airport was established and the communication protocol presented. The bi-directional communication between the infrastructure and the mobile receiver was analysed. Two cellular networks were tested and compared: square and hexagonal. The main results show that, for both topologies, the location of a mobile receiver, concomitant with data transmission is achieved. The LED-aided VLC navigation system makes possible to determine the position of a mobile target inside the network, to infer the travel direction as a function of the time and to interact with the received information.

Minding the benefits of VLC, it is expected that this type of communication will have an important role in positioning applications. Moving towards real implementation, the performances of such systems still need to improve. As a future goal, we plan to finalize the embedded application for experimenting in several network layouts. Effects such as synchronization, shadowing and ambient light noise will be minimized by distributing lighting sources (MIMO techniques) to optimize the coverage.

ACKNOWLEDGEMENTS

This work was sponsored by FCT – Fundação para a Ciência e a Tecnologia, within the Research Unit CTS – Center of Technology and systems, reference UID/EEA/00066/2019 and projects reference IPL/2018/II&D_CTS/UNINOVA_ISEL and by IPL/IDI&CA/2018/LAN4CC/ISEL.

REFERENCES

[1] C. Yang and H. R. Shao, "WiFi-based indoor positioning," IEEE Commun. Mag., vol. 53, no. 3, pp. 150–157, Mar. 2015.

[2] C. H. Huang, L. H. Lee, C. C. Ho, L. L. Wu, and Z. H. Lai, "Real-time rfid indoor positioning system based on Kalman filter drift removal and heron-bilateration location estimation," IEEE Trans. Instrum. Meas., vol. 64, no. 3, pp. 728–739, Mar. 2015.

[3] N. U. Hassan, A. Naeem, M. A. Pasha, T. Jadoon, and C. Yuen, "Indoor positioning using visible led lights: A survey,"ACM Comput. Surv., vol. 48, pp.1–32, 2015.

[4] E. Ozgur, E. Dinc, and O. B. Akan, "Communicate to illuminate: State-of-the-art and research challenges for visible light communications," Physical Communication 17 72–85, 2015.

[5] D. Tsonev et al., "A 3-Gb/s single-LED OFDM-based wireless VLC link using a Gallium Nitride μLED," IEEE Photon. Technol. Lett. 26 (7), pp. 637–640, 2014.

[6] D. O'Brien et al., "Indoor visible light communications: challenges and prospects," Proc. SPIE 7091, 709106, 2008.

[7] M. Vieira, P. Louro, M. Fernandes, M. A. Vieira, A. Fantoni and J. Costa "Three Transducers Embedded into One Single SiC Photodetector: LSP Direct Image Sensor, Optical Amplifier and Demux Device," Advances in Photodiodes InTech, Chap.19, pp. 403-425, 2011.

[8] M. A. Vieira, P. Louro, M. Vieira, A. Fantoni, and A. Steiger-Garção, "Light-activated amplification in Si-C tandem devices: A capacitive active filter model," IEEE sensor journal, 12, NO. 6, pp. 1755-1762, 2012.

[9] A. Jovicic, J. Li, and T Richardson, "Visible light communication: opportunities, challenges and the path to market," Communications Magazine, IEEE, vol. 51, no. 12, pp. 26–32, 2013.

[10] M. Vieira, M. A. Vieira., P. Louro, P. Vieira, and A. Fantoni, "Fine-grained indoor localization: optical sensing and detection," Proc. SPIE 10680, Optical Sensing and Detection V, 106800H, 9 May 2018.

[11] M. Vieira, M. A. Vieira, P. Louro, P. Vieira, and A. Fantoni, "Light-emitting diodes aided indoor localization using visible light communication technology," Opt. Eng. **57**(8), 087105, 2018.

[12] M. Vieira, M. A. Vieira, P. Louro, P. Vieira, and A. Fantoni, "Light-Fidelity (Li-Fi) Optical Sensing and Detection in Large Indoor Environments," The Ninth International Conference on Sensor Device Technologies and Applications, SENSORDEVICES, 2018.

Real-Time Failure and Reliability Analysis of Agricultural Sprayers Based on Sensors, Arduino Architecture, and Controller Area Bus Protocol

Paulo E. Cruvinel[1,2], Elmer A. G. Penãloza [1,4], Pedro B. Andrade[1], Heitor V. Mercaldi[1,3]
[1]Embrapa Instrumentation Brazilian Agricultural Research Corporation, Sao Carlos, SP, Brazil
[2] Post-Graduation Programs in Computer Science - Federal University of São Carlos, SP, Brazil
[3]Department of Electrical Engineering – Federal University of São Carlos, SP, Brazil
[4]Engineering Center - Federal University of Pelotas, RS, Brazil
Emails: paulo.cruvinel@embrapa.br, eagpenaloza@ufpel.edu.br, pedro_borghi@hotmail.com, heitor.mercaldi@gmail.com

Abstract—**In this study, a solution for the operational analysis of agricultural sprayers based on their sensor devices for measurements, surveillance, signal conditioning, and interfacing circuits is proposed. The agricultural electronics-based machinery industry has significantly expanded during the past 10 years, and performance and cost advances have enabled the feasibility of operations for decision-making capabilities for food production. However, it is becoming increasingly necessary to study the system reliability, which is one of the major concerns in real agricultural machinery during field operation. A method is presented for the verification of the failure and reliability of an agricultural spraying system using a microcontroller, operating in an Arduino-based architecture, a controller area network protocol for communication and data analysis, and sensors for pressure, flow, and temperature, which are frequently used in such agricultural machinery for the spray quality control. All these sensors play an important role to support the variables control, and they must not only be operating correctly but must also ensure the verification of the application quality, which depends on the correct rate of pesticide application for pest control. Such a system allows to verify, in real time and at a low cost, the sensors' calibration in addition to the evaluation of the whole operation, including the indication for corrections and sensor replacement, if necessary. In other words, it is possible to periodically check the sensor and sprayer reliability. Thus, the knowledge of sensors has become imperative for such applications in agriculture. Furthermore, the establishment of computational procedures for the evaluation of correct operation is equally important, which plays a strategic role, so that users can appropriate such knowledge and decrease measurement errors in variables that are directly related to the efficiency of pest control, as well as reduce the impact on the environment.**

Keywords—failure and reliability of sensors; calibration of sensors; agricultural application quality; decision-making support; CAN bus; precision farming.

I. INTRODUCTION

Agriculture is essential for the production of food, and this production has become even more necessary because of the continuous growth of the world population [1]. Because of the resource constraints and the need to feed 9 billion people globally by 2050, it has been argued that more food should be produced but that, at the same time, production should become more sustainable regarding people, planet, and profit [2]. Today, the whole world is seeking food security, and agricultural machinery plays in this context a very important role.

Without agricultural mechanization and its advanced automation, it will be practically impossible to meet such needs and provide solutions to achieve food and nutrition safety [3]-[5]. Automation of agricultural mechanization is an intensive area of research and development, with emphasis on enhancement of food quality, preservation of operator comfort and safety, precision application of agrochemicals, energy conservation, and environmental control, among others. Automation applications are today oriented toward and assist in the attainment of environmentally friendly and more-sustainable systems of agricultural and food production [6][7]. The mechanization of farming practices throughout the world has revolutionized food production, enabling it to keep pace with population growth [8][9].

In terms of technology development for agriculture today, there are requests for more investments, system innovation, and a better understanding of how people and machines must interact. In addition, almost every piece of agricultural equipment has sensors and controls these days, and a number of sensing technologies are used in agriculture, providing data that help farmers monitor and optimize crops. In such a context, the assessment of sensor failure and reliability is important for the machinery designers' engineers and researchers.

The methodology for assessing sensor reliability has adaptive aspects and should be customized as a function of their application. In agriculture, for instance, the design of embedded electronic-sensor-based systems in machinery for the field has been shown to require the inclusion of failure and reliability. In such a way, three general approaches can be considered: system failure because of uncalibrated sensors, system failure-rate prediction, and physics-of-failure reliability assessment [10]-[13].

In general, the sensors in an agricultural sprayer are organized in sensor networks. If using redundancy, the failure of a single device may not be critical to the applications. However, when failures occur in sensors, the consequences are likely to be disastrous, particularly for critical applications, such as the application of pesticides for pest control. The impact of an incorrect application of pesticides is well known, not only in terms of the economic aspects and on the plant's health, but also on the environment. The cause of such a failure must be determined as soon as possible; otherwise, the negative consequences could become more widespread [14].

According to records, isolated component evaluations of sprayers have been carried out since the 1940s, but only in the 1970s did technical inspection programs emerge [15]. Around 1960, the implementation of the first Sprayer Inspection Project in Germany began. In 1969, other countries, such as Italy, began to carry out inspections and, from there, the quality improvement and the reduction of the negative impacts obtained through the applications [16] were noticed. There are reports that, in Norway, agricultural sprayers have been inspected since 1991 [17]. The periodic inspection projects of sprayers implemented in Europe, besides verifying the working condition and adequacy of the equipment, show the importance of the educational process [18]. Belgium has performed obligatory inspections on agricultural sprayers in use since 1995, setting as main objectives the maintenance of equipment and the education of applicators [19][20]. In a project carried out in Spain's Valencia region, the inspected sprayers were divided into operative or not operative as a function of their condition of use [21]. In Argentina, a survey conducted in the 1990s showed the need for technical maintenance of spraying machines, because the majority of them were in trouble [22]. In Brazil, the first sprayer inspection was performed in 1998, where an evaluation was done in the State of Paraná, finding inadequate working conditions of the pressure gauges of some sprayers [23]. Today, several countries are performing periodic sprayer inspections, and various groups of researchers have reported in the literature that the best conditions of the use of sprayers are closely related to their constant maintenance. In such a context, the uniformity of the spray distribution applied by the sprayer boom, the working pressure, the temperature of the mixture, and the volume of the pesticide, which must be adjusted for effective pest control [24]-[27], play important roles.

Currently, through technical-support programs, machinery companies have been providing such periodic maintenance service; however, it is still based on an external diagnostic toolkit [28].

Today, agricultural spraying is used with a focus on precision agriculture, where control, supervision, and the highest quality of the application process are sought, to increase the safety and efficiency of the application processes. These aspects are also related to the minimization of the environmental impacts resulting from these agrochemical application processes. In such work, which quantifies the economics of the localized application (variable rate), it is quite common to observe improvements in the cost/benefit relation [29][30]. Variables, such as temperature, flow, and pressure, have a direct influence on these results, affecting the volume and distribution of the drops in the plantation, which directly influence the efficiency of the application. If there is no control of the pesticide drops, waste can occur. Extremely fine drops can be carried by the wind, spreading and contaminating the environment, which characterizes the drift phenomenon. Extremely thick droplets, although reducing the drift, provide less coverage of the application target, because the pesticide volume that leaves can hold is limited by their size [31][32]. Therefore, it is important to know precisely the values of the variables of temperature, pressure, and flow to have a greater control of the application of these agricultural products. For the automation of these sprayers' processes, embedded computer systems are currently being used.

The innovation presented in this report is based on the inclusion of the concept of on-the-go periodic measurements for operational surveillance based on the monitoring of flow, pressure, and temperature of the mixture to obtain in real time not only the information regarding the operational failure, but also the sprayer reliability analysis.

When done properly, a periodic evaluation of the sensors' calibration, or even a verification of the electronics used for signal processing, can correct mistakes, and network robustness can be established. In addition, selection of a reliability assessment approach is of fundamental importance, because it is related to the effective design of strategies for the operation of reliable sensors.

Furthermore, research on sensors and their effects on the reliability and response characteristics when operating in agricultural sprayer devices is presented. The presented concept and the results can be used in various sprayers' modalities and make increasing reliability possible in relation to the sensor calibration, which defines the quality of the application of pesticides. Because the control circuits rely on the feedback from voltage/current sensors, the whole system for pesticide application has performance that is likely to be affected by the sensors' failure rates, their dynamic characteristics, and the signal-processing circuits. This approach proactively incorporates reliability into the process by establishing a way to verify the calibration of the sensors, i.e., including verification modules for important variables of the spraying process in an unsupervised and automated interface.

In the rest of this work, in Section 2, the materials and methods used are described. In Section 3, the results obtained are discussed, and the conclusions are presented in Section 4.

II. MATERIALS AND METHODS

To design the development of the module for the virtual verification of the calibration of the sensors in a spraying system, the use of a low-cost Arduino architecture was considered. For validation, the platform developed at the Brazilian Agricultural Research Corporation (Embrapa Instrumentation) in partnership with the School of Engineering of São Carlos University of São Paulo (EESC-USP) was used [33]. This platform is used for sprayer development and analyzes and operates as an Agricultural Sprayer Development System (ASDS). It uses a National Instruments embedded controller, NI-cRIO, which works on the platform LabVIEW. The NI-cRIO architecture integrates four components: a real-time processor, a user-programmable field-programmable gate array, modular I/O, and a complete software tool chain for programming applications. This ASDS has an advanced development system that makes possible the design of architectures involving the connections of hydraulic components and devices, mechanical pumps, and electronic and computer algorithms. Such a system also has hydraulic devices used to make any configuration of commercial agricultural sprays and new prototypes of sprayers, a user interface for system monitoring and control, and an electromechanical structure that emulates the movement of the agricultural sprayer in the field (Figure 1).

Figure 1. Agricultural Sprayer Development System (ASDS) dedicated to the application of liquid agricultural inputs.

The ASDS platform has the following components: (1) spray nozzle, (2) system that emulates the movement of the sprayer, (3) pesticide disposal tank, (4) user interface for the development system, and (5) spray booms. In such a platform, the data are presented by a graphical user interface (GUI), where the user can interact with the digital devices by graphical elements with icons and visual indicators, thereby being able to select and manipulate symbols to obtain the practical result.

The Controller Area Network (CAN) bus was also used. It is a synchronous serial communication protocol. Modules connected to a network send messages to the bus at known time intervals, so synchronization is done. The CAN bus was developed by Bosch [34] as a multimaster, message broadcast system that specifies a maximum signaling rate of 1 Mbps, where the modules can act as masters and slaves, depending on the use [35]. This protocol works with multicast messages, where all modules connected to a network receive all messages sent. The connected modules check the status of the bus and analyze whether another module with a higher priority is not sending messages; if this is noticed, the module whose message has the lowest priority interrupts the transmission and allows the highest-priority message to be sent.

For the organization of a reference database with correct values, calibrated and high-precision sensors were used. They were subjected to known temperature, pressure, and flow conditions to obtain voltage values related to these conditions.

The method to obtain and approximate the model was based on the use of polynomial regression. In addition, such a concept can be used to estimate the expected value of a variable (y), given the values of another variable (x). This type of regression is used for models that obey polynomial and nonlinear behavior, as in the previous case. For these types of model, it is necessary to adjust for a higher-degree polynomial function [36]. This technique follows the same steps of linear regression, but using a concept based on Eq. (1).

$$y = a_0 + a_1 x + a_2 x^2 + \cdots + a_m x^m + e \quad (1)$$

where (y) is a polynomial function in which a represents real numbers (sometimes called the coefficients of the polynomial), m is the degree, and (e) represents an error. In this case, the mathematical procedure is the same as in the least-squares method, but the error is now represented by a function of degree greater than 1, such as in Eq. (2).

$$\sum_{i=1}^{m} e_i^2 = \sum_{i=1}^{n} \left(y_i - a_0 - a_1 x_i - a_2 x_i^2 + \cdots + a_m x_i^m\right)^2 \quad (2)$$

Thus, Eq. (2) must be derived in parts from the terms that accompany x_i and be equated to zero to find a system of equations, which makes it possible to calculate its values.

In addition, after the construction of a database with precalibrated values together with a mathematical model obtained as mentioned earlier, an intelligent calibration and correction system can be applied by using such a dataset as a reference to compare the results obtained from the sensors operating in real time. Such sensors have their calibrations checked periodically with the results obtained from the use of the models. Thus, using this comparison method, the system can identify whether a sensor is calibrated, i.e., the same concept can be replicated for each monitored variable. Additionally, either a real-time recalibration can be performed or the sensor can be replaced, if necessary.

The methods of comparison are relative change, Euclidean Distance (ED), Root-Mean-Square-Error (RMSE), and percent error, as among others [37]-[39]. The ED and the RMSE methods were used in the developed solution. The ED for comparison of the measured values of the variables takes into account the distance between two points that can be calculated by the application of the Pythagorean Theorem. In the algorithm, the ED is primarily calculated as the square root of the sum of the squares of the arithmetic difference between the corresponding coordinates of two points, as in Eq. (3).

$$d(x, y) = \sqrt{(x - x_{ref})^2 + (y - y_{ref})^2} \quad (3)$$

where, $d(x, y)$ is the ED, (x) is the measured point, (x_{ref}) is the measured variable at the reference point, (y) is the variable at the measured point, and (y_{ref}) is the variable obtained at the reference point. In addition, as a second verification, the RMSE is used. It represents the standard deviation of the residuals (prediction errors). Residuals are a measure of how far the data points are from the regression line, and RMSE is a measure of how spread out are these residuals values. In other words, it indicates how concentrated the data are around the line of best fit, as in Eq. (4).

$$RMSE = \sqrt{(x_{ref} - x)^2} \quad (4)$$

where (x_{ref}) is the reference variable, and (x) is the measure variable.

In addition, an accurate power supply is used, because such a system is going to be used not only for the verification of the sensors' calibration, but also their possible failure and reliability. For calibration, it is necessary to consider one power supply that generates a precise and high-stability reference voltage. Such a voltage serves as a parameter for the intelligent calibration and correction system, and it is also responsible for feeding each of the electronic devices used.

Most analog-to-digital and digital-to-analog converters internally have voltage references that are used in the process of converting the signal, either to quantize its analog signal or to convert its digital signal to analog [40]. At this point, the accuracy and stability of the reference directly influence the conversion performance.

In agricultural spraying systems, the most commonly used sensors are: (1) temperature sensors, used to measure the temperature of the syrup, which is formed by the addition of the pesticides to water, as well as the temperature of the environment where the spraying occurs; (2) pressure sensors, used to measure the pressure in the spray bar near the spray nozzles; and (3) flow sensors, which measure the flow in the tubes and spray bar, and are used to measure and feed back these values to the spray quality control system.

Figure 2 shows the integration of the Arduino-based architecture and a CAN with the sensors (temperature, pressure, and flow) in the sprayer system. The module that has the Arduino platform is a low-cost device, functional, and easily programmable. The Arduino Uno is a board consisting of an ATMEL ATMEG328 microcontroller and input and output circuits, and it can be easily connected to a computer via a USB cable and is programmed through free software called Arduino IDE (integrated development environment) using a language based on C/C++.

Figure 3 depicts the software structure for the sensors' monitoring, as well as the spraying process for failure and reliability analysis. First, all sensors are tested in relation to failure. Then, the process to monitor the operation of the agricultural sprayer in real time starts and is repeated periodically. The flags are used to alert the operator of the operational status. Either the group of sensors or any single one of them can fail during an operation. For this reason and because of the probability of its occurrence, a previous routine is used to verify the operation based on the use of previously calibrated values and references of electrical voltage. The reference modules receive an electrical signal from the Arduino architectures using the controller area bus protocol and determine whether they are calibrated or must be replaced. Additionally, as a function of the measured values of the variables, such as flow, pressure, and temperature, verification is performed periodically to determine whether the sprayer is operating adequately or if there is need for adjustments of these variables. Such verification can also indicate whether parts of the circuits related to each variable must be replaced when the correction of a failure cannot be made by software. To obtain information regarding the operational conditions, a set of flags is used for the signaling by the GUI. In addition, if a sensor needs to be recalibrated, the system performs the necessary correction to deliver the appropriate information to a CAN bus, where the control and processing unit collects the sensors' information of all the modules.

Furthermore, CAN has been used because its advantages involve data communication and the use of only two wires, which reduces the cost and facilitates the physical implementation.

To communicate between the Arduino and the CAN bus, two important elements that are not directly found in the standard Arduino Uno were used. For this, a CAN transceiver (TJA1050) and a CAN microcontroller module (MCP2515) dedicated to translating the signal made available serially by the transceiver were used (Figure 4).

The transceiver used was manufactured by NXP-Philips Semiconductors. It was used because it is fully ISO11898 compatible and supports high-speed CAN. It also can act as the entire interface between the network and the physical bus [41]. The inputs/outputs (pins 6 and 7) for the transceiver can be directly connected to the CAN L and CAN H lines of the CAN bus used. A 5-V voltage from a power supply is used, pin 2, and pin 3 for the ground potential (GND). Pin 8 of the transceiver is called "silent mode," where, if a 5-V voltage is applied, the mode is activated, preventing the component from sending CAN messages to the bus. If no voltage is applied to this pin, the transceiver operates normally. Pin 5, Reference Voltage (VREF), provides the average CAN bus voltage, and pins 1 and 4, named Transmit Data (TXD) and Receive Data (RXD), respectively, are responsible for receiving or sending the serial signal that is used to decode CAN messages by the CAN controller.

At each decoded dominant bit, the transceiver sends a 1-bit serial via the TXD pin, and, at each recessive bit, the transceiver sends a 0 bit. In this way, the messages are transferred bit by bit from the transceiver to the MCP2515 CAN controller, which decodes the sequence according to the CAN protocol. Figure 5 shows how the communication between the transceiver and the microcontroller is performed. The transceiver RXD pin receives the CAN message sent by the microcontroller. In addition, when a full message is received, it is passed to the CAN bus via the CAN H and CAN L pins.

The MCP2515, manufactured by Microchip, is a stand-alone CAN controller that implements the CAN specification, Version 2.0B. It can transmit and receive standard and extended data frames, with 11 or 29 bits as message identifiers (frame IDs), respectively. The MCP 2515 was used, because it makes the serial peripheral interface bus communication with another microcontroller possible, and its manufacturer, Microchip, provides necessary instructions for writing and reading the registers. Each register has a byte for address that is used by some instructions to make the necessary settings. The addressing of each register is different from its content, that is, the initial setting of the bits for a register is not equal to the numerical value of its addressing.

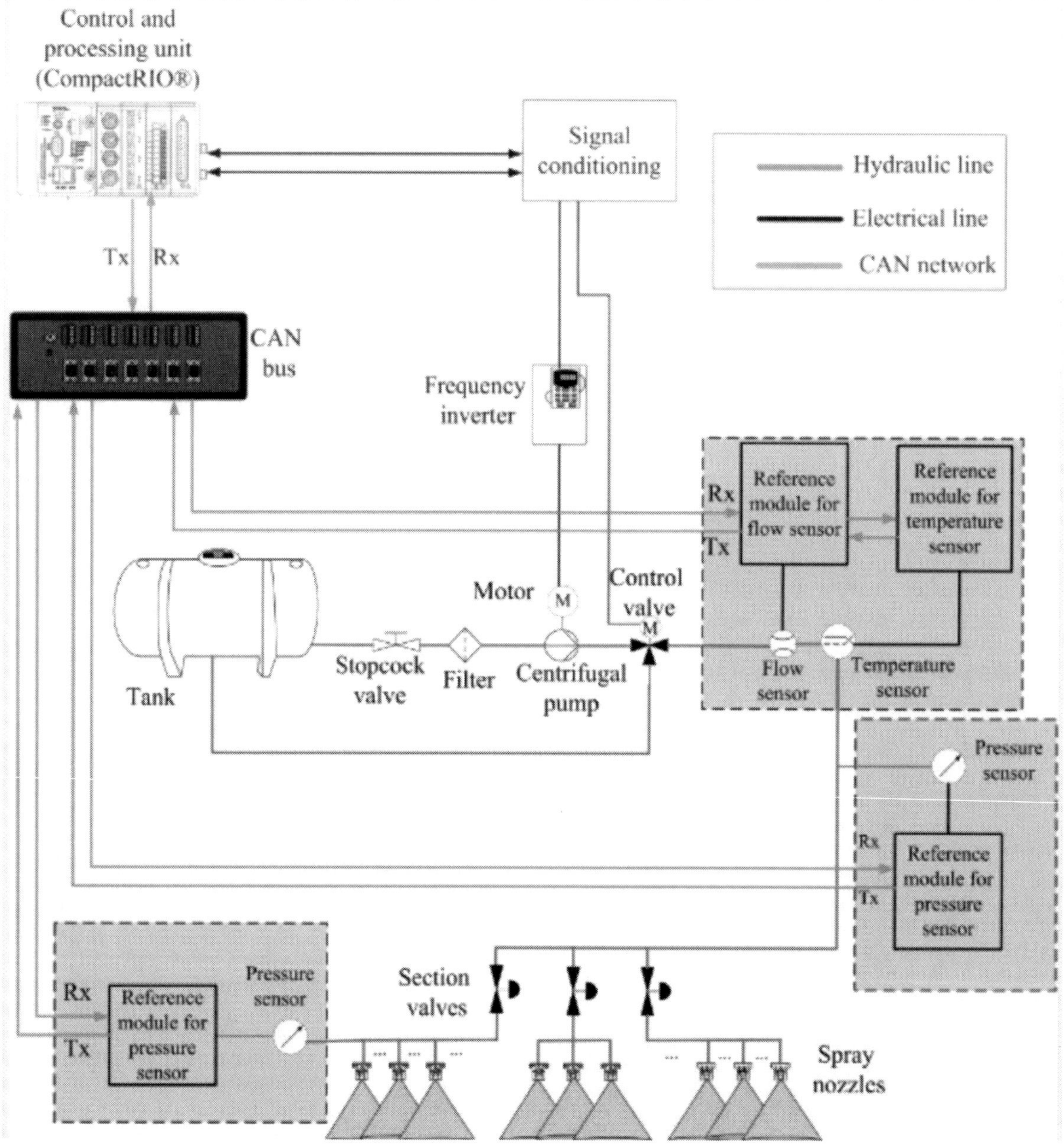

Figure 2. Block diagram of the sprayer system, in which the electrohydraulic configuration and the CAN network can be seen: in the red blocks are the modules based on the Arduino architecture, one for each sensor's modalities, for measurements of flow, pressure, and temperature.

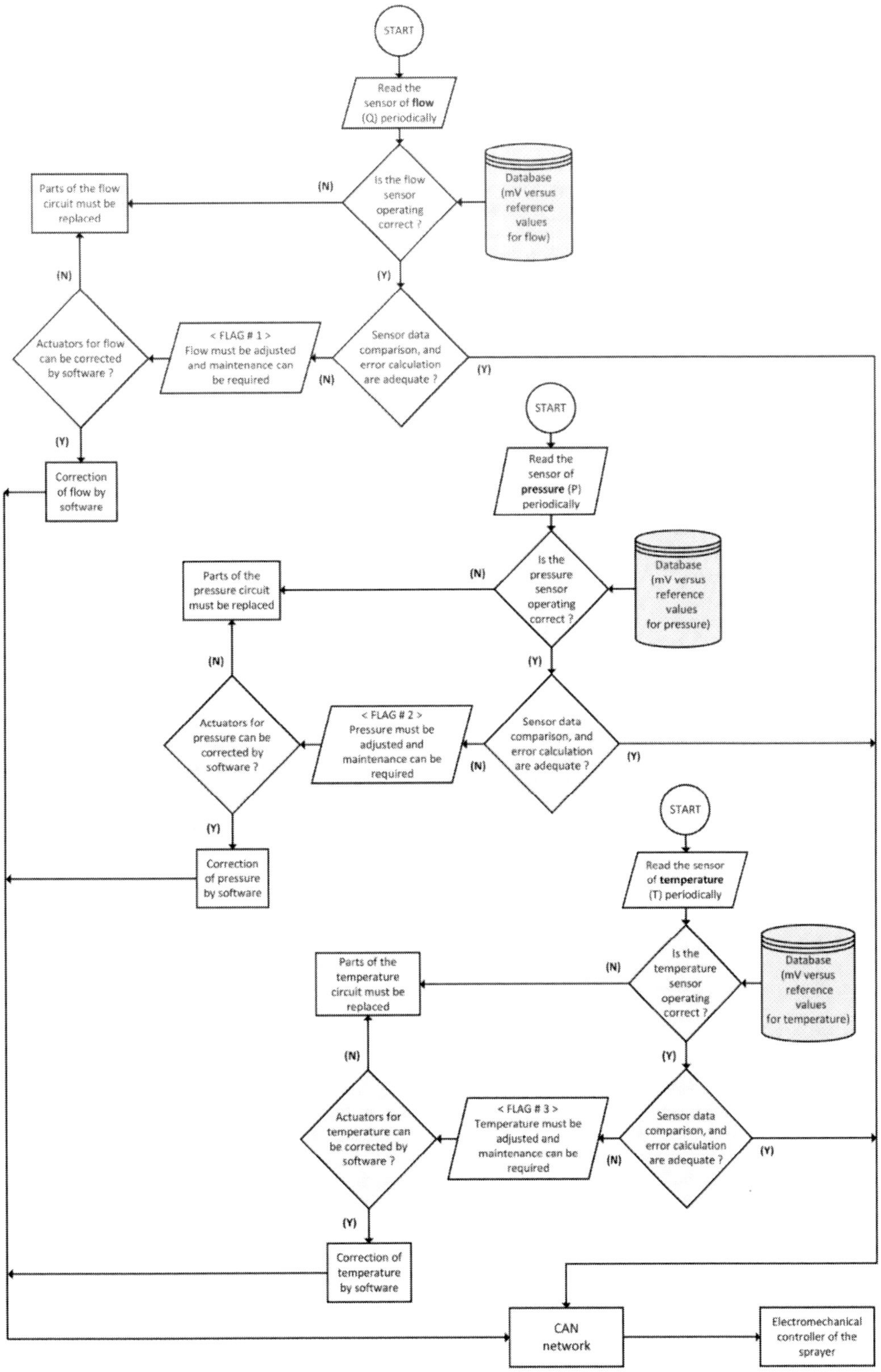

Figure 3. Software structure to monitor the sensors used for measurements, as well as the process for spraying for failure and reliability analyses.

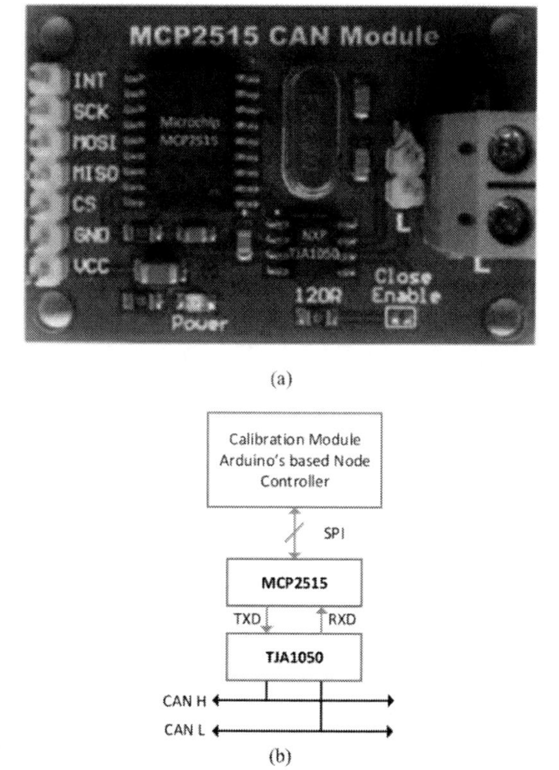

Figure 4. (a) Arduino CAN bus shield (MCP 2515) and (b) the structural architecture for operation in block diagram.

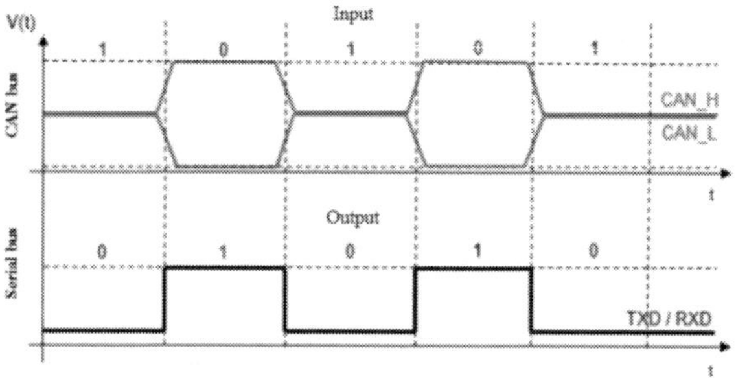

Figure 5. Input and output diagram of the TJA1050 transceiver

III. Results and Discussion

The sensors, which generate analog signals, were connected directly to the calibration module, which analyzed and corrected the data obtained through the algorithms. Then, the data were sent to the CAN network, which used the control and processing unit for presenting the information with the values calibrated by the supervision software. The implementation for the intelligent calibration and correction was carried out by means of the Arduino-based architecture and the algorithms, which used the mathematical models. When the algorithm started, it received the values of the sensor with the parameter to be analyzed, or temperature, pressure, or flow, and then this value was compared with the reference model, which was constructed using the database. If the result of the comparison was satisfactory, this value was sent to the CAN bus; otherwise, this value was corrected by the software through emulation, and only then was the value sent to the bus. When the read values were out of the typical range of the sensors, there was an indication for sensor replacement, and the user was informed by means of a flag. There was a specific flag for each kind of sensor, i.e., FLAG#1, FLAG#2, and FLAG#3, respectively, for the sensors being used for flow, pressure, and temperature measurements.

Reliability is an important performance index of agricultural sprayers. A paradigm shift in reliability research on agricultural sprayers has left a simple handbook based on a constant failure rate for the smart-system sensor-based and the support real-time decision-making approaches. Based on this, for each flag, the structure was considered to be that presented in Figure 6.

Destruction level	**Design specification/ performance tests**	**Robustness margin**	**Safety and approval tests**	**Optimal Operating point**

Figure 6. Structure of the flags, in which the operational conditions of the sprayers based on flow, pressure, and temperature, as well as constraints, can be observed.

For the flag structure, the context of sensitivity and specificity summarized the performance of a diagnostic test with outcomes that determined the level of a standard for operation. When the test was quantitative, receiver operating characteristic curves were used to display the performance of all possible cut points of the quantitative diagnostic marker. Here, it was being used for both the reference curve of the sensors and the polynomial regression method. Attention was given to determining an optimal decision rule, which is also called the optimal operating point. Such a point provides a graphical interpretation for decision making. The construction of the databases for the three different sensors, which were related to the calibration and correct operation of the agricultural sprayer in a specific range of use, was organized previously.

Table I shows results as evidence of the operation of the algorithms applied for a commercially available sprayer´s inspection based on the system for real-time failure and reliability analysis.

Safety and approval tests are related to finding and guaranteeing that an approved safety element of an agricultural sprayer reliably or consistently functions in accordance with manufacturer specifications. Furthermore, the robustness margin is related to the formulation for robustness requirements in the agricultural industry. They do not require specific, detailed uncertainty models, and, hence, these margins can be evaluated based on the experience and interpretation of the analysis results. They are, in general, evaluated in the frequency domain, or even by using the information related to the safety margin of a machine's operation, without loss of its hydraulic characteristics and purpose. Likewise, the design specification and performance tests are typically related to performance specifications. They are written in projects and should be observed when implemented. The design's specifications for a piece of machinery are straightforward related to its purpose and application.

TABLE I. RESULTS FOR A REAL-TIME FAILURE AND RELIABILITY ANALYSIS.

FLAG # 1	Destruction level (Q_6 and Q_7)	Design Specification/ Performance tests (Q_4 and Q_5)	Robustness margin (Q_2 and Q_3)	Safety and approval tests (Q_1)	Optimal operating point (Q_0)
[l/m]	$3.00 \leq F_6 < 6.00$ $19.00 < F_7 \leq 21.50$	$6.00 \leq F_4 < 8.25$ $16.90 < F_5 \leq 19.00$	$8.25 \leq F_2 < 10.25$ $14.00 < F_3 \leq 16.90$	$10.25 \leq F_1 \leq 14.00$	12.25

FLAG #2	Destruction level (P_6 and P_7)	Design Specification/ Performance tests (P_4 and P_5)	Robustness margin (P_2 and P_3)	Safety and approval tests (P_1)	Optimal operating point (P_0)
[bar]	$0.00 \leq P_6 < 0.38$ $2.12 < P_7 \leq 2.49$	$0.38 \leq P_4 < 0.63$ $1.81 < P_5 \leq 2.12$	$0.63 \leq P_2 < 1.00$ $1.50 < P_3 \leq 1.81$	$1.00 \leq P_1 \leq 1.50$	1.25

FLAG #3	Destruction level (T_6 and T_7)	Design Specification/ Performance tests (T_4 and T_5)	Robustness margin (T_2 and T_3)	Safety and approval tests (T_1)	Optimal operating point (T_0)
[°C]	$0.00 \leq P_2 < 10.00$ $75.00 < P_3 \leq 87.50$	$10.00 \leq T_4 < 22.50$ $65.00 < T_5 \leq 75.00$	$22.50 \leq T_2 < 31.25$ $55.00 < T_3 \leq 65.00$	$31.25 \leq T_1 \leq 55,00$	42.50

Therefore, information's contained in the structures of the flags are used to evaluate the range of the feedback variables used in the control of the agricultural machines to support decision making for a correct and adequate operation. In the same way, the concept behind the destruction level is related to the region where one can find risks for the machinery lifetime and that must be avoided.

For the acquisition of a reference curve for the flow sensor, an ORION electromagnetic flowmeter, model Orion 4621A300000, installed at the outlet of the water pump of the ASDS was used [42]. The electromagnetic flowmeter had a measuring range from 5 to 100 l/min for pressures up to 4000 kPa. The calibration constant of this flowmeter, according to the manufacturer, was 600 pulses per liter, and the flow rate in liters per minute was obtained from reading a related frequency in Hertz. With the aid of LabVIEW software, a group of reference flows in liters per minute was sent to the sensor, and a set of values was obtained from the sensor flow (Figure 7).

Also, for the acquisition of a reference database with pressure values, a WIKA model A-10 pressure sensor was used. The voltage signals of the A-10 sensor varied from 0 to 10 V, proportional to their pressure measurement ranges from 0 to 16 bar, and this sensor had a reading error and a maximum linearity of 0.016 bar. With the aid of LabVIEW software, reference pressure values considering intervals of 0.15 bar for a useful operating range from 0.5 to 3.0 bar were sent to the pressure sensor, and the values obtained were recorded (Figure 8). In addition, to obtain a reference database with correct temperature values, a calibrated sensor, type PT 100 of the Mit-Exact brand, was used, which was initially dipped in a beaker with water and ice. This water was heated, with the aid of a mixer, to 95°C. As the temperature values increased, the internal resistance of the sensor also increased. For a better perception of the variation of the values of the sensor's resistance, a Wheatstone bridge was used. In this way, it was possible to measure the unknown resistance of the sensor. The values were recorded considering intervals of 5°C, i.e., taking into account an experimental range for evaluation of different levels of the sprayer operation (Figure 9).

According to the flag structure for each variable, it is possible to carry out, in real time, the agricultural sprayer's diagnosis, as well as, if actions are required, to find its prognostic and corrections based on the actuation by its control circuit, or even recommendation for any sensor's replacement.

Then, based on such a context, the prognostics and fault-tolerant strategies for reliable field operation can be obtained.

However, joint efforts from engineers and researchers in a transdisciplinary way are still required to fulfill the needs in such a field of knowledge and promote completely the new paradigm shift in reliability of agricultural machinery.

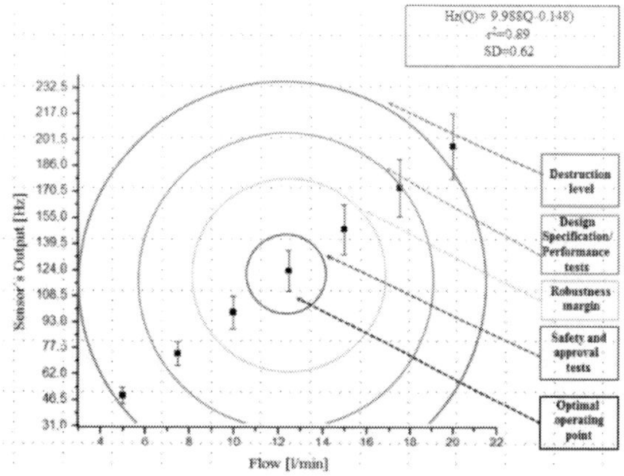

Figure 7. Reference curve for the flow sensor (Electromagnetic flowmeter, model Orion 4621A300000) installed at the outlet of the water pump, and the experimental range results obtained for an agricultural sprayer's operation.

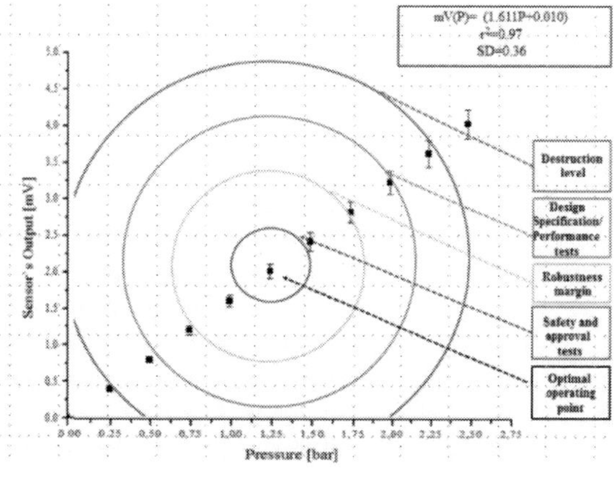

Figure 8. Reference curve for the pressure sensor (WIKA model A-10) installed at the boom, and the experimental range results obtained for an agricultural sprayer's operation.

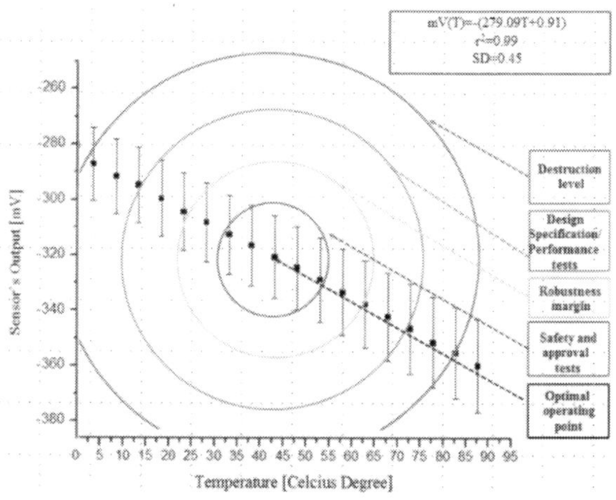

Figure 9. Reference curve for the temperature sensor (PT 100 of Mit-Exact) used to measure the temperature of the syrup, which is formed by the pesticides added to water, and the experimental range results obtained for an agricultural sprayer's operation.

IV. CONCLUSIONS

An intelligent system for evaluation of the failure and reliability of agricultural sprayers, based on the sensors' information and a smart support decision-making architecture, was presented.

Results showed that it is possible to observe real-time prognostics, as well as help with robustness, to ensure quality aggregation in pest control processes based on agricultural spraying systems. In addition, such a system enabled the configuration of a sensor's recalibration using an unsupervised algorithm considering the use of a CAN bus protocol operating with the measurements of the flow rate, pressure, and temperature in the controlled circuit process of an agricultural sprayer.

Furthermore, there are opportunities for a condition of real-time monitoring and fault-tolerant design that can enable an extended lifetime and reduced failure rate, as well as a better understanding of failure mechanisms, because more failure-mechanism-specific accelerated testing can be designed, which can lead to improved reliability predictions for sensor-based agricultural machinery and its applications.

ACKNOWLEDGMENT

This research was supported by the Brazilian Corporation for Agricultural Research (Embrapa), Process SEG – No. 11.14.09.001.05.06.

REFERENCES

[1] Food Security Information Network (FSIN): *Global Report on Food Crises (GRFC 2019)*, pp. 202, 2019. [retrieved: August, 2019]. Available from: http://www.fsinplatform.org/sites/default/files/resources/files/GRFC2019FullReport.pdf.

[2] Food and Agriculture Organization of the United Nations: "Global agriculture towards 2050", FAO, Rome, 2009.

[3] J. K. Schueller, "Automation and control". In: CIGR Handbook of Agricultural Engineering, Information Technology, vol. VI, ed. by A. Munack (CIGR, Tzukuba) pp. 184–195, Chap. 4, 2006.

[4] T. Stombaugh, E. Benson, and J. W. Hummel, "Automatic guidance of agricultural vehicles at high field speeds", ASAE Paper No. 983110 (ASAE, St. Joseph), 1998.

[5] M. Yitayew, K. Didan, and C. Reynolds, "Microcomputer based low-head gravity-flow bubbler irrigation system design", Computer and. Electronics in Agriculture, vol. 22, pp. 29–39, 1999.

[6] F. R. Miranda, R. E. Yoder, J. B. Wilkerson, and L. O. Odhiambo, "An autonomous controller for site-specific management of fixed irrigation systems, Computer and. Electronics in Agriculture, vol. 468, pp. 183–197, 2005.

[7] S. Fountas *et al.*,"Farm management information systems: current situation and future perspectives", Computer and. Electronics in Agriculture, vol. 115, pp. 40-50, 2015.

[8] C. G. Sørensen *et al.*,"Conceptual model of a future farm management information system", Computer and Electronics in Agriculture, vol. 72, Issue 1, pp. 37-47, 2010.

[9] A. Kaloxylos *et al.*, "Farm management systems and the future internet era", Computer and Electronics in Agriculture, vol. 89, pp. 130-144, 2012.

[10] M. Pecht and V. Ramappan, "Are components still the major problem: a review of electronic system and device field failure returns", IEEE Transaction on Components, Hybrids, Manufacturing Technology, vol, 15, pp 1160-1164, 1992.

[11] C. T. Leonard, "Mechanical engineering issues and electronic equipment reliability: Incurred costs without compensating benefits", Journal of Electronic Packaging, vol. 113, pp 1-7, 1991.

[12] A. Bar-Cohen, "Reliability physics vs reliability prediction", IEEE Transaction on Reliability, vol. 37, p. 452, 1988.

[13] P. D. T. O'Connor, "Reliability prediction: Help or hoax?", Solid State Technology, vol. 33, pp 59-61, 1990.

[14] H. V. Mercaldi, E. A. G. Peñaloza, R. A. Mariano, V. A. Oliveira, and P. E. Cruvinel, "Flow and Pressure Regulation for Agricultural Sprayers Using Solenoid Valves", In: International Federation of Automatic Control (IFAC), Elsevier, vol. 50, Issue 1, 2017, pp. 6607-6612, doi.org/10.1016/j.ifacol.2017.08.693.

[15] D. L. Reichard, H. E. Ozkan, and R.D. Fox, "Nozzle wear rates and test procedure", Transaction of the ASAE, St. Joseph, vol.34, n.6, pp.2309-2316, 1991.

[16] H. Ganzelmeier and S. Rietz, "Inspection of plant protection in Europe". In: International Conference on Agricultural Engineering. Part II, Oslo. Proceedings..., Eurageng, pp.597-598, 1998.

[17] N. Bjugstad, "Controlo of crop sprayers in Norway", Oslo: Ageng, Eurageng, 1998.

[18] M. A. Gandolfo, "Periodic inspection of agricultural sprayers" (original title: Inspeção periódica de pulverizados agrícolas). Doctoral Thesis, Faculty of Agronomic Sciences, São Paulo State University (UNESP), SP, Brazil, 92 pp., 2002.

[19] B. Huyghebaert *et al.*, "Compulsory inspection of crop sprayers already in use Belgium", Selection of control method, Madrid: Ageng, CD-ROM, 1996.

[20] P. Braekman *et al.*, "Organisation and results of the mandatory inspection of crop sprayers in Belgium", Belgium: Ministry of Small Enterprises, Traders and Agriculture, 9 pp., 2005.

[21] L. M. Val, "Programs for the formation of the applicators and equipment's maintenance" (original title: Programas de formación de aplicadores y programa de revisión de equipos. In: Jornada Internacional en Tecnologia de Aplicacion, 2007, Proceedings... Montevidéo: Republic University, CD-ROM, 2007.

[22] J. C. Magdalena and A. P. Di Prinzio, "Calibration service for fruit growing sprayers in Black River and Neuquén" (original title: Servicio de calibración de pulverizadoras fruticolas en Río Negro y Neuquén), In: Congreso Argentino de Ingenieria Rural, Córdoba. Proceedings.... Argentina: National Cordoba University, vol. 2, pp. 137-148, 1992.

[23] E. Fey, "State of the art in relation to the spray process of the associates from the COOPERVALE" (original title: Estado de arte do processo de pulverização junto a associados da COOPERVALE), Supervised Internship Report Ponta Grossa State University, Maripá – PR, Brazil, 26 pp., 1998.

[24] J. Langenakens and M. Pieters, "The organization and first results of the mandatory inspection of crop sprayers in Belgium", In: Aspects of applied Biology - Optimizing pesticide application, Agricultural Research Centre Ghent, pp. 233-240, 1997.

[25] S. Sartori, "Sprayers for tractor ground application" (original title: Pulverizadores para aplicação terrestre tratorizada), In: Simpósio Brasileiro sobre Tecnologia de Aplicação de Defensivos Agrícolas, Jaboticabal, SP, Brazil, Proceedings... FUNEP, vol. 1, pp. 46-79, 1985.

[26] G. F. Dedordi *et al.*, "Technical-operational evaluation of bar sprayers in Pato Branco region" (original title: Avaliação técnica-operacional de pulverizadores de barras na região de Pato Branco), Acta Iguazu, Cascavel, PR, Brazil, vol.3, n.1, pp.144-155, 2014.

[27] J. F. Schlosser, "Application technology and machine use: use of agrochemicals" (original title: Tecnologia de aplicação e uso de máquinas: uso de agroquímicos), Federal University of Santa Maria, Textbook - Technical Series, Module 5, 2002.

[28] F. Olivi and A. Simão, "In order to speed up the maintenance of sprayers, the diagnostic case provides technical support and spare parts" (original title: Com o objetivo de agilizar a manutenção dos pulverizadores, a maleta de diagnóstico dá suporte técnico e na reposição de peças). Agricultural News. [retrieved: September, 2019]. Available from: https://noticiasagricolas.com.br/videos/ma-quinas-e-tecnologias/.

[29] K. R. Felizardo, H. V. Mercaldi, P. E. Cruvinel, V. A. Olivei-ra, and B. L. Steward, "Modeling and model validation of a chemical injection sprayer system", Applied Engineering in Agriculture, vol. 32, Issue 3, pp. 285-297, 2016.

[30] X. Wei, S. Jian, and H. Sun, "Design and Test of Variable Rate Application Controller of Intermittent Spray Based on PWM", Journal of agricultural machinery vol. 43, Issue 12, pp. 87-129, 2012.

[31] H Liu, H Zhu, and Y Shen, "Development of digital flow control system for copy multi-channel variable-rate sprayers", Journal Transactions of the ASABE, vol. 57, Issue 1, pp. 273-281, 2014.

[32] American Society of Agricultural and Biological Engineers (ASAE) Standards: "S572 - Spray nozzle classification by droplet spectra", no. 99, St. Joseph USA, pp. 389-391, 2000.

[33] P. E. Cruvinel, V. A. Oliveira, H. V. Mercaldi, E. A. G. Penaloza and K. R. Felizardo, "An advanced sensors-based platform for the development of agricultural sprayers," In: Sergey Y. Yurish (Ed.). Sensors and Applications in

Measuring and Automation Control Systems. [S. l.]: IFSA, pp. 181-204. (Advances in Sensors: Reviews; vol. 4), 2016.

[34] K. Etschberger, "Controller Area Network. Basics, Protocols, Chips and Applications", IXXAT, ISBN 3-00-007376-0, 2001.

[35] R. B. GmbH, "CAN Specification, Version 2.0", Postfach 50, D-7000 Stuuugart 1, 1991. Imported into Framemaker 4 by Chuck Powers, BOSCH, Motorola MCTG Multiplex Applications, April 3, 1995.

[36] J. R. Edwards, "Polynomial regression and response surface methodology," In: C. Ostroff & T. A. Judge (Eds.), Perspectives on organizational fit, pp. 361–372. San Francisco: Jossey-Bass, 2007.

[37] L. Tornqvist, P. Vartia, and Y. Vartia, "How should relative changes be measured?" The American Statistician, vol. 39, Issue 1, pp. 43–46, 1985.

[38] P. E. Danielsson, "Euclidean distance mapping," Computer Graphics Image Processing, vol. 14, pp. 227-248, 1980.

[39] T. Chai and R. R. Draxler, "Root mean square error (RMSE) or mean absolute error (MAE)? - arguments against avoiding RMSE in the literature," Geoscience Model Development, vol. 7, pp. 1247–1250, 2014.

[40] R. H. Walden, "Analog-to-digital converter survey and analysis", IEEE Journal on Selected Areas in Communication, vol. 17, no. 4, pp. 539–550, 1999.

[41] TJA 1050 Data Sheet – High speed CAN transceiver. Product specification, Integrated Circuits, Philips Semiconductors, pp. 18, 2003.

[42] ORION Electro-Magnetic Flow Meter. [retrieved: November, 2019]. Available from: mcpheeenterprises .com/orion-electromagnetic-flowmeter/.

Advanced Mathematical Calibration Procedure for Sensor Systems Measuring Multi Component Gas Mixtures

Rolf Seifert
HybridSensorNet e.V. (HSN)
D-76131 Karlsruhe, Germany
e-mail: rolf.seifert@partner.kit.edu

Hubert B. Keller
Institute of Automation and Applied Informatics (IAI)
Karlsruhe Institute of Technology
D-76344 Eggenstein-Leopoldshafen, Germany
e-mail: hubert.keller@kit.edu

Abstract—**Although sensor chips for multi gas sensors are usually batch wise fabricated, each sensor chip has to be individually calibrated to yield a high analytic performance. For multi gas applications, a sensor chip normally has to be measured for calibration at least at 3 calibration points for every component. An advanced mathematical procedure for batch wise calibration called ProCal2.0 is introduced to reduce the calibration effort nearly by a factor of three even for multi gas-analysis. By application of the procedure to sensitivity data sampled at binary Ethanol/H_2 gas mixtures, it is demonstrated that, with this efficient calibration procedure, the analysis results are very close to those which are obtained when each sensor chip is individually calibrated.**

***Keywords* - multi gas sensors; batch wise calibration; multi gas applications; multi gas analysis; analysis error.**

I. INTRODUCTION

Economic online and in-situ field analyses applications like discriminated alarming of smouldering fire or toxic gas leakages, monitoring of volatile components in chemical and biochemical processes, quality monitoring in food processing, etc., rely on reliable and economic analytical solutions by sensor systems.

In this context, the isothermally operated Metal Oxide Gas sensors (MOGs) with tin oxide as base material have been introduced due to their high sensitivity, long term stability and low price. Their sensitivity to specific gas components, however, cannot be cultivated with high discrimination to others. Therefore, other approaches are necessary like a gas sensor array of MOGs [1][2] or a thermo-cyclic operation of the MOG and simultaneous sampling of the conductance which finally leads to the mathematical analysis of the so called Conductance-over-Time-Profiles (CTPs) [3]. These CTPs show characteristic profile shapes reflecting gas composition and gas component concentrations depending on the choice of additives. It can be shown that, using this approach, valuable signal information can be extracted to be numerically analyzed for substance identification and concentration determination even in the case of varying environmental conditions (e.g. humidity) [4].

The effort for calibration of the sensor elements is very time consuming and costly. Sensor elements are usually batch wise fabricated. But, unavoidable production inaccuracies of the sensor elements lead to unreproducibilities of the gas analytic attributes. Therefore, although the signal patterns of the various sensor elements of a production batch are quite similar, each sensor element has to be calibrated, in order to yield high analytic performance, and this can be very costly. The number of components to be simultaneously analyzed determines the dimension of the calibration field and, for good analysis results, as was experimentally shown, about three to five or even more calibration points for every dimension are necessary depending on the accuracy demands of the analysis.

In this report, an advanced mathematical calibration procedure called ProCal2.0 is introduced which is able to drastically reduce the calibration effort of batch wise fabricated sensor chips measuring multi component gas mixtures.

In Section 2, the considered application field is briefly described. A short outline of the advanced calibration procedure ProCal2.0 is given in Section 3. Different calibration models to compare the performance of the procedure are introduced in Section 4. In Section 5, the analysis results are presented. Section 6 summarizes the results of this report.

II. APPLICATION: BINARY ETHANOL/H_2 GAS MIXTURES

The application, on which the outline of ProCal2.0 is described and the analysis results are presented, is measuring binary Ethanol/H_2 gas mixtures. The measurements are performed using the sensor system, which is described in detail in [5]. The sensor system is armed with batch wise fabricated sensor chips and runs in the above mentioned thermo-cyclic mode.

III. OUTLINE OF PROCAL2.0

As mentioned above, even if the sensor chips are fabricated in a batch wise manner, each sensor chip has to be individually calibrated to gain reasonable analysis results. To calibrate a sensor chip, calibration measurements have to be performed, which are very time consuming and, therefore, costly. In the case of binary Ethanol/H_2 gas mixtures, the gas mixture has to be measured at least at three concentration levels of each component and all concentration combinations. That leads to at least 9 calibration measurements to determine a reasonable mathematical calibration model.

Table I shows the considered calibration field.

TABLE I. CALIBRATION FIELD OF 9 CONCENTRATION POINTS (CP) AND RELATED APPROXIMATION FUNCTIONS

Ethanol H_2 in ppm		Ethanol H_2 in ppm		Ethanol H_2 in ppm	
50-10	CP1	50-20	CP4	50-30	CP7
100-10	CP2	100-20	CP5	100-30	CP8
175-10	CP3	175-20	CP6	175-30	CP9
Function f(i,10)		Function f(i,20)		Function f(i,30)	

ProCal2.0 is an extension of the procedure ProCal [6], which was only designed for calibrating single gases.

ProCal2.0 is developed to drastically reduce the calibration effort for multi component gas mixtures.

Therefore, one sensor chip of the batch wise fabricated sensor chips is chosen as the so-called reference chip. Using this reference chip, the binary Ethanol/H_2 gas mixture is measured at all 9 calibration points.

With all the other sensor chips of the batch, the binary Ethanol/H_2 gas mixture is measured only at the calibration points CP2, CP5 and CP8, the so-called reference calibration points, which are written in red in the calibration field in Table I.

Next, approximation functions are determined which map the signal patterns, in our case the CTPs, of the reference chip in a best manner to the signal patterns of the other, non-reference, sensor chips at the reference calibration points. That means, we get 3 approximation functions for each non-reference chip.

For example, function f(i,10) in Table I is the best approximation function for mapping the signal pattern of CP2 of the reference chip to the corresponding signal pattern of sensor chip i. The signal pattern of sensor chip i at CP1 is calculated by mapping the signal pattern of the reference chip at this calibration point, using this approximation function f(i,10).

This procedure is performed in a similar way for all non-reference sensor chips and for all calibration points.

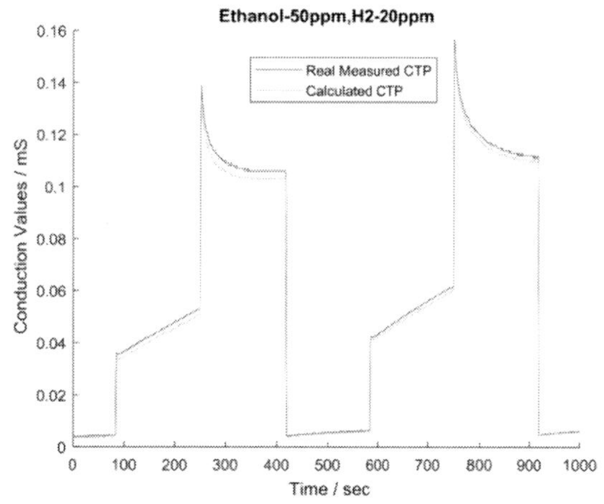

Figure 1. Comparison of real measured CTP and calculated CTP.

Therefore, we get all the needed signal patterns to determine the related mathematical calibration models. However, only 3 instead of 9 calibration measurements are needed for all non-reference chips. This reduces the calibration effort by factor of 3.

It can be shown that ProCal2.0 is also able to determine the best choice of the reference chip and also to detect outliers. That means, ProCal2.0 can identify chips of the production batch which cannot be reasonably calibrated using this procedure.

IV. MATHEMATICAL CALIBRATION MODELS

To demonstrate the performance of the above described procedure ProCal2.0, three mathematical calibration models are established. The "individual model of each chip" means that each sensor chip of the batch is individually calibrated. This is a very costly and time consuming calibration process and leads to the best possible analyses results. Using the "class reference model", only one sensor element of a batch (here, the reference chip) is completely calibrated and the calibration model of this sensor chip is assigned to each one of the other chip of the batch. This leads to very poor analysis results will be shown later in the paper. The third calibration model is the above mentioned "batch wise calibration model" using procedure ProCal2.0 with reduction of the complete calibration effort by a factor of 3.

The data analysis is performed with the calibration and evaluation program ProSens [7].

V. ANALYSIS RESULTS

In this section, we consider 4 sensor chips of a batch, called S1, S2, S3 and S4. Sensor chip S4 was chosen as reference chip.

Binary Ethanol/H_2 gas mixtures at the concentration points given in Table II are measured using the 4 chips and the concentration determination is performed using the 3 calibration models mentioned above.

TABLE II. CONTRATION POINTS FOR DATA ANALYSIS

Ethanol-H_2 in ppm	Ethanol-H_2 in ppm	Ethanol-H_2 in ppm
50-10	50-20	50-30
100-10	100-20	100-30
135-10	135-20	135-30
175-10	175-20	175-30

The red marked line is additionally measured for data analysis.

A. *Analysis Results of Sensor Chip S1*

The following tables show the analysis results of sensor chip S1 using the 3 calibration models. Table III shows the analysis results using the individual calibration model, Table IV the results using the class reference model and Table V using the batch wise calibration model. The bold values are the dosed values and the values in the table are the calculated values (all values in ppm).

TABLE III. ANALYSIS RESULTS USING THE INDIVIDUAL MODEL

Ethanol/H_2	10	20	30
50	50.3-10.1	47.9-20.1	54.6-27.6
100	95.1-11.1	111.3-18.9	92.7-32.8
135	127.0-11.1	139.9-20.2	134.5-31.2
175	175.1-9.7	168.5-21.0	179.4-28.7

TABLE IV. ANALYSIS RESULTS USING THE CLASS REFERENCE MODEL

Ethanol/H_2	10	20	30
50	60.2-4.5	59.3-18.3	69.7-26.1
100	106.4-9.9	121.7-18.5	114.0-30.7
135	141.3-10.4	149.6-20.1	156.4-28.7
175	156.4-28.7	177.6-20.7	202.2-25.6

TABLE V. ANALYSIS RESULTS USING THE BATCH WISE CALIBRATION MODEL

Ethanol/H_2	10	20	30
50	46.2-11.7	48.0-19.6	54.8-26.5
100	89.2-11.3	110.5-18.6	84.3-32.3
135	119.6-11.2	138.9-20.4	120.0-31.7
175	163.8-10.0	165.7-21.7	157.3-30.4

Tables VI to VIII show the relative analysis errors.

TABLE VI. RELATIVE ANALYSIS ERRORS IN % USING THE INDIVIDUAL MODEL

Ethanol/H_2	10	20	30
50	0.6-0.8	4.1-0.7	9.3-7.9
100	4.9-11.1	11.3-5.7	7.3-9.3
135	5.9-10.9	3.6-1.1	0.4-3.8
175	0.1-2.5	3.7-5.0	2.5-4.5

TABLE VII. RELATIVE ANALYSIS ERRORS IN % USING THE CLASS REFERENCE MODEL

Ethanol/H_2	10	20	30
50	20.3-55.1	18.7-8.5	39.4-12.9
100	6.4-0.9	21.7-7.6	14.0-2.2
135	4.6-4.4	10.8-0.3	15.9-4.4
175	11.5-6.3	1.5-3.7	15.5-14.8

TABLE VIII. RELATIVE ANALYSIS ERRORS IN % USING THE BATCH WISE CALIBRATION MODEL

Ethanol/H_2	10	20	30
50	7.6-17.5	4.0-2.1	9.6-11.5
100	10.8-12.6	10.5-6.9	15.7-7.6
135	11.4-11.9	2.9-1.8	11.1-5.5
175	6.4-0.1	5.3-8.5	10.1-1.3

The red marked numbers indicate the largest relative analysis errors in the related tables.

It can be clearly seen that, as expected, the best the analysis results are obtained using the individual calibration model. The analysis results using the batch wise calibration are very close to these best results but the calibration effort is reduced by the factor of 3. Using the class reference model, the analysis results are very poor.

B. *Analysis Results of the Other Sensor Chips*

The analysis results of the other sensor chips based on the 3 calibration models are very similar to those of sensor chip S1.

The following Tables IX to XI show the maximum analysis errors of the components Ethanol and H_2 using the sensors S1, S2 and S3 and the related calibration models.

TABLE IX. MAXIMAL ANALYSIS ERRORS IN % FOR SENSOR S1

Maximal Analysis Errors in %	Ethanol	H_2
Individual Model	11.3	11.1
Batch wise Calibration Model	15.7	17.5
Class Reference Model	39.4	55.1

TABLE X. MAXIMAL ANALYSIS ERRORS IN % FOR SENSOR S2

Maximal Analysis Errors in %	Ethanol	H_2
Individual Model	14.8	13.1
Batch wise Calibration Model	19.3	13.3
Class Reference Model	44.5	17.4

TABLE XI. MAXIMAL ANALYSIS ERRORS IN % FOR SENSOR S3

Maximal Analysis Errors in %	Ethanol	H_2
Individual Model	14.2	12.4
Batch wise Calibration Model	14.2	13.9
Class Reference Model	34.5	17.1

It can be clearly seen that in all considered cases the analysis results obtained by the batch wise calibration model are very close to the best possible analysis results.

VI. CONCLUSION

Using the calibration procedure ProCal2.0, the very time consuming and expansive calibration of batch wise fabricated sensor elements can be reduced almost by the factor of 3. ProCal2.0 is able to determine the class reference chip, which best represents the chips of the batch and can exclude outliers, i.e, chips which cannot be calibrated with this procedure. It was shown that the calculated signal patterns are close to the sampled signal patterns and the analysis errors using this calibration model are very close to the best possible ones using the very time-consuming individual model, but dramatically better than those using the class reference model.

The same procedure can also be applied for cost effective and time saving recalibration.

REFERENCES

[1] P. Althainz, J. Goschnick, S. Ehrmann, and H. J. Ache, "Multisensor Microsystem for Contaminants in Air", Sensors and Actuators B: Chemical, 33, 1-3, 1996, pp. 72-76.

[2] V. V. Sysoev, I. Kiselev, M. Frietsch, and J. Goschnick, "Discrimination Power of a Metal-Oxide Thin-Film Sensor Microarray", Sensors, 4, 2004, pp. 37-46.

[3] A. Jerger, H. Kohler, F. Becker, H. B. Keller, and R. Seifert, "New applications of tin oxide gas sensors II. Intelligent sensor system for reliable monitoring of ammonia leakages", Sensors and Actuators B: Chemical, 81, 2-3, 2002, pp. 301-307.

[4] K. Frank et al., "Chemical Analysis with Tin Oxide Gas Sensors:Choice of Additives, Method of Operation and Analysis of Numerical SignalSensors", Letters 6, pp. 908-911 2008.

[5] R. Seifert, H. B. Keller, T. Conrad, and J. Peter, "Alcohol Control: Mobile Sensor System and Numerical Signal Analysis", Sensors and Transducers, (ISSN: 2306-8515, e-ISSN 1726-5479), Vol. 205, Issue 10, October 2016, pp.10-15

[6] R. Seifert, H. B. Keller, K. Frank, and H. Kohler, "ProSens— An Efficient Mathematical Procedure forCalibration and Evaluation of Tin Oxide Gas Sensor Data", Sensor Letters, Vol. 9/2, pp. 621-624, 2011

[7] R. Seifert, H. B. Keller, K. Frank, and H. Kohler, "Batch-Wise Mathematical Calibration of Thermo-Cyclically Operated Tin Oxide Gas Sensors", Sensor Letters 9, pp. 621-624, 2011.

Digital Sensing Platform with High Accuracy Time Synchronization Function for Management of Buildings and Cities

Narito Kurata
Faculty of Industrial Technology
Tsukuba University of Technology
Tsukuba City, Ibaraki, Japan
e-mail: kurata@home.email.ne.jp

Abstract - **In this paper, a diverse and robust digital sensing platform is proposed as a practical smart sensing system for maintenance management of ageing buildings and cities. High-accuracy time information is added to measurement data to obtain sets of digital sensing data with time synchronization for use in multimodal analysis of risk. As a first step, this paper describes the development of a sensor device for performing high accuracy time synchronization sensing on civil infrastructure, such as bridges and building structures using a digital high-accuracy acceleration sensor. An ultra high-accuracy clock, such as a Chip Scale Atomic Clock (CSAC) is mounted in the sensor device, and using its time measurement accuracy, a mechanism is implemented for time stamping the output of the digital sensor. The measurement accuracy of the chip scale atomic clocks is too high, so if the CPU of the sensor device adds the time stamp, tracking cannot be performed. Therefore, a dedicated Field-Programmable Gate Array (FPGA) for adding the time stamp is provided. Tests were performed on the developed sensor device using a shaking table, and the time synchronization performance was checked by comparing the measurement results of multiple sensor devices and a servo type acceleration sensor.**

Keywords-Time Synchronization; Chip Scale Atomic Clock; Earthquake Observation; Structural Health Monitoring; Micro Electro Mechanical Systems.

I. INTRODUCTION

Aging of civil infrastructure, such as bridges, expressways, and high-rise buildings, is advancing, and automation of inspection for maintenance and management of these structures is an important civil task. Also, Japan is subject to natural disasters, such as earthquakes, so it is necessary to detect the damage to structures and identify the damage status immediately after occurrence of a disaster. To automate the detection of such abnormal events, it is effective to collect and analyze data from groups of sensor devices.

The authors have developed sensor devices for earthquake observation and structural health monitoring by applying wireless sensor network technology, and have verified the performance on high-rise buildings [1][2]. One of the important tasks in this verification was time synchronization between sensor devices. Ensuring time synchronization between sensor devices is essential for analysis of sets of data measured by multiple sensor devices to evaluate the structural safety of a structure. In a wireless sensor network system, time synchronization is realized by transmitting and receiving wireless packets between the sensor devices [2]. However, wireless sensor network technology cannot cover large structures, such as buildings and bridges or a wide urban area.

On the other hand, if the sensor devices installed at the various locations can autonomously maintain accurate time information, this problem can be resolved. The use of Global Positioning System (GPS) signals is effective outdoors, but within a building, underground, on the substructure of a bridge, in a tunnel and others, this is not possible. Therefore, a prototype sensor device autonomously maintaining accurate time information using an ultra high-accuracy clock, namely a Chip Scale Atomic Clock (CSAC) [3]-[8], was produced [9][10]. Next, improvements were made to increase the performance and stability of the prototype sensor device, and a device for practical use was developed [11]. In addition, in order to apply the developed practical sensor device to earthquake observation, the logic for the detection of occurrence of earthquakes and storage of data for seismic events was implemented, and the performance was checked using shaking table tests. From these, the performance of the sensor device capable of autonomously maintaining accurate time information was confirmed, indicating that the sensor device can be applied to seismic observation and structural health monitoring of civil infrastructures and buildings. Furthermore, the developed sensor device was installed on actual buildings and bridges, and applied to seismic observation and evaluation of structural health [12]. However, a Micro Electro Mechanical Systems (MEMS) acceleration sensor was mounted in the developed sensor device, so it was difficult to measure down to microtremors with high accuracy. The developed sensor device is equipped with an external analog input interface, through which any analog sensor can be connected. High-performance servo acceleration sensors can also be connected, but the risk of noise being mixed into the analog signal remains. Therefore, it was decided to mount a digital acceleration sensor in the sensor device, to eliminate the risk of noise. A camera sensor can be connected to the digital sensor device described in this paper, with the aim of developing a diverse digital sensor platform.

In this paper, Section II shows the existing time synchronization methods and describes their problems and achievement of the development of the digital sensing platform proposed in this research. Section III describes the mechanism for providing ultra-high accurate time information to digital sensor data by the CSAC, and explains the configuration of the digital sensing platform and the development of the actual sensor device. Further, Section IV describes the performance confirmation tests on the time synchronization of the developed sensor device, and it is confirmed that time synchronization among the developed digital sensor devices is achieved.

II. STATE OF THE ART

Methods for ensuring time synchronization between measurement data from multiple sensors include the method of transmitting and receiving wireless packets [13][14], the method using a network, such as IEEE 1588 [15], the method using a GPS signal, and the Network Time Protocol (NTP) [4] designed for time synchronization on the Internet. However, these have the restrictions that they cannot be used without wireless communication, cable network connections, and an environment where GPS signals can be received, respectively. When sensors are installed on high-rise buildings or civil infrastructure, it is difficult to cover all the installations with a single method. For example, with the method of transmitting and receiving wireless packets, the convenience is high as cables are not required, and if a multi-hop ad hoc wireless function is implemented it is considered that this can be used on structures within a single building [2]. However, if multiple sensors are deployed over long and large structures, such as high-rise buildings and bridges or a wide area urban space, it is not possible to ensure long term stable operation with wireless technology. It is likely that the most stable system can be constructed with cable network connections, but laying dedicated cables for time synchronization is difficult from the cost point of view. Also, the method of GPS signals can be easily used outdoors, but GPS signals cannot be used in such places as indoors, on bridge substructures, underground and in tunnels.

Even if GPS signals cannot be used, wireless transmission and reception is unstable, and cable network connections are not possible, in order to stably acquire sets of sensor data with time synchronization, the ideal method is to enable each individual sensor itself to autonomously maintain accurate time information. In other words, if it is possible to add accurate time information (time stamp) to the measurement data from each sensor, sets of data with time synchronization can be acquired. Therefore, it was decided to develop a sensing system that autonomously maintains accurate time information, by applying high-accuracy clocks, namely CSAC [3]-[8]. The size of CSACs has been miniaturized so that they can be mounted in boards, and they can realize ultra high-accuracy time measurement in the order of several tens of picoseconds. Development commenced in 2001 with support from the Defense Advanced Research Projects Agency (DARPA) of the USA, and in 2011 the commercial product was put on the market. Applications include countermeasures against obstruction of GPS positioning using jamming signals, high-accuracy positioning by mounting the product in such devices as smartphones, and high-level identification of disaster status, and it is expected that the cost will be further reduced as the use spreads. The error in time measurement by CSACs is 4 to 8 orders of magnitude smaller than the error in time measurement by crystal oscillators or the error in time synchronization by NTP or GPS signals. If this CSAC is mounted in each sensor device and a mechanism for adding a high-accuracy time stamp to measurement data that is sampled individually is implemented, sets of sensor data with time synchronization can be acquired even when GPS signals cannot be used, wireless transmission and reception is unstable, and cable network connections are not possible.

In previous developments, the sensor device was equipped with a MEMS acceleration sensor and an external input interface that can connect to any analog sensor. However, the accuracy of a built-in MEMS acceleration sensor is not high and it cannot measure microtremors. High-accuracy servo acceleration sensors can be used via the external input interface, but a risk that noise will be mixed into the analog signal remains. Therefore, in this research, it is decided that a fully-fledged digital sensing platform shall be developed. Specifically, a high-accuracy digital acceleration sensor will be mounted in the sensor device to enable accurate acceleration measurements with no risk of noise being mixed in, and technology has been developed to add an accurate time stamp to the digital sensor output using CSACs. In addition, it is intended for a camera sensor to be connected in the next development step, with the aim of developing a diverse digital sensing platform.

III. DESIGN OF DIGITAL SENSING PLATFORM

The sensor device normally consists of a CPU that controls the measurement, sensors, a memory device, a network interface, etc., and the CPU uses a crystal oscillator. When a CSAC is mounted in this device, the CPU of the sensor device is corrected using the time information of the CSAC as-is, and when measurement is performed, a delay occurs due to the high-accuracy time measurement of the CSAC. Therefore, a mechanism provided with a dedicated integrated circuit, Field-Programmable Gate Array (FPGA), was developed for directly adding the CSAC time information to the digital sensor measurement data at the hardware level. In this way, the measurement data with the CSAC time information added by the FPGA is stored in memory without load on the CPU, and the data can be collected via a network. Also, the FPGA is programmable, so logic for detecting abnormal events using the measurement data can be incorporated while handling the CSAC time information. In the development to date, it has been assumed that analog sensors will be used, but in this paper the development of a mechanism for adding an accurate time stamp from the CSAC to the output of digital sensors is described.

The sensor device developed in this research consists of a CSAC board, an FPGA board, and a sensor board, as shown in Figure 1. The CSAC board is equipped with the CSAC, GPS, etc., and it generates accurate time information. The FPGA board controls the measurement by each sensor while adding the ultra high-accuracy time information from the CSAC, and after the measurement data is stored in memory, the data is transmitted to a network through Ethernet, Wi-Fi, or 3rd generation mobile communication system (3G). Two types of data are stored: always measured data, and data that is only measured in an event, such as an earthquake. The former is constantly stored on a Secure Digital Memory Card (SD card), and, when a certain quantity is exceeded, old data is deleted to leave space for overwriting with new data. In the case of the latter, logic for detecting the start and end of an earthquake is incorporated in the FPGA, and, after an earthquake, the data for the earthquake event only is immediately transmitted to the network. The sensor board performs the measurements by the sensors in accordance with instructions from the FPGA. The sensors mounted are a digital high-accuracy acceleration sensor and a temperature sensor (-50℃ to +150℃). For checking the time synchronization performance, an external analog sensor interface is provided to which any external analog sensor can be connected via a Sub Miniature Type A (SMA) connector. Table 1 shows the specifications of the digital high-accuracy acceleration sensor mounted in the sensor board. An A/D converter having 16-bit resolution is mounted in the sensor board, and data from signals that have passed through the A/D converter is branched and amplified by a factor of 10, so analog sensors that require a wide dynamic range can also be connected. This has been packaged and developed as a digital sensing platform. Figure 2 shows the produced digital sensor device in which the CSAC is mounted. The CSAC board, the FPGA board, and the sensor board are shown in Figures 3 to 5, respectively.

The autonomous time synchronization digital sensing system is constructed using the developed digital sensor device. The digital sensor devices in which a CSAC is mounted each keep accurate time independently of each other, but, in order to construct a sensing system consisting of multiple devices, it is necessary to define absolute time information in one device as the master device, and synchronize the other devices as slaves. Each main board contains an input output connector for 1 Pulse Per Second (PPS) signal from the CSAC. Using this connector, a 1 PPS signal is output from the master device and input to each slave device for synchronization, so that the phases of the CSAC clocks of the slave devices can be aligned with the master.

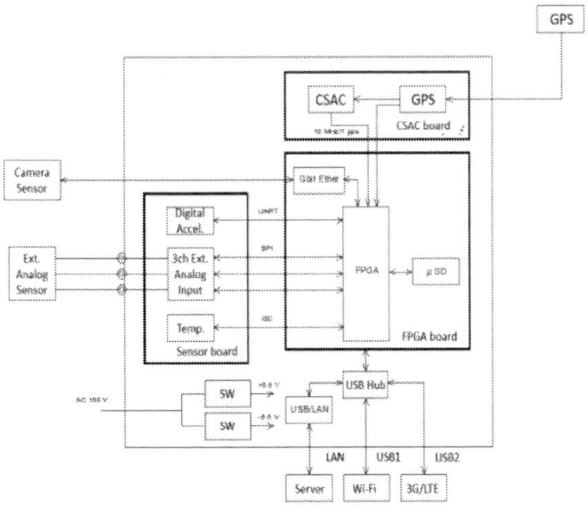

Figure 1. Configuration of digital sensing platform.

TABLE I. SPECIFICATIONS OF DIGITAL ACCELERATION SENSOR

Model	EPSON M-A351AS
Range	±5G
Noise Density	0.5 µG/√Hz (Average)
Resolution	0.06 µG/LSB
Bandwidth	100 Hz (selectable)
Output Range	1000 sps (selectable)
Digital Serial Interface	SPI
Outside dimensions (mm)	24 × 24 × 19
Weight	12 grams
Operating Temperature	-20 °C to +85 °C
Power Consumption	3.3 V, 66 mW
Output Mode Selection	Acceleration, Tilt Angle, or Tilt Angle Speed

Figure 2. Internal configuration of sensor device.

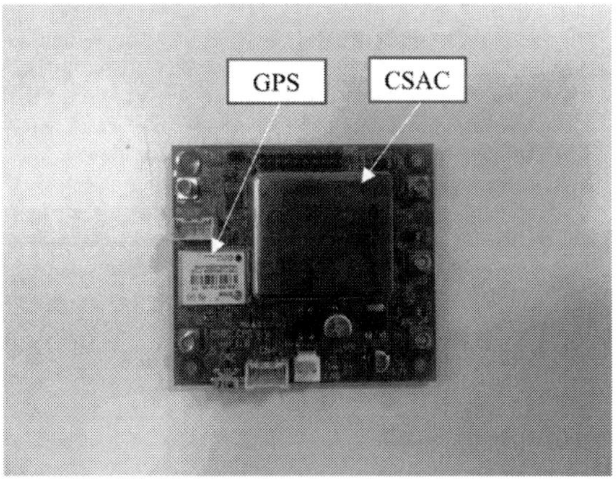

Figure 3. CSAC board.

Figure 4. FPGA board.

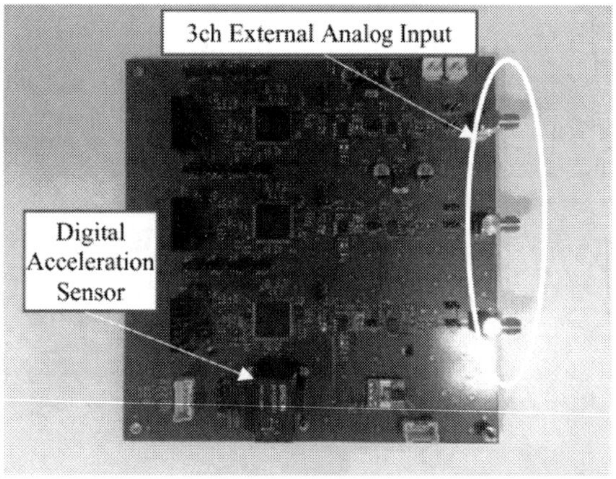

Figure 5. Sensor board.

The time measurement accuracy of the CSACs is advanced, but they do not have absolute time information from the start, so it is necessary that this be separately defined. For this purpose, the GPS device mounted in the main board may be used, or such information may be manually input. Also, during initial setting, all sensor devices may acquire the absolute time using their GPS device and they can be synchronized together. When all the sensor devices from which the sensing system is constituted are initially synchronized in this way, they subsequently continue to autonomously maintain high-accuracy time information, so they can be installed in any location and the measurement data can be streamed or can be stored on an SD card and retrieved at any time. An accurate time stamp is recorded during each sampling process of the measurement data, so a data acquisition method, such as Ethernet, Wi-Fi and 3G, can be selected. Also, even in places where GPS signals or network connection is not available, since just measurement and data collection are required, this system is suitable for mobile measurement or for use as a transportable sensing system.

IV. Performance Confirmation Tests on the Time Synchronization Function of Digital Sensing Platform

Tests were performed using a shaking table to confirm the performance of the developed digital sensor device. The objective was to confirm the measurement performance and time synchronization performance of the digital sensor device. Three sensor devices and a servo acceleration sensor for comparison were fixed on a shaking table, as shown in Figures 6 and 7. The same vibrations were applied in one horizontal direction and the results were compared. The analog output of the comparative servo acceleration sensor was input to the sensor devices via the external input interface. In the test, a sweep wave of 2 to 20 Hz, as shown in Figures 8 and 9, was applied to excite the shaking table as an input wave, and the measurement sampling frequency of the sensor devices was set to 1,000 Hz.

Figure 6. Experimental setup.

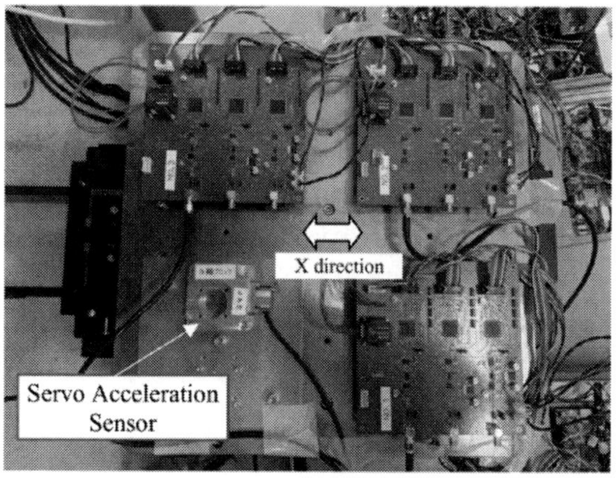

Figure 7. Sensor boards on shaking table.

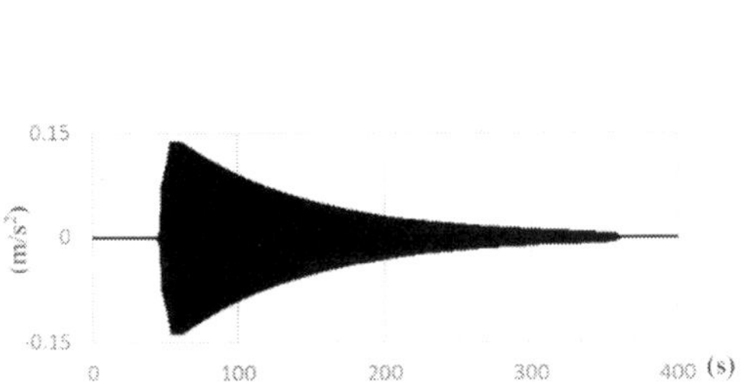

Figure 8. Input swept sine wave (2 to 20 Hz).

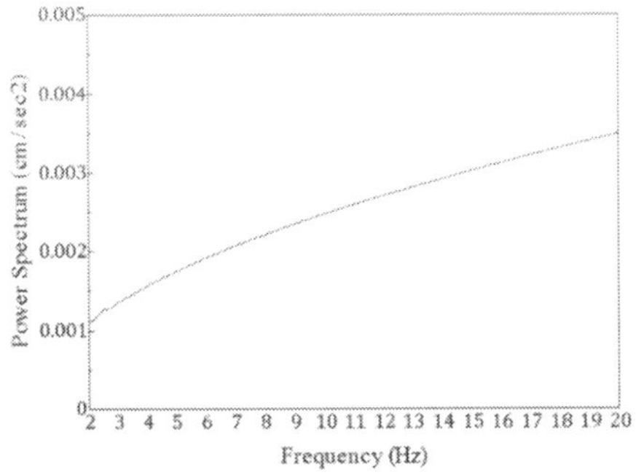

Figure 9. Power spectrum of input swept sine wave

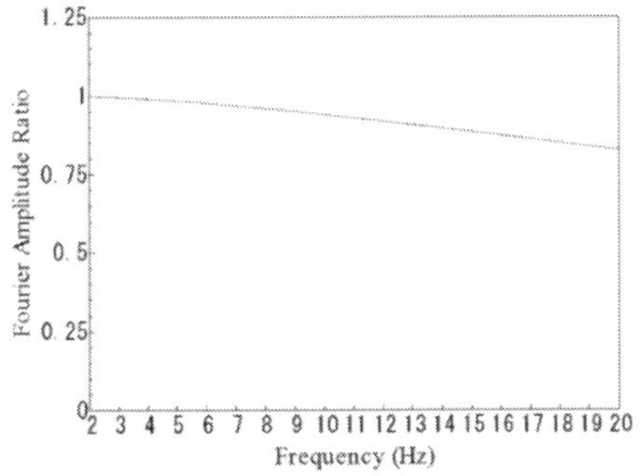

Figure 10. Spectrum ratios of Fourier amplitudes of three sensor modules to servo-type acceleration sensor (X direction).

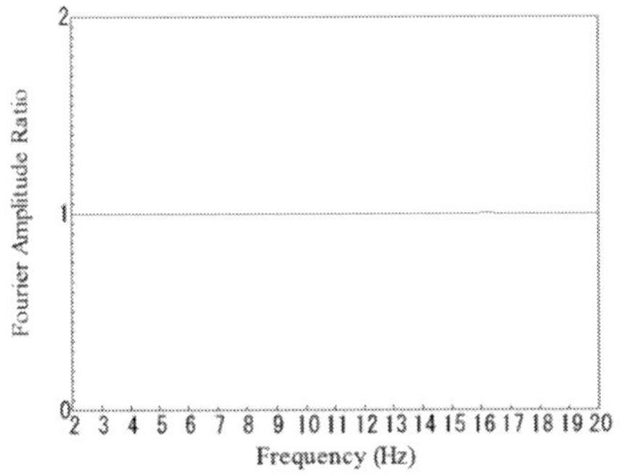

Figure 11. Spectrum ratios of Fourier amplitude of two slave modules to master module (X direction).

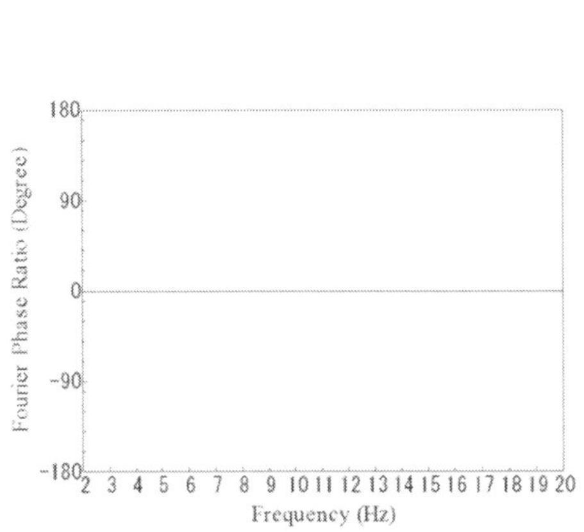

Figure 12. Spectrum ratios of Fourier phase of two slave modules to master module (X direction).

Excitation was applied in the X-direction of the sensor devices, and measurement was performed by the sensor devices and the comparative servo acceleration sensor. Figure 10 shows the results of calculation of the Fourier amplitude spectrum ratios of the acceleration time history measured by the three sensor devices and the comparative servo acceleration sensor. The amplitude of the former three devices relative to the latter reflected the low pass filter characteristics of the digital sensors, so it can be seen that the digital acceleration sensor mounted in the sensor boards have good performance.

Next, Figure 11 shows the results of obtaining the Fourier amplitude spectrum ratios for the acceleration time history from two sensor devices (slaves) on the shaking table when the other sensor device was used as the master. The amplitude of the former two devices relative to the latter was flat over the frequency band 2 to 20 Hz. In addition, Figure 12 shows the results of obtaining the Fourier phase spectrum ratios for the acceleration time history from two sensor devices (slaves) on the shaking table when the other sensor device was used as the master. There is no phase delay between the sensor devices, and, if the time synchronization was maintained, it would be expected that it should be about zero over the frequency band 2 to 20 Hz. From the figure, it can be seen that time synchronization has been achieved between the sensor devices.

V. Conclusion

This paper has reported on research into a digital sensing platform that autonomously maintains high-accuracy time information, by applying CSACs. First, the issues with a system that was developed assuming analog sensors were pointed out, and a system based on digital sensors was proposed and developed as a method of resolving these issues. Autonomous time synchronization using CSACs was described, and the mechanism for adding ultra high-accuracy time information to digital sensor data using a CSAC and the development of the sensor devices was described in detail. In addition, the results of tests performed to confirm the time synchronization performance of the sensor device were reported. Three sensor devices were mounted in a shaking table and tests were performed by applying vibrations simultaneously, and by checking the phase properties of the measurement results it was confirmed that time synchronization was achieved for sampling at 1000 Hz.

In the next development step, we intend to additionally connect a camera sensor, with the aim of developing a diverse digital sensing platform. For absolute time synchronization of the camera sensor, a digital input interface will be additionally installed to the developed sensor device as a digital sensor platform so that a camera sensor can be connected. A function for adding the time stamp to the output of the camera sensor will be added, the same as for the output of the built-in digital acceleration sensor. The developed diverse digital sensing platform will be applied to actual structures, to acquire acceleration and image data with accurate time information.

Acknowledgment

This research was partially supported by the New Energy and Industrial Technology Development Organization (NEDO) through the Project of Technology for Maintenance, Replacement and Management of Civil Infrastructure, Cross-ministerial Strategic Innovation Promotion Program (SIP). This research was also partially supported by JSPS KAKENHI Grant Number JP16K01283 and JP19K04963.

References

[1] N. Kurata, M. Suzuki, S. Saruwatari, and H. Morikawa, "Actual Application of Ubiquitous Structural Monitoring System using Wireless Sensor Networks," Proc. 14th World Conference on Earthquake Engineering (14WCEE), Beijing, China, Oct. 2008, Paper ID:11-0037, pp. 1-8.

[2] N. Kurata, M. Suzuki, S. Saruwatari, and H. Morikawa, "Application of Ubiquitous Structural Monitoring System by Wireless Sensor Networks to Actual High-rise Building," Proc. the 5th World Conference on Structural Control and Monitoring (5WCSCM), Tokyo, Japan, July 2010, Paper No. 013, pp. 1-9.

[3] M. Maroti, B. Kusy, G. Simon, and A. Ledeczi, "The Flooding Time Synchronization Protocol," Proc. the 2nd International Conference on Embedded Networked Sensor Systems (SenSys '04), Baltimore, USA, Nov. 2004, pp. 39-49, ISBN:1-58113-879-2.

[4] D. L. Mills, "Internet Time Synchronization: the Network Time Protocol," IEEE Transactions on Communications, vol. 39, Issue 10, pp. 1482-1493, Oct. 1991, doi:10.1109/26.103043.

[5] B. W. Parkinson and J. J. Spilker Jr. eds, "Global Positioning System: Theory and Applications," Vol. I & II, American Institute of Aeronautics and Astronautics (AIAA), 1996, ISBN: 978-1-56347-106-3.

[6] S. Knappe et al., "A Microfabricated Atomic Clock," Applied Physics Letters, vol. 85, Issue 9, pp. 1460-1462, Aug. 2004, doi:10.1063/1.1787942.

[7] Q. Li and D. Rus, "Global Clock Synchronization in Sensor Networks," IEEE Transactions on Computers, vol. 55, Issue 2, pp. 214-226, Jan. 2006, ISSN: 0018-9340.

[8] R. Lutwak et al., "The Chip-Scale Atomic Clock - Prototype Evaluation," Proc. the 39th Annual Precise Time and Time Interval (PTTI) Meeting, Long Beach, USA, Nov. 2007, pp. 269-290.

[9] N. Kurata, "Disaster Big Data Infrastructure using Sensing Technology with a Chip Scale Atomic Clock," World Engineering Conference and Convention (WECC2015), Kyoto, Japan, Dec. 2015, pp. 1-5.

[10] N. Kurata, "Basic Study of Autonomous Time Synchronization Sensing Technology Using Chip Scale Atomic Clock," Proc. the 16th International Conference on Computing in Civil and Building Engineering (ICCCBE2016), Osaka, Japan, July 2016, pp. 67-74.

[11] N. Kurata, "An Autonomous Time Synchronization Sensor Device Using a Chip Scale Atomic Clock for Earthquake Observation and Structural Health Monitoring", The Eighth International Conference on Sensor Device Technologies and Applications (SENSORDEVICES 2017), pp.31-36, Rome, Italy, 2017.

[12] N. Kurata, "Improvement and Application of Sensor Device Capable of Autonomously Keeping Accurate Time Information for Buildings and Civil Infrastructures," The Ninth International Conference on Sensor Device Technologies and Applications (SENSORDEVICES 2018), pp. 114-120, Venice, Italy, 2018.

[13] J. Elson, L. Girod, and D. Estrin, "Fine-Grained Network Time Synchronization using Reference Broadcasts," Proc. 5th Symposium on Operating Systems Design and Implementation (OSDI'02), Boston, Massachusetts, Dec. 2002, pp. 147-163.

[14] S. Ganeriwal, R. Kumar, and M. B. Srivastava, "Timing-sync Protocol for Sensor Networks," Proc. the 1st International Conference on Embedded Networked Sensor Systems (SenSys '03), Los Angeles, California, Nov. 2003, pp. 138-149.

[15] K. Romer, "Time Synchronization in Ad Hoc Networks," Proc. the 2nd ACM International Symp. on Mobile Ad Hoc Networking & Computing (MobiHoc'01), Long Beach, California, Oct. 2001, pp. 173-182.

Integrated Sensor System for Signal Conditioning, Digitization and Interfacing for Terahertz Bolometric Camera

Tomo Markočič and Janez Trontelj
University of Ljubljana, Faculty of Electrical Engineering
Ljubljana, Slovenia
tomo.markocic@student.uni-lj.si; janez.trontelj1@guest.arnes.si

***Abstract*—This work is about designing an integrated system to capture, partially process and digitalize data from a terahertz bolometric antenna array. Different techniques for achieving the required operation are presented, including a low noise amplifier with a custom lateral bipolar p-n-p structure as input stage and other strategies to reject noise, and integration of analogue signal processing into Analogue-to-Digital Converter (ADC). The results of the bipolar structure characterization are presented in great detail, demonstrating the feasibility of using them in an amplifier.**

Keywords-lateral bipolar transistor; low-noise amplifier; terahertz bolometric camera; custom CMOS structure.

I. INTRODUCTION

The one-dimensional terahertz camera uses a pulsed 50% duty cycle source of electromagnetic waves with frequency between 0.08 and 1 THz and in-house designed and manufactured bolometers, precisely designed resistors bonded to THz micro antennas, that are sensitive to these frequencies [1][2]. The camera is designed for industrial applications where high image rate is required. Typically, objects are flying past the camera at speeds up to 20 m/s and need to be imaged with precision in the range of millimetres, requiring sample rates in the range of 20 kS/s [3].

Due to the nature of bolometers, sensor value acquisition must be synchronised with the terahertz source duty cycle to correctly detect peak-to-peak values (between source being on and off). The effective pixel value is the difference between these two acquired values.

The currently used system uses an Application-Specific Integrated Circuit (ASIC) with custom designed Low-Noise Amplifiers (LNA), Successive Approximation Register (SAR) ADCs for early digitalization and Field-Programmable Gate Array (FPGA) unit for processing and interfacing. Early digitalization is a trend in the sensor industry but, with the ever-increasing number of pixels, the data rates and processing power requirements are becoming too high and too expensive. It currently takes 8 16-bit ADC conversions per one pulse of terahertz source, which are then averaged and subtracted to get one sample value for one pixel. With several hundred sensors at 20 kS/s, it becomes a costly challenge for the FPGA interface.

Designing a single chip sensor interface as for regular complementary metal–oxide–semiconductor (CMOS) camera sensors is not feasible; pixels are a couple of millimetres apart, stretched over wide areas and we can only interface a few pixels with one chip. Therefore, distributed processing is required, to minimise the amount of data that goes to the interface unit.

Section 2 of this work describes the proposed updates of the system; Section 3 demonstrates some preliminary results of system simulations and test structures measurements and Section 4 summarizes the findings.

II. UPDATED SYSTEM DETAILS

The novel proposed system joins an improved LNA, a circuit for analogue processing of the amplified signal and an integrated capacitive SAR ADC on a single ASIC. The camera would be composed of several ASICs which would be interfaced through a simplified central system with a microprocessor or FPGA (Fig. 1).

The LNA is improved by introducing a bipolar input stage, as it is not a victim to 1/f shot noise and helps in reducing the white noise level. Unlike for CMOS transistors, noise is not dependent on the bipolar transistor size. Therefore, the new LNA is expected to utilize a fraction of the silicon area used by the existing LNA. Designing a bipolar stage is, however, a challenge of its own as a regular bipolar transistor cannot be fabricated in the preferred 0.35 μm CMOS technology due to layer availability, or has the collector permanently connected to the substrate, making it useless. Fortunately, there is an option to create a lateral p-n-p structure which has two collectors, one (horizontal) still permanently connected to substrate and the other (lateral) available for active load connection (Fig. 2). Initial Spice simulation model parameters for the structure have been borrowed from a similar CMOS technology of a different

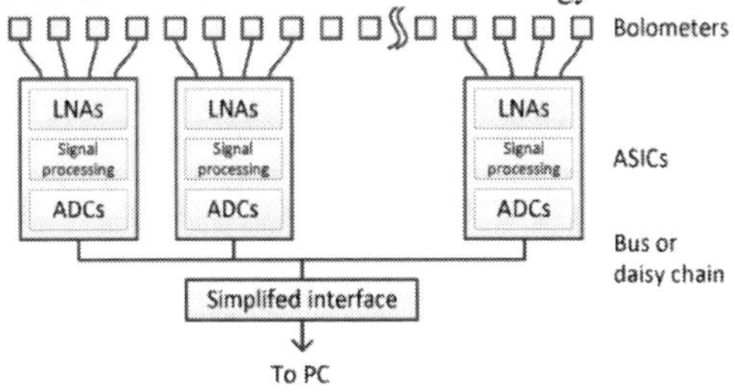

Figure 1. Proposed system

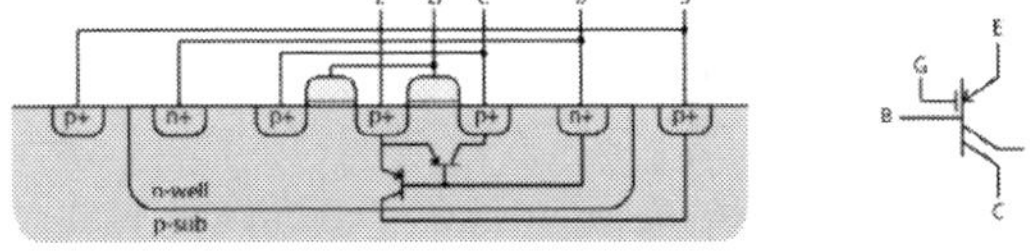

Figure 2. Lateral p-n-p structure

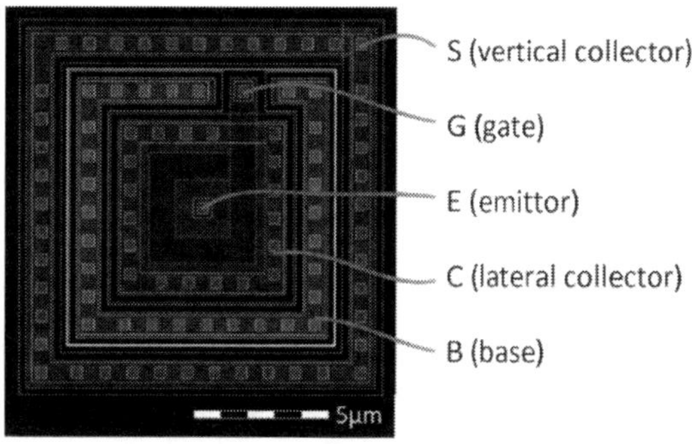

Figure 3. Layout diagram for lateral p-n-p structure

semiconductor foundry and will be later updated to better match the results of the test structures (Fig. 3) to be then used in simulations of LNA.

The analogue signal processing circuit is partially integrated into ADC and allows it to directly digitize peak-to-peak values of the amplified signal from the bolometers. A SAR ADC usually samples signal and reference simultaneously in its capacitors, while here it is set to sample the bottom peak as reference in the first half of the period and the top peak as signal in the second half. The rest of the processing circuit is a configurable low-pass filter, used to minimise noise with lowest impact on signal, so that we can avoid oversampling and possibly lower requirements for the number of bits.

III. Results and Discussion

Testing of lateral p-n-p test structures showed promising results compared to the existing Spice model (Fig. 4). We tried two slightly different layouts of which one (Q1) appears to be more stable over V_{BC} voltage with beta factor around half of expected value, while the second (Q2) shows much better beta factors at higher currents, but varies a lot with V_{BC}. In an amplifier, a number of transistors would be connected in parallel, allowing utilisation of higher beta factors at lower currents through single transistors. The grey area in Fig. 4 marks the planned single-transistor collector current – it would be a compromise between total collector current, silicon area and highest beta. The samples still require more detailed characterisation, but designing a third layout that is between these two seems as a reasonable idea to get a better compromise.

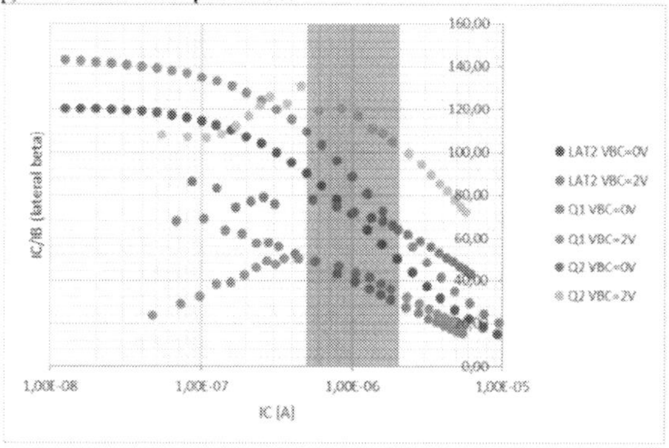

Figure 4. Measurement results for beta of lateral transistor

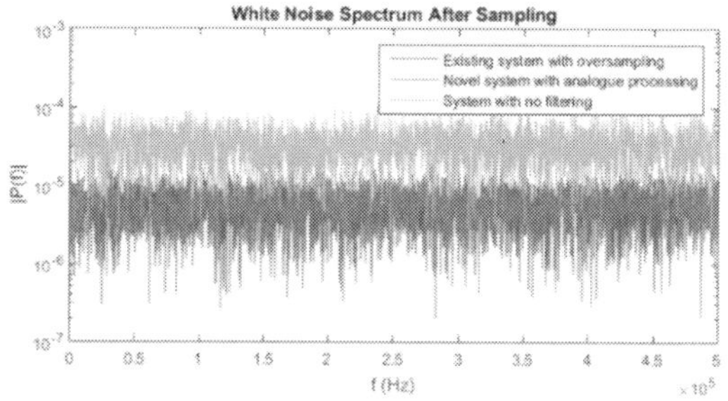

Figure 5. Noise comparison of systems with digital and analogue signal processing, and with no filtering

Noise results are incomplete at this point, but we are expecting white noise with level inversely proportional to the collector current.

Simulink simulations of analogue processing show noise levels comparable to digital with oversampling. The correct settings of analogue low-pass filter are required. By varying the filter edge frequency, we could either let more noise pass through, lower the signal, or even introduce pixel retention noise. When the filter is set correctly, the noise rejection in our proposed system is very similar to the digital system, when we compare them to a system with no filtering, as seen in Fig. 5.

Our findings suggest that we will need to trim these filters to adapt them to the desired sample rate and possibly compensate for the process spread of integrated components (resistors, capacitors).

IV. Conclusion

With this work, we have demonstrated that the novel system with analogue processing is feasible and would significantly reduce hardware cost of the terahertz camera. This is done by more means: integrating ADCs on chip, reducing the amount of digital data, optimizing data connections to the interface and replacing powerful FPGA with a simpler interface.

At the same time, we have shown that the performance of the system will not be compromised but rather improved with better noise characteristics of the new LNA.

References

[1] A. Sešek, I. Kašalynas, A. Žemva, and J. Trontelj, "Antenna-Coupled Ti-Microbolometers for High-Sensitivity Terahertz Imaging," Sens. Actuators Phys., Vol. 268, pp. 133–140, Dec. 2017.

[2] I. Kašalynas et al. , "Performance of the Antenna Coupled Microbolometers Characterized by the Quasi-Optical Measurements at Frequencies 0.1–1.0 THz," 38th International Conference on Infrared, Millimeter, and Terahertz Waves (IRMMW-THz), 2013, pp. 1–2.

[3] S. Boppel, A. Lisauskas, A. Max, V. Krozer, and H. G. Roskos, "CMOS Detector Arrays in a Virtual 10-kilopixel Camera for Coherent Terahertz Real-Time Imaging," Opt. Lett., 37, February 4, 2012, pp. 536–538.

Thermoelectric Energy Harvesting Circuit for Variable Temperature Gradients

Martin Lenzhofer
Silicon Austria Labs GmbH
Villach, Austria
e-mail: Martin.Lenzhofer@silicon-austria.com

Abstract—**In this paper, a thermoelectric energy harvesting circuit that starts up at very low input voltages and harvests the very little energy of a variable temperature gradient is presented. It is based on a commercially available step-up converter Integrated Circuit (IC), with an adopted wiring scheme and some additional components to guarantee a stable operation for a sensor unit over a certain time. As a result, it turns out that load matching is suboptimal for the start up of the Thermo-Electric Generator (TEG) system in the case of small temperature gradients.**

Keywords-energy harvesting; small temperature gradient; step-up converter; thermoelectric generator.

I. INTRODUCTION

One main resource used for generating electrical power is thermal energy. There are many applications, which focus on the usage of thermoelectric devices exploiting temperature differences, but there are rarely any of them dealing with harvesting energy from temperature gradients [1]-[3]. There are two main reasons for that: on one hand, the little energy potential within a gradient does not seem to be attractive and, on the other hand, it is a reliability issue for stable operations of autonomous systems. Nevertheless, there are a plenty of applications that show small temperature gradients, for example in wearable systems and in systems for environmental and infrastructure monitoring.

The presented paper describes in Section 1, a thermal harvesting circuit that is capable to start up at very low voltage levels and to harvest all disposable energy within a thermal gradient to supply a sensor node in an oven application. In Section 2, the main results are briefly discussed and an outlook for future work is given.

II. DEVELOPMENT OF THE HARVESTER CIRCUIT

A commonly used IC to build up a thermal energy harvesting device is the LTC3108 from Linear Technology Corp. [4]. It is intended for low power wireless sensor nodes and other low power applications and, therefore, contains additional to the power management unit, several output voltage regulators that can either be switched on independently, on demand or sequentially, to supply a controller core and a transmitter or sensor unit. The power-up sequence of the circuit is fixed and hard coded, if thermal energy is applied to the TEG and will be described next.

After some energy is collected, the voltage at the low voltage regulator starts to increase until it reaches a level of 2.2 V. This regulator is intended to supply a controller unit. As the thermal energy is still available at the input, the voltage at the output VOUT still increases to 3.3 V. If this level is reached, the Power-Good (PGD) indicator pin activates, indicating the controller that a valid voltage level is available for other components. Due to the still applied energy at the input, now a transistor in the LTC3108 activates another output to charge an additional external storage capacitor.

Based on this short functional description, it can be recognized that the power up sequence is only useful if a constant energy is present at the input. If working with thermal gradients, in worst case also limited in time and additionally at varying rates, some problems will occur with this setup. One major problem is that the thermal energy within such gradients is very limited. In the case of constant heat transfer in the TEG, load matching is targeted to guarantee maximal power transfer. This configuration is suboptimal for the start up of a TEG system from small temperature gradients. The reason is that, if a load like a Microcontroller (MCU) core is already present at the Low-Dropout Regulator (LDO) output, the current flow will lead to a decrease of voltage level at the input. Tests showed that even for very low power MCUs, a valid start up of the controller core is impossible. Therefore, another strategy must be implemented; meaning, first to harvest all available energy within the thermal gradient and just at a certain point where enough power is available to initially activate the controller circuit.

If investigating in the different units implemented in the LTC3108, [3], all necessary building blocks can be found that are suitable to change the originally intended sequence, by just adding a few external components and adopting the connection scheme shown in Figure 1. The presented circuit just considers temperature gradients, which result in a positive voltage on the TEG system.

The start up procedure, for example of an oven, results in a temperature gradient, which proportionally increases the generated voltage of the TEG in the self-sustaining sensor system. If a level of 20 mV is reached, the dc-dc converter of the LTC3108 starts, leading to a corresponding voltage at the pin VOUT. To avoid a constant current flow and perform voltage matching, just a capacitor as load is connected to this pin. The reason is that it is slowly charged and, therefore, harvests all the available power at the input. The value of this capacitance must be matched to the slope of the thermal gradient, because if it continues to heat up the system, the voltage at the TEG will decrease at a certain time and will deactivate the dc-dc converter again if turning below 20 mV. In the case of a too high value, even the expected output voltage level at VOUT will not be reached anymore. The stored energy in this capacitor can then be used to supply the sensor electronics. The IC internally generates a PGD signal if the programmed output level at VOUT reaches 2.235 V. In the presented application, the load formed by a MCU is connected to the pin VOUT2. The reason for that is that this pin is switchable by an internal low leakage transistor. For enabling VOUT2, the PGD signal is used and connected to the respective input pin with a low voltage Schottky diode D1. This diode D1 represents another key aspect of the presented circuit, because it forms together with the second one an OR-gate controlled by an output of the MCU. This method is necessary due to the load case at output VOUT2. The MCU current at start up, refer to Figure 2 a.) (A), leads to a voltage drop at VOUT (B), where the energy flows from the capacitor C7 over the internal transistor of IC1 to the MCU. The PGD condition is tied to an internal not access- and adjustable hysteresis setting, which leads to switch off again if the voltage level decreases by 7.5% of the nominal set value (B). This happens quite rapidly, because the start up current even of a low power MCU is quite high. If the voltage is switched off by the PGD signal again, the electronics would never be supplied sufficiently. After switching off (B) again, the current is almost zero again, causing an increase in voltage at VOUT and switching on the voltage regulator once more (C). So, this effect of switching on and off the load leads to some kind of ringing, refer to Figure 2 a.), which has to be prohibited. Therefore, the energy stored in the capacitor C7 must be high enough to hold the voltage level during start up, configuration and switching on the diode D1 over the rated voltage minus 7.5% (internally fixed hysteresis value). After that, a further decrease in voltage level is not critical anymore, due to the lock of the high level of the MCU pin, resulting in Figure 2 b.). In the presented application, the output level is 2.235 V, therefore, the start up procedure including the output pin set is not allowed to decrease beyond 2.174 V. As an MCU with a supply rating of 1.8 V is used, still a margin for a further approximately 0.4 V voltage drop is guaranteed for valid operation. Depending on the stored energy, the permitted voltage drop and the current demand of the electronic circuit for the active operation time of the system, can be calculated.

III. RESULTS AND CONCLUSION

This paper describes a thermal harvesting circuit that can start up at very low input voltages, generated by thermal gradients and supply a circuit over a certain time. As a result, it must be mentioned that the presented solution is just meant for applications where the temperature gradient is exploited in one direction. Furthermore, if harvesting energy from small thermal gradients load matching of the TEG is not suitable, then additional changes to the standard circuitry, provided by the manufacturer, are presented and evaluated to proof the concept. Future work will focus on the improvement of the matching of the used components to increase the efficiency of the circuit and to extend the active time for the sensor application.

ACKNOWLEDGMENT

The COMET Centre ASSIC Austrian Smart Systems Integration Research Center/ COMET Project XX is funded by BMVIT, BMDW, and the Austrian provinces of Carinthia and Styria, within the framework of COMET - Competence Centres for Excellent Technologies. The COMET programme is run by FFG.

REFERENCES

[1] V. Leonov, P. Fiorini, S. Sedky, T. Torfs, and C. Van Hoof, "Thermoelectric MEMS generators as a power supply for a body area network", Proc. IEEE Transducers 2005, pp. 291-295, 2005

[2] Y. Meydbray, R. Singh, and A. Shakouri, "Thermoelectric module construction for low temperature gradient power generation", Proc. 24th Int. Conference on Thermolectrics, pp. 348-351, 2005

[3] P. Woias, "Thermoelectric Energy Harvesting from small variable Temperature Gradients", Proc. 12. Dresdener Sensor-Symosium, pp. 83-88, DOI 10.5162/12dss2015/5.6, 2015

[4] Linear Technology Corp., datasheet LTC3108. [Online]. Available from: https://www.analog.com/media/en/technical-documentation/data-sheets/LTC3108.pdf , [accessed Oct. 2019]

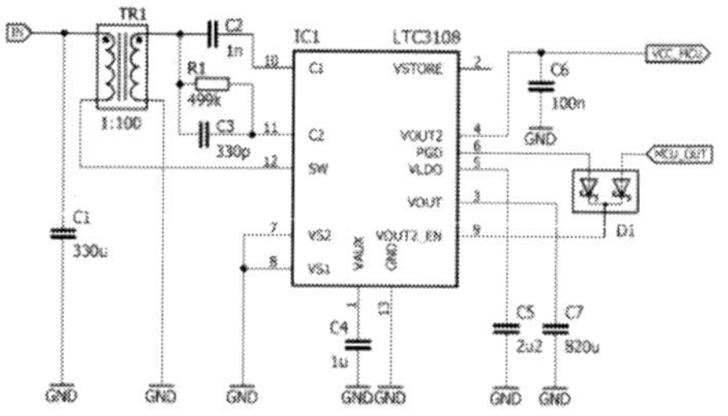

Figure 1. Developed circuit of the thermal harvester unit.

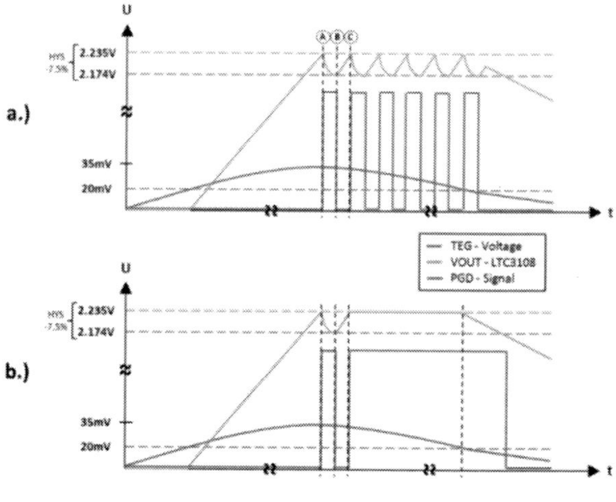

Figure 2. a.) Ringing phenomena due to different load conditions at VOUT, b.) Avoidance of the effect through self locking circuitry

Energy Capture Methods by Piezoelectric Sensors

Irinela Chilibon
National Institute of Optoelectronics, INOE 2000
Bucharest-Magurele, Romania
e-mail: qilib@yahoo.com

Abstract—**This paper presents different energy capture methods with application to the piezoelectric sensors. The piezoelectric material elements of sensors convert mechanical energy into electrical charges due to the direct piezoelectric effect. Collecting energy from the environment is a major area of interest to the development of unconventional renewable energy sources. Electrical energy is created in a way similar to the classic one. Potential energy sources from the environment could be successfully used.**

Keywords-piezoelectric sensor; supercapacitors; renewable energy; low-power.

I. INTRODUCTION

Capturing energy from the environment has shown considerable interest in recent research [1]-[4]. Piezoelectric material elements are able to convert mechanical energy into electrical charges, due to the direct piezoelectric effect. These electric charges could be used in low-power electronic circuitry that use electrically charged high-capacity capacitors. The mechanical sources could be vibrations, pulses and shocks. Piezoelectric sensors are suitable to convert small mechanical deformations directly into electricity, which can be used in small power electrical sources in applications such as: supercapacitors, battery packs, interferometric lasers, etc.

Collecting energy from the environment is a major area of interest with extensive applications in the development of unconventional renewable energy sources. This study clarifies mechanisms for converting mechanical energy into electricity in a highly efficient way. The *mechanical energy* could come from *environmental sources* such as: *wind, vibrations, shocks, rotary movements, wheel rotations, car engines, human breathing, blood flow, body movements, free or lost mechanical energy or acoustic and ultrasonic vibrations.*

This paper is organized as follows. Section II describes the piezoelectric materials and structures used. Section III discusses an overview of Energy Capture Methods in low-power electronics. Section IV presents a summary of low-power electronics. The conclusions, future work and acknowledgement close the article.

II. PIEZOELECTRIC MATERIALS AND STRUCTURES

Piezoelectric materials, usually crystals or ceramics, have the capability to generate a small amount of current, when they are subjected to mechanical pressure, such as pushing, bending, twisting, and turning. Multiple such materials placed near each other could increase the electrical energy.

The process of energy conversion in a piezoelectric material is based on the principle of the piezoelectric effect. The piezoelectric element stores the energy in two forms, as an electric field (electrical energy) and as a strain (mechanical energy). The *piezoelectric effect* exists in two domains, the first is the *direct piezoelectric effect* that describes the material's ability to transform mechanical strain into electrical charge, and the second form is the converse effect, which is the ability to convert an applied electrical potential into mechanical strain energy, as shown in Figure 1. When a piezoelectric element is mechanically stressed, it generates a charge.

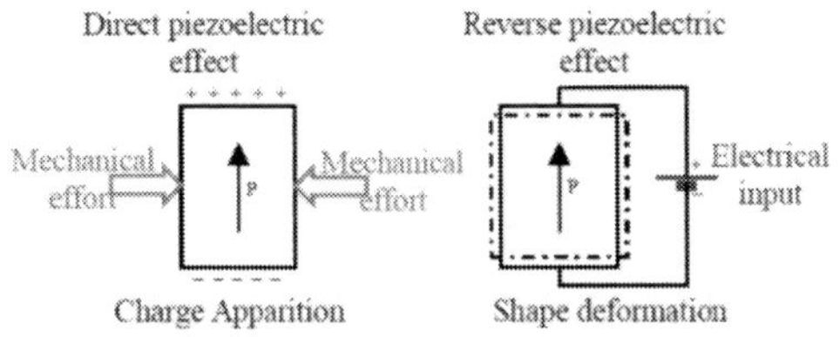

Figure 1. Electromechanical conversion via piezoelectricity phenomenon

The most common type of piezoelectric used in *power harvesting applications* is lead zirconate titanate, a piezoelectric ceramic, or piezoceramic, known as PZT. Although PZT is widely used as a power harvesting material, the piezoceramic's extremely brittle nature causes limitations in the strain that it can safely absorb without being damaged. Lee et al. [1] note that piezoceramics are susceptible to fatigue crack growth when subjected to high frequency cyclic loading. In order to eliminate the disadvantages of piezoceramic materials and improve upon their efficiency, researchers have developed and tested other, more flexible, piezoelectric materials that can be used in energy harvesting applications.

Another common piezoelectric material is *poly(vinylidene fluoride) (PVDF).* PVDF is a piezoelectric polymer that exhibits considerable flexibility when compared to PZT.

Mohammadi et al. [2] developed a *fiber-based piezoelectric (piezofiber) material* consisting of PZT fibers of various diameters (15, 45, 120, and 250 μm) that were aligned, laminated, and molded in an epoxy [3]. *Piezofiber power harvesting materials* have also been investigated by Churchill et al. [4], who tested a composite consisting of unidirectionally aligned PZT fibers of 250 μm diameter embedded in a resin matrix. It was found that, when a 0.38 mm thick sample of 130 mm length and 13 mm width was subjected to a 180 Hz vibration that caused a strain of 300 με in the sample, the composite was able to harvest about 7.5 mW of power.

The last years have seen the birth of many new types of piezoelectric materials or transducers (PZT- lead zirconate titanate, PT-lead titanate, PVDF- polyvinylidene fluoride-trifluoroethylene, piezoceramic/polymer composites, Macro Fiber Composite - MFC, etc.). The schematic of the cross section of an Active Fiber Composite (AFC) actuator [5] is presented in Figure 2. If optimized geometrically, a piezoelectric generator associated with a well suited electronic is likely able to produce the standard 3 Watts required for the lighting system, with all the benefits that it provides.

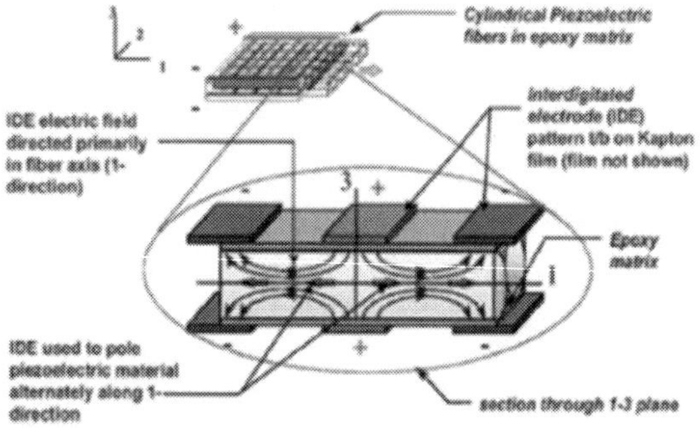

Figure 2. Schematic of the cross section of an Active Fiber Composite (AFC) actuator [5].

Piezoelectric materials exhibit the property that if they are mechanically strained, they generate an electric field proportional to the strain [6]. Conversely, when an electric field is applied, the material undergoes strain. These anisotropic relationships are described by the piezoelectric strain constant, *d*, which gives the relationship between applied stresses while the electro-mechanical coupling coefficient, *k*, describes the efficiency with which energy is converted between mechanical and electrical forms. This latter coefficient is important in determining the efficiency of a resonant generator since the overall efficiency of a piezo element clamped to a substrate and cyclically compressed at its resonant frequency is (1):

$$\eta = \frac{\dfrac{k^2}{2(1-k^2)}}{\dfrac{1}{Q} + \dfrac{k^2}{2(1-k^2)}} \qquad (1)$$

where Q is the quality factor of the resonator. As Q becomes larger, the efficiency tends towards unity but, for typically achievable Q factors, the efficiency increases significantly for higher values of k.

Lee et al. [1][7] developed a PVDF film that was coated with poly(3,4-ethylenedioxy-thiophene)/poly(4-styrenesulfonate) [PEDOT/PSS] electrodes. They compared *the PEDOT/PSS coated films* to films coated with the inorganic electrode materials, *indium tin oxide (ITO)* and platinum (Pt). When subjected to vibrations of the same magnitude over varying frequencies, it was found that the films with Pt electrodes began to show fatigue crack damage of the electrode surface at a frequency of 33 kHz. The ITO electrodes became damaged when operating at a frequency of 213 Hz. The PEDOT/PSS film, however, ran for 10 h at 1 MHz without electrode damage. One can conclude that, by utilizing a more durable electrode layer, a piezoelectric device can operate under more strenuous conditions. This may give the device the ability to harvest more power throughout its lifespan; however, the exact effect of a stronger electrode layer may vary depending on the specific application.

III. OVERVIEW OF ENERGY CAPTURE METHODS IN LOW-POWER ELECTRONICS

Piezoelectric generators are appropriate to convert the smallest mechanical deformations directly into electrical energy. This solid-state effect is free of degradation in a wide operation range. Therefore, a very high lifetime and availability can be guaranteed.

Piezoelectric materials and transducers are available commercially. Thus, new piezoelectric generators could be produced cost-efficiently in large quantities and can be easily exploited. Nowadays, it is *possible to generate renewable electricity* using piezoelectric materials and transducers placed in special structures that allow the amplification of the direct piezoelectric effect.

Several techniques have been proposed and developed to extract energy from the environment. The most common available sources of energy are: wind, solar, temperature and stress (pressure). In general, *vibration energy* could be converted into electrical energy using one of *three techniques: electrostatic charge, magnetic fields*, and *piezoelectric materials.*

A number of sources of harvestable ambient energy exist, including waste heat, vibration, electromagnetic waves, wind, flowing water, and solar energy. While each of these sources of energy can be effectively used to power remote sensors, the structural and biological communities have placed an emphasis on scavenging vibrational energy with piezoelectric materials [8]. A piezoelectric material transforms electrical energy into mechanical strain energy, and likewise to transform mechanical strain energy into electrical charge [9].

As piezo energy harvesting has been investigated only since the late '90s, it remains an *emerging technology*. With the recent surge of microscale devices, piezoelectric power generation can provide a *convenient alternative to traditional power sources* used to operate certain types of *sensors/actuators, telemetry,* and Microelectromechanical systems, *MEMS* devices. Scavenging energy from ambient vibrations, wind, heat or light could enable *smart sensors* to be functional indefinitely.

Now it is necessary to develop the structures of materials with high piezoelectric coefficients and an optimal architecture for increasing the electrical efficiency of specialized devices for the production of cheap alternative energy to replace traditional energy sources.

Advances in low-power electronics and in energy harvesting technologies have enabled the conception of truly self-powered devices [10]. Cantilevered piezoelectric energy harvesters have been investigated in the literature of energy harvesting [6][16].

The concept of *"harvesting"* is recent and involves capturing the energy normally lost around a system and converting it into electricity that can be used to extend the life of the system or to provide an endless source of energy to a system [11].

IV. OVERVIEW OF LOW-POWER ELECTRONICS

The methods of accumulating and storing the energy generated, until sufficient power has been captured, is the *key to developing completely self-powered systems*. Piezoelectric transduction has received great attention for vibration-to-electric energy conversion over the last five years [12]. Future applications may include high power output devices (or arrays of such devices) deployed at remote locations to serve as reliable power stations for large systems, *wearable electronics*.

Among *challenges* is the electronic circuitry needed to capture, accumulate and store energy from energy harvesting energy sources. The circuitry must then switch the power from an energy storage device and then supply it to the application. In general, energy can be stored in a *capacitor, super capacitor,* or *battery*. Piezoelectric generators are appropriate to convert the smallest mechanical deformations directly into electrical energy. Among *alternative energy sources*, we recall, water energy, solar, wind, heat, etc. It needs to find other methods and possible ways of using energy sources such as mechanical energy converted into electrical energy.

Many conventional systems consist of a single piezoceramic in bending mode (*unimorph*) or two bonded piezoelectric in bending mode (*bimorph*), but upon the experimental, the validating model had 4.61 % maximum error [9]. Some structures can be tuned to have two natural frequencies relatively close to each other, resulting in the possibility of a *broader band energy harvesting system* [12] [13]. The energy produced by these materials is in many cases far too small to directly power an electrical device [11][14]. Recent studies present the ability to take the energy generated through the vibration of a piezoelectric material and use it to recharging a discharged battery [9].

Bimorph actuators consist of two independent flat piezoelectric elements, stacked one on top of the other. By driving one element to expand while contracting the other one, the actuator is forced to bend, creating an out-of-plane motion and vibrations [15]. *Cantilevered* piezoelectric energy harvesters have been investigated in the literature for energy harvesting [12]. An attractive configuration is to form the piezoceramic into a cantilever arrangement, as shown in Figure 3, where layers of piezoceramics are bonded to a substrate, typically made from a suitable metal. This structure allows a lower resonant frequency to be achieved while producing large strains in the piezoceramic. Where two layers of piezo material are used, the structure is referred to as a *bimorph*. In this case, the piezo layers may either be connected in series or parallel. If only a single piezo layer is used, the structure is referred to as a *unimorph* [6].

A. Piezoelectric devices

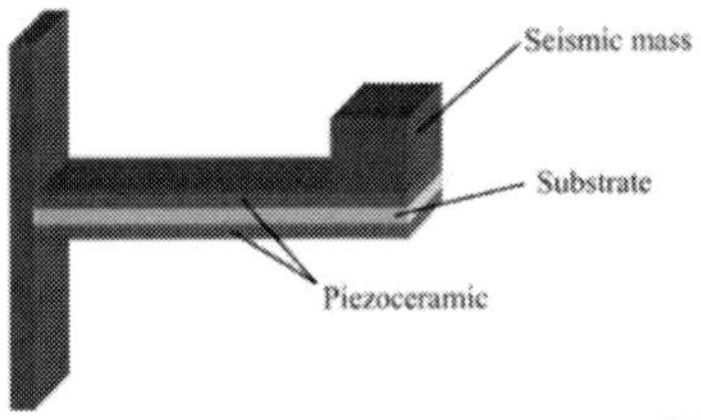

Figure 3. Piezoceramic cantilever resonator [6].

Figure 4 presents a power generator array prototype, realized by small cantilevers of different lengths, in order to obtain a larger broadband [16].

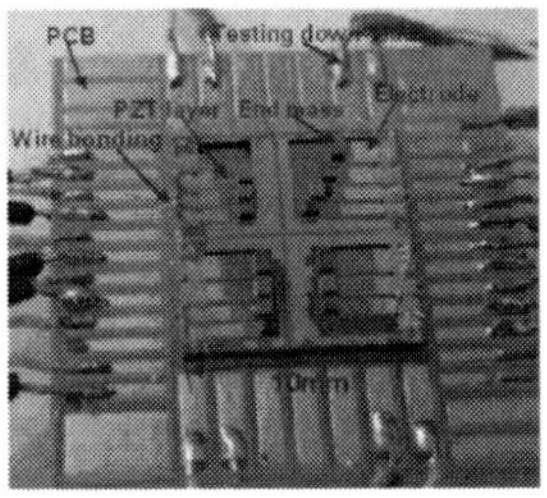

Figure 4. Picture of power generator array prototype [16].

The main steps of the fabrication process of a micro piezoelectric power generator are presented in Figure 5 and they are: (1) Functional films preparation: SiO_2/Ti/Pt/PZT /Ti/Pt, (2) functional films pattern, (3) silicon slot etching by RIE, (4) back silicon deep etching by KOH solution, (5) cantilever release by RIE, and (6) metal mass micro fabrication and assemblage [17].

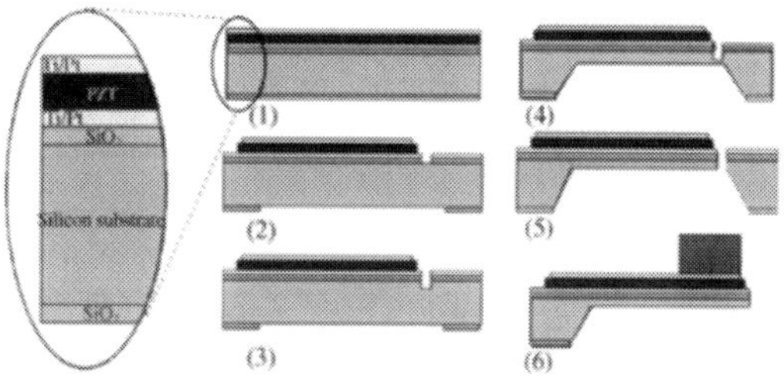

Figure 5. Fabrication process of micro piezoelectric power generator [17].

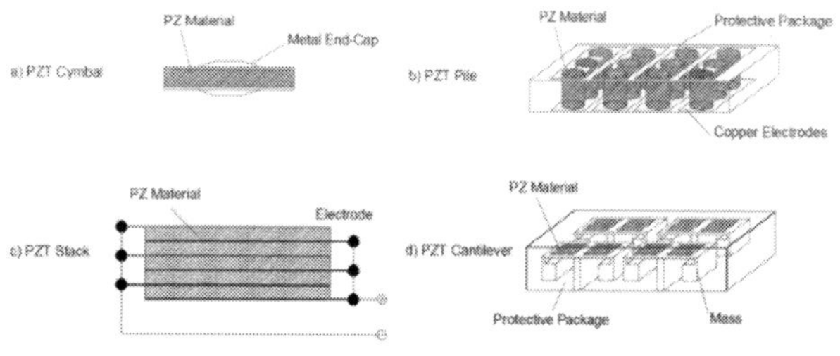

Figure 6. Types of PZT energy harvesters in pavement [18].

Studies about the piezoelectric effects for energy harvesting pavement can be found in [18], using different structures of Piezoelectric Sensors, like: PZT cymbal, PZT pile, PZT stack and PZT cantilever, as shown in Figure 6.

B. Energy harvesting piezoelectric circuitry

Piezoelectric generators are appropriate to convert the smallest mechanical deformations directly into electrical energy. This solid-state effect is free of degradation in a wide operation range. A vibrating piezoelectric device differs from a typical electrical power source in that it has capacitive rather than inductive source impedance, and may be driven by mechanical vibrations of varying amplitude, as shown in Figure 7. A PZT disc, for example, compressed between two metal surfaces, will never be able to expand in the radial direction as would a long, thin cylinder, which is only constrained at its ends and assumes a barrel shape on radial expansion. So, the way in which the material is mounted will directly affect the energy conversion per unit volume. The general rule, therefore, is to allow the PZT body some freedom to expand radially since charge generation is directly coupled to deformation.

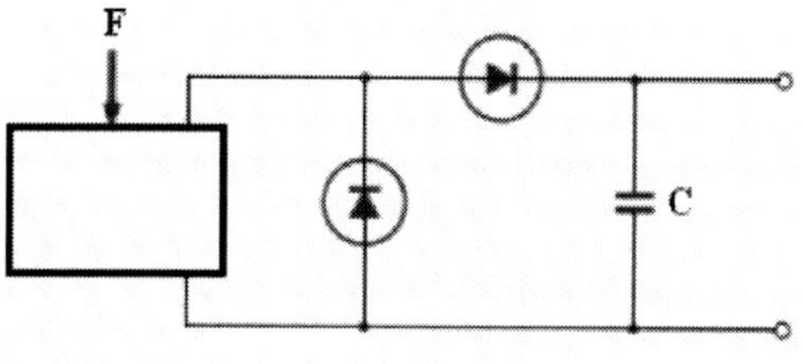

Figure 7. PZT element generator with 2 diodes as DC converter and a parallel capacitor C.

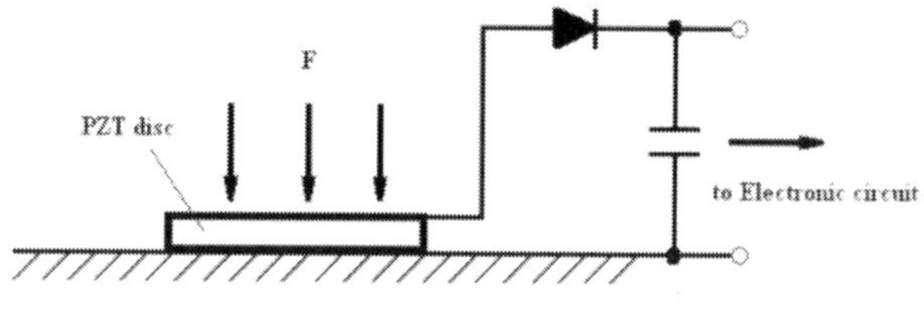

Figure 8. Electronic circuit with PZT disc strained by F force, and one diode DC converter.

The principles of charge generation by a PZT disc to an electronic circuit performance are the shape of the PZT transducer, the manner in which the transducer is mounted and, of course, the nature of the electrical load, as shown in Figure 8.

Typical energy harvesting circuitry consists of voltage rectifier, converter and storage, as shown in Figure 9.

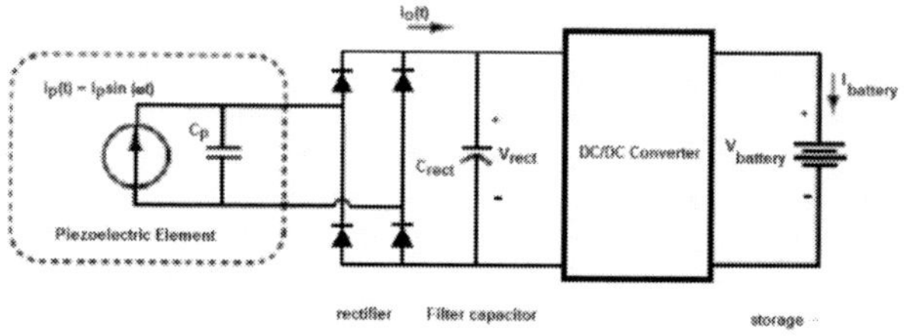

Figure 9. Typical energy harvesting circuitry

Energy harvesting sources that generate power from ambient sources present problems in generating a predictable flow of electricity for the operation of electronic circuits. At times, these sources generate zero power. At other times, they generate trace amounts of power that are unusable. Then, there are times when the power generated is so great that a charge from an energy harvesting source could burn out the circuitry. Therefore, electronics with energy harvesting intelligent piezoelectric transducer should be used. In Wireless Sensor Networks (WSNs), one of the major hurdles is the limited battery power that is unable to meet long-term energy requirements. Energy harvesting, conversion of ambient energy into electrical energy has emerged as an effective alternative to powering WSNs [19].

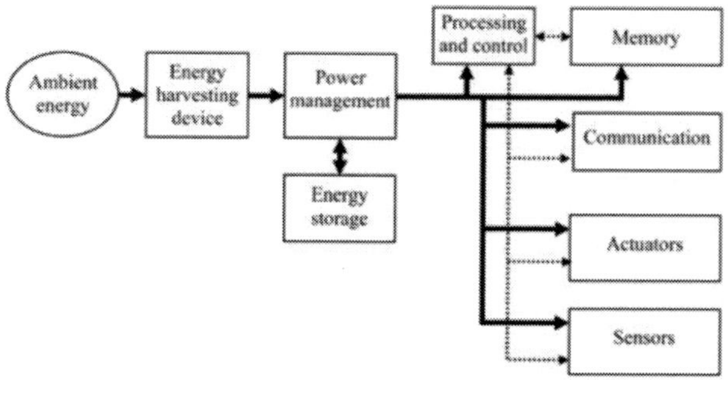

Figure 10. A generic sensor network node with energy harvesting device [6].

The idea of harvesting ambient energy from the immediate surroundings of the deployed sensors is to recharge the batteries and to directly power the sensor nodes. The power consumed by a network node can be split between the various functions it has to perform, as shown in Figure 10.

V. CONCLUSION AND FUTURE WORK

Collecting energy from the environment is a major area of interest with extensive applications in the development of unconventional renewable energy sources. This study clarifies mechanisms for converting mechanical energy into electricity with a high efficiency conversion rate.

Energy harvesting is an attractive concept because so many energy sources such as light, heat, and mechanical vibration that exist in our ambient living could be converted into usable electricity. The technical progress in the *field of extremely low energy electronics* opens up the chance to use *harvested energy* from the environment. Most piezoelectric electricity sources produce power in the order of milliwatts, too small for system application, but enough for hand-held devices such as some commercially available self-winding wristwatches. The methods of accumulating and storing the energy generated, until sufficient power has been captured, is the *key to developing completely self-powered systems*.

WSNs are crucial in supporting continuous environmental monitoring, where sensor nodes are deployed and must remain operational to collect and transfer data from the environment to a base-station. Further development of such energy circuitry and piezoelectric materials with various structures will facilitate the progression of power harvesting methods from a research topic to a useable technology in practical devices.

ACKNOWLEDGMENT

This work was financed by the Romanian Ministry of Research and Innovation (MCI), 2019 Core Program, Contract nr. PN19-18.01.02/2019, Stage I, Stage II, and the 19 PFE-PDI/2018 Project, Stage II/2019.

REFERENCES

[1] C. S. Lee, J. Joo, S. Han, J. H. Lee, and S. K. Koh, "Poly(vinylidenefluoride) transducers with highly conducting poly(3,4-ethylenedioxythiophene) electrodes," Proc. Int. Conf. on Science and Technology of Synthetic Metals, 2005, vol. 152, pp. 49–52.

[2] F. Mohammadi, A. Khan, and R. B. Cass, "Power generation from piezoelectric lead zirconate titanate fiber composites," Proc. Materials Research Symp. 2003, pp. 736.

[3] A. A. Bent, N. W. Hagood and J. P. Rodgers, "Anisotropic actuation with piezoelectric fiber composites," J. Intell. Mater. Syst. Struct., vol. 6, pp. 338–349, 1995

[4] D. L. Churchill, M. J. Hamel, C. P. Townsend, and S. W. Arms, Strain energy harvesting for wireless sensor networks," Proc. Smart Struct. and Mater. Conf., Proc. SPIE 5055, 2003, pp. 319.

[5] W. K. Wilkie et al., "Low-cost piezocomposite actuator for structural control applications," Proc.7th Int. Symp., 2000.

[6] J. M. Gilbert and F. Balouchi, "Comparison of Energy Harvesting Systems for Wireless Sensor Networks," International Journal of Automation and Computing, vol. 05(4), pp. 334-347, Oct. 2008.

[7] C. S. Lee, J. Joo, S. Han, and S. K. Koh, "Multifunctional transducer using poly(vinylidene fluoride) active layer and highly conducting poly(3,4-ethylenedioxythiophene) electrode: actuator and generator," Appl. Phys. Lett., vol 85, pp. 1841–3, 2004.

[8] S. R. Anton and H. A. Sodano, "A review of power harvesting using piezoelectric materials (2003–2006)", Smart Mater. Struct., vol. 16, pp. R1–R21, 2007, doi:10.1088/0964-1726/16/3/R01.

[9] H. A. Sodano, D. J. Inman, and G. Park, "A Review of Power Harvesting from Vibration using Piezoelectric Materials," The Shock and Vibration Digest, pp. 197-205, May 2004.

[10] M. Lallart, S. Priya, S. Bressers, and D. J. Inman, "Small-scale piezoelectric energy harvesting devices using low-energy-density sources," Journal of the Korean Physical Society, vol. 57(41), pp. 947-951, Oct 15 2010.

[11] H. Sodano and D. Inman, "Generation and Storage of Electricity from Power Harvesting Devices," Journal of Intelligent Material Systems and Structures, vol. 16(1), pp. 67-75, Jan. 2005, doi: 10.1177/1045389X05047210.

[12] A. Erturk and D. J. Inman, "An experimentally validated bimorph cantilever model for piezoelectric energy harvesting from base excitations," Smart Mater. Struct., vol. 18, pp. 025009 (18pp), 2009, doi:10.1088/0964-1726/18/2/025009.

[13] A. Erturk and D. J. Inman, "A Distributed Parameter Electromechanical Model for Cantilevered Piezoelectric Energy Harvesters", J. Vib. Acoust, vol. 130(4), pp. 041002 (15 pages), June 2008, doi:10.1115/1.2890402.

[14] N. M. White, P. Glynne-Jones, and S. P. Beeby, "A novel thick-film piezoelectric micro-generator," Smart Materials & Structures, *10*(4), pp. 850-852, 2001.

[15] I. Chilibon, C. Dias, P. Inacio, and J. Marat-Mendes, "PZT and PVDF bimorph actuators," Journal of Optoelectronics and Advanced Materials, vol. 9, Issue 6, pp. 1939-1943, Jun 2007, ISSN: 1454-4164.

[16] J-Q. Liu et al., "A MEMS-based piezoelectric power generator array for vibration energy harvesting," Microelectronics Journal, vol. 39, pp. 802–806, 2008.

[17] H-B Fang et al., "Fabrication and performance of MEMS-based piezoelectric power generator for vibration energy harvesting," Microelectronics Journal, vol. 37, pp. 1280–1284, 2006.

[18] L. Guo and Q. Lu, "Potentials of piezoelectric and thermoelectric technologies for harvesting energy from pavements," *Renewable and Sustainable Energy Reviews*, vol. 72, pp. 761-773, May 2017, doi: 10.1016/j.rser.2017.01.090.

[19] K. Singh and S. Moh, "Comparative Survey of Energy Harvesting Techniques for Wireless Sensor Networks," Advanced Science and Technology Letters, vol.142, pp. 28-33, GDC 2016, http://dx.doi.org/10.14257/astl.2016.142.05.

A Highly Sensitive Interdigital Biosensor for Cancer Cells Dielectric Characterization Using Microwave Frequencies

Marwa Rezeg
Research Laboratory Smart Electricity & ICT, SEICT
National Engineering School of Carthage
University of Carthage
Tunis, Tunisia
e-mail: rezegmarwa@enicar.u-carthage.tn

Hassen Zairi
Research Laboratory Smart Electricity & ICT, SEICT
National Engineering School of Carthage
University of Carthage
Tunis, Tunisia
e-mail: hassen.zairi@gmail.com

Abstract— **This paper describes the design and assessment of a highly sensitive micro biosensor functioning at microwave frequencies. The proposed technique allows single step dielectric characterization and measurement of human cells. In this work, two resonators are etched on the center of the planar device. Their microscopic sensing area is an Inter-Digital Capacitor (IDC) used to guarantee an intense electric field, especially between 15 and 35 GHz. Hence, the inter resonators detection capabilities are demonstrated on normal (HaCaT) and cancerous (Glial) biological cells, which are shaped as solid octagonal with the electrical proprieties found in the literature. Experimental results on human cells are presented showing the biosensor's ability to differentiate at least two particular cell types by means of frequency.**

Keywords - biosensors; inter-digital; capacitor; planar resonator; biological cell.

I. Introduction

In electrical approaches, the term dielectric spectroscopy, which describes the interaction of an electromagnetic field with biological elements, has become a topic of increasing research interest in many fields, including biological and medical fields [1][2].

Dielectric spectroscopy is therefore highly important in non-invasive characterization of living biological cells [3]. Moreover, microwave frequencies can be used in different biological researches for investigating the properties of living matter by means of electromagnetic waves. Thus, at high frequency, the electric field penetrates biological elements unimpeded so that significant induced that wavelengths are roughly equal to the dimensions of living matter [4]. Also, dielectric proprieties which are related to biological parameters of tested cells are ideally done in a label-free manner and with electromagnetic readout.

Moreover, water is the single most abundant chemical fund in cells, accounting for 70 % or more of the total cell mass [5]. It shows relaxation (γ) dispersion that is suitable for microwaves, with a corresponding frequency located around 20 GHz [6], by means of its molecular reorientation dynamic. It is now possible in this range to better understand cancer mechanisms that constitute strong challenges to the biologists and physicians communities.

Several kinds of bio-detection methods have been adapted for the development of tools dedicated to both manipulation and analysis, even with a low number of cells. In particular, we mention the high sensitivity mechanical method [7][8], optical (using fluorescence properties) [9][10] or even electrical method. Nevertheless, specific markers are used in order to have an efficient way to discriminate cells, which can strongly modify cell properties and damage them. Contrarily, electronic detection methods [11][12] become interesting as they can be label-free.

Based on similar sensor topology, this paper presents a CoPlanar Waveguide (CPW) resonator based on IDC structure. The CPW-fed IDC biosensor has been designed using standard microelectronics technologies which permits to attain cell scale. In order to integrate the IDC sensor on lab-on-chip, its planar configuration makes it a good candidate for this system approach which is used also for microfluidic method [13].

We propose an original biosensor design based on microwave frequency impedance measurement for biological cells. The biosensor is designed and simulated using a full-wave electromagnetic simulation tool. Thanks to its structure, this bio detection technique presents the advantage of working with a very limited number of cells. The presented biosensor successfully discriminates between different cell types by means of frequency shifts.

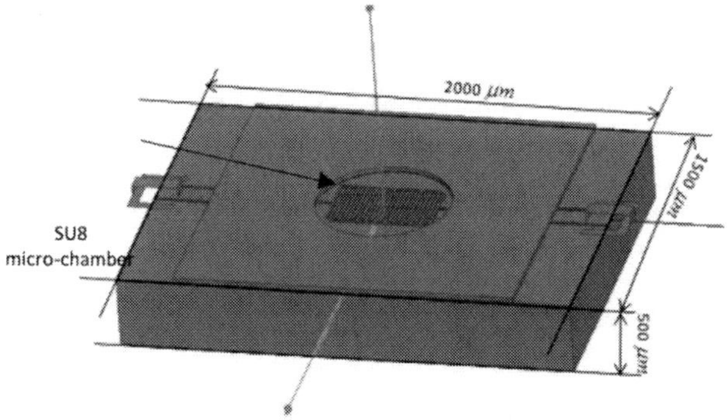

Figure 1. 3D view of proposed biosensor

After a review of the analysis, the modeling and the characterization of this microwave resonator (Section 2), the simulation results on the two types of human cells, normal (HaCaT) and cancerous (Glial) cells are shown in Section 3 and the dielectric parameters are extracted. Finally, conclusions are given in Section 4.

II. Biosensor Design

A. RF design

Using the electromagnetic simulation software High Frequency Structure Simulator (HFSS), the biosensor was designed to have several structural resonances between 15 and 35 GHz when a biological cell was present.

Hence, the proposed cell biosensor design is based on a coplanar resonator structure made with an inter-digital capacitor. The sensor is designed on a 500 um thick fused silica substrate for its low loss properties in the RF frequency domain and its transparency that allows easy observation of cells through it. Indeed, molecular properties of pure glass substrate provide a suitable and comfortable surface for cell growth and colonization. Moreover, metal lines are made of gold for its biocompatibility and its fast conductivity, with thickness up to 7μm. As shown in Figure 1, a 20 um thick SU8 resist layer is deposited on the sensor surface to delimitate the micro-culture chambers in order to allow locating cells only in the areas where the EM field is strongly concentrated (between comb capacitor fingers).

The dimensions of the proposed coplanar resonator biosensor, as shown in Figure 2 and Table I, are optimized to resonate at microwave band frequency.

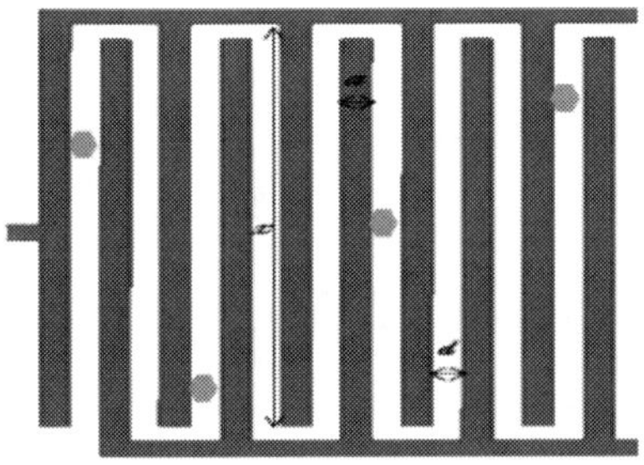

(a)

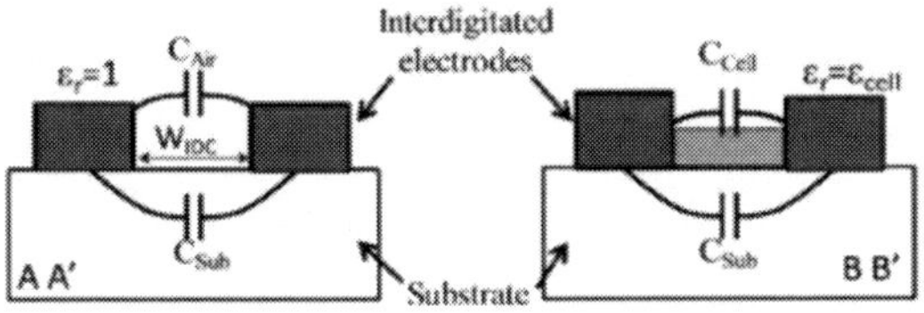

(b)

Figure 2. (a) Top view and (b) cross view of IDC structure

TABLE I. Dimension details of proposed structure

x	Length of finger	270
a	Width of finger	10
d	Spacing between fingers	10
n	No of finger	24
h	Height of substrate	500
ε_{sub}	Dielectric constant of a substrate	3.78
ε'_r	Dielectric constant of a test cell	--

As illustrated in Figure 3(a), at resonance frequency the IDC lines concentrate on most of the electric field. The electric field between fingers is 9.749×10^5 V/m and near inductor is 6.097×10^4 V/m. On the contrary, the magnetic field, as shown in Figure 3(b), is minimum at the IDC area at 5.315×10^3 A/m and near the inductor is 2.048 A/m.

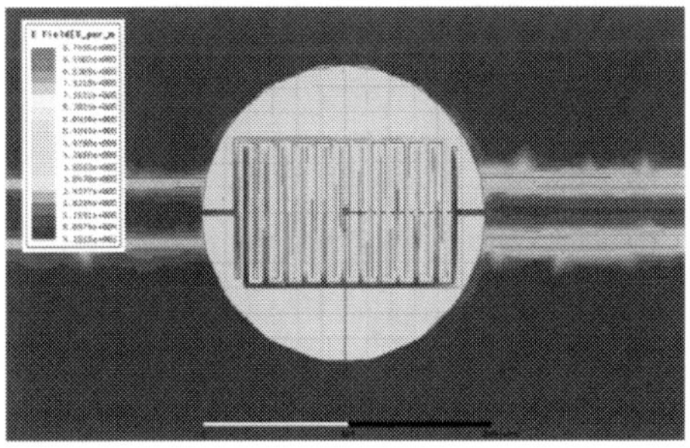

(a)

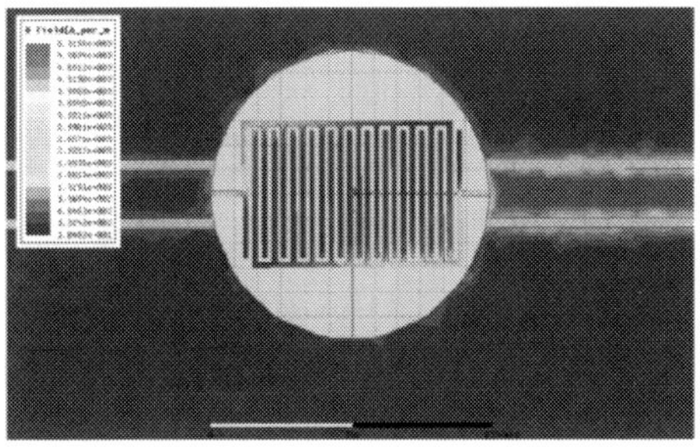

(b)

Figure 3. (a) Electric and (b) magnetic field distribution in the coupling comb capacitor.

Accordingly, these areas will be highly sensitive to any dielectric perturbation and have to be carefully designed to efficiently interact with cells. So, spaces between these metal lines are set to 10 um that represent dimensions in the same range than cell size offering a better interaction with the microwave signal.

B. IDC Structure

IDC is the main constituent of the proposed design, and each element is discussed as follows. The dimensions of the IDC structure are shown in Figure 2. The coplanar geometry can be transformed into a parallel plate geometry using a conformal transformation technique [14]. The capacitance of the IDC (C_{IDC}) can now be calculated as:

$$C_m = nx(C_{air} + C_{sub})pF\,, \tag{1}$$

where x is the length of the IDC finger, n the total number of fingers, and C_{air} and C_{sub} are the line capacitance of coplanar strip with air and dielectric substrate, respectively. C_{air} and C_{sub} are given as [15]:

$$C_{air} = 4\varepsilon_0\varepsilon'_r \frac{K(k'_1)}{K(k_1)} {pF}/{cm}, \tag{2}$$

$$C_{sub} = 2\varepsilon_0(\varepsilon_{sub} - 1)\frac{K(k'_2)}{K(k_2)} {pF}/{cm}, \tag{3}$$

$$k_1 = \left(1 + \frac{2a}{2d+a}\right)\left(\sqrt{\frac{1}{1+\frac{2a}{d}}}\right), \tag{3}$$

$$k'_1 = \sqrt{1-k_1^2}, \tag{4}$$

$$k_2' = \frac{\sinh\left(\frac{\pi a}{4h}\right)}{\sinh\left(\frac{\pi}{2h}\left(\frac{a}{2}+d\right)\right)} \times \sqrt{\frac{\sinh^2\left(\frac{\pi}{2h}\left(\frac{3a}{2}+d\right)\right) - \sinh^2\left(\frac{\pi}{2h}\left(\frac{a}{2}+d\right)\right)}{\sinh^2\left(\frac{\pi}{2h}\left(\frac{3a}{2}+d\right)\right) - \sinh^2\left(\frac{\pi a}{4h}\right)}}, \tag{5}$$

$$k_2 = \sqrt{1 - k_2'^2}, \tag{6}$$

$$\frac{K(k)}{K(k')} = \frac{2}{\pi}\ln\left(2\sqrt{\frac{1+k}{1-k}}\right) \tag{7}$$

III. Simulation Results

In this section, we present the frequency response of the designed sensor before and after addition of a sample with different permittivities and losses at different positions on the sensor.

A. Exprements verification and Discussion

After modeling the sensor, the resonance frequency of the biosensor in this work is chosen to be between 15 and 35 GHz and two peaks in the microwave frequency band are observed, as frequencies above 10 GHz allow penetrating the intrinsic content of biological cells. It is the case that biological cells of interest are too small with an average diameter about ~10 µm. As the sensor sensitivity is concerned, the region of the resonator is, therefore, optimized to increase interaction between the EM fields and cells. In the present sensor design, 10 µm gaps have been used.

The investigations focued on two cell types: HaCaT cell, which represents normal cells with measured relative effective permittivity of 42 ± 3 and conductivity of 1.8 ± 0.3 S/m at 18 GHz and Glial cell, which represent tumor cells with measured relative effective permittivity of 36 ± 3 and conductivity of 0.1 ± 0.02 S/m at 18 GHz [15].

For all simulation results, we suppose that the cells are in dry condition. This supposition is deemed fundamental because signal absorption losses at high frequencies present by aqueous saline solutions, which degrade RF performances of the device.

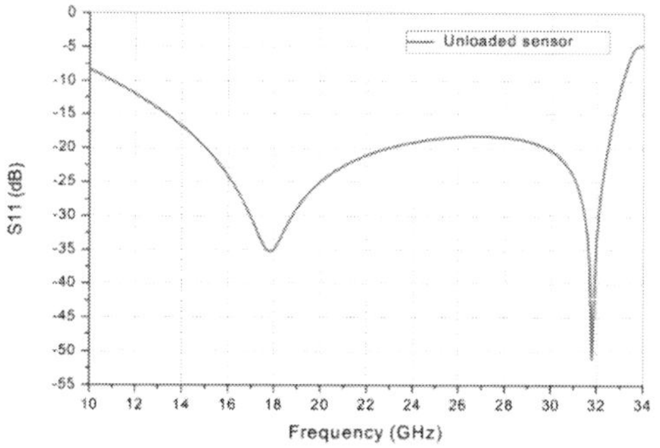

Figure 4. The simulated magnitude of the transmission coefficient (S11) of the resonator biosensor is unloaded.

Cancer cells are modeled as solid octagonal (Figure 2), with a radius of 10 µm and the implemented medium is equivalent to ≈ 8 cells. As shown in Figure 4, the simulated reflection spectrum (S11) presents two peak frequencies at 17.8 GHz and 31.8 GHz, respectively, when the detection area is empty (unloaded). Figure 5 illustrates the simulated magnitude of the reflection coefficient (S11) of the coplanar resonator biosensor when the interdigital capacitor lines are loaded with a single normal (HaCaT) cells. Figure 6 depicts the simulated reflection spectrum (S11) of the biosensor, when the gaps between sensitive lines are loaded with cancerous (Glial) cells. The interaction (field/cells) in this region creates an electromagnetic perturbation frequency shift in S11 response, whose amount varies from a cell type to another.

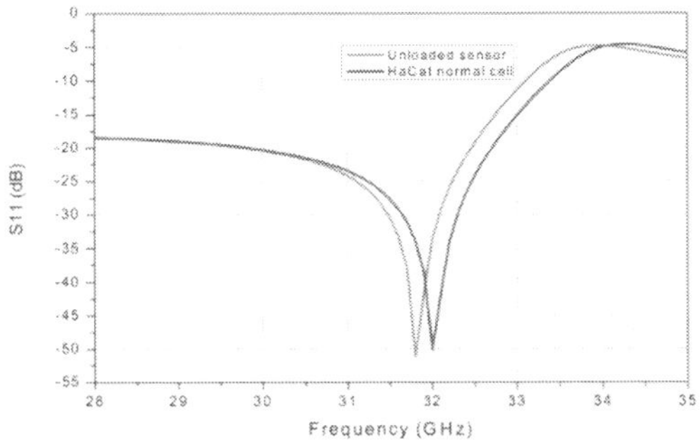

Figure 5. The simulated magnitude of the transmission coefficient (S11) of the biosensor when is loaded with a normal (HaCaT) cell

Hence, the effect of eight living HaCaT cells on the biosensor have been observed resulting in a frequency shift of about 200 MHz and an increase of the S11 parameter of about 0.7 dB while Glial cells show a frequency downshift of 200 MHz and a slight decrease of 11.7dB in the S11 parameter.

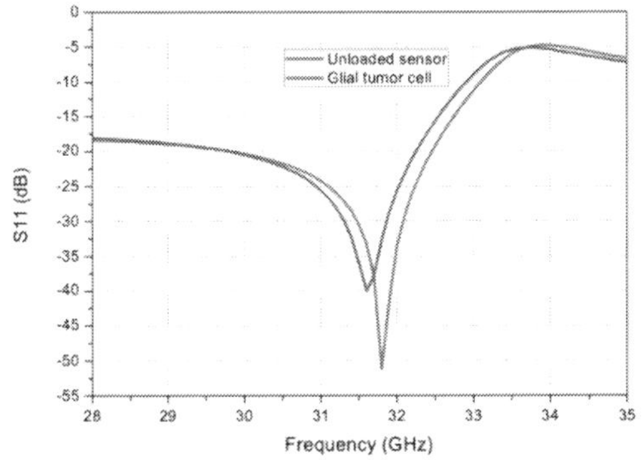

Figure 6. The simulated magnitude of the transmission coefficient (S11) of the biosensor when is loaded with a cancerous (Glial) cell

Nevertheless, according to these simulation results, the biosensor can discern between the two cell types. In practice, the cell's global permittivity can be extracted with a good accuracy probably on a large frequency band around the sensor resonance frequency.

IV. CONCLUSION

The developed sensor model has the advantage of differentiating permittivity based on the resonant frequencies and is well adapted for low concentration conditions. The results confirm the hypothesis that the electrical characteristics of normal and cancerous cells are different. These preliminary simulation results can be used for other cell types discrimination. It was also highlighted that these simulations can become a relevant alternative to conventional labeling techniques and could be more suitable for complex and sensitive biological samples studies. The practical realization of these sensors always remains a challenge for us, especially as it requires a very high level technology. Another interesting direction will be to develop analytical modeling of the sensor resonant frequency versus the biological media permittivity, based on graphene substrate.

REFERENCES

[1] H. P. Schwan, "Electrical properties of tissues and cell suspensions: Mechanism and models," in Proc. 16th Annu. IEEE Int. Conf., vol. 1, pp. A70–A71, 1994.

[2] W. E. Moerner and M.Orrit, "Illuminating single molecules in condensed matter," Science, New Series, Vol. 283, pp. 1670-1676, Mar. 1999.

[3] T. Hanai, K. Asami and N. Koizumi, "Dielectric theory of concentrated suspension of shell-spheres in particular reference to the analysis of biological cell suspensions," Bull. Inst. Chem. Res., Kyoto University 57 , pp. 297-305, 1979.

[4] A.D. Shaw et al., "Rapid analysis of high-dimensional bioprocesses using multivariate spectroscopies and advanced chemometrics," Adv Biochem Eng Biotechnol. book series, vol. 66, pp. 83-113, 2001.

[5] GM. Cooper, The Cell: A Molecular Approach. 2nd edition Sunderland (MA): Sinauer Associates; 2000. THE Molecular Compositon of Cells. Available from: https://www.ncbi.nlm.nih.gov/books/NBK9879/ retrieved: 09, 2019.

[6] K. Grenier et al., "Recent advances in microwave-based dielectric spectroscopy at the cellular level for cancer investigations," IEEE Trans. Microw. Theory Techn., vol. 61, no. 5, pp. 2023–2030, 2013.

[7] P. M. Kosaka et al., "Detection of cancer biomarkers in serum using a hybrid mechanical and optoplasmonic nanosensor," Nature nanotechnology, vol. 9, no. 12, pp. 1047, 2014.

[8] W. Shuaipeng, W. Jingjing, Z. Yinfang ,Y. Jinling and Y. Fuhua., "Cantilever with immobilized antibody for liver cancer biomarker detection," Journal of Semiconductors, Vol. 35, no. 10, pp. 104008, 2014.

[9] Y. Fang, "Label-Free Cell-Based Assays with Optical Biosensors in Drug Discovery," ASSAY and Drug Development Technologies, Volume 4, no. 5, pp. 583-595, 2006.

[10] A. J. Haes, S. Zou, G. C. Schatz, and Richard P. Van Duyne, "A Nanoscale Optical Biosensor: The Long Range Distance Dependence of the Localized Surface Plasmon Resonance of Noble Metal Nanoparticles," The Journal of Physical Chemistry B, vol. 108, no. 1, pp. 109-116, 2004.

[11] C. Dalmaya, M. Cherayb, A. Pothiera, F. Lalloueb, M.O. Jauberteaub and P. Blondya, "Ultra sensitive biosensor based on impedance spectroscopy at microwave frequencies for cell scale analysis," Sensors and Actuators A: Physical 162, pp. 189-197, 2009.

[12] P. Porwal, S. Azeemuddin, P. Bhimalapuram, and T. K. Sau, "Design of RF Sensor for Simultaneous Detection of Complex Permeability and Permittivity of Unknown Sample," Progress In Electromagnetics Research C, Vol. 79, pp. 159-173, 2017.

[13] J. Kilpijärvi, N. Halonen, J. Juuti and J. Hannu, "Microfluidic Microwave Sensor for Detecting Saline in Biological Range," Sensors, 19(4), 819, 2019.

[14] J. W. Kim, "Development of Interdigitated Capacitor Sensors for Direct and Wireless Measurements of the dielectric Properties of Liquids," Electrical and Computer Engineering, University of Texas Libraries, 2008.

[15] C. Dalmay, A. Pothier, P. Blondy, F. Lalloue and M. O. Jauberteau, "Label free biosensors for human cell characterization using radio and microwave frequencies," 2008 IEEE MTT-S International Microwave Symposium Digest, Atlanta, GA, USA, pp. 911-914, 2008.

2D In-plane Sensitive Hall Device

Siya Lozanova
Institute of Robotics
Bulgarian Academy of Sciences
Sofia, Bulgaria
email:lozanovasi@abv.bg

Avgust Ivanov
Institute of Robotics
Bulgarian Academy of Sciences
Sofia, Bulgaria
email: avgust@ir.bas.bg

Chavdar Roumenin
Institute of Robotics
Bulgarian Academy of Sciences
Sofia, Bulgaria
email: roumenin@bas.bg

Abstract—**A new single-chip silicon 2D in-plane sensitive Hall-effect device having the form of a Greek-cross surrounded by a deep *p*-zone is proposed. In each of the four ends of the *n*-Si cross, one ohmic contact is available. Through the original design and circuitry, two independent currents with non-standard topology sharing the same active region are formed. The contacts are connected to one load resistor each, whereas the resistors with the opposite contacts are fed into one supply terminal, and the resistors with the other two contacts are connected to the other supply terminal. The pairs of opposite contacts are the outputs for the two orthogonal in-plane magnetic-field components at sensitivities $S_{RI} \approx 110$ V/AT. The channel offsets are fully compensated by trimming and the contact numbers are only 4. The non-linearity is small and does not exceed 0.5 % within the range + 0.6 T ÷ - 0.6 T. The cross-talk is very promising and is no more than 2.3% at induction B = 1.0 T, the spatial resolution is high compared to the standard solutions, reaching 70 x 30 x 40 μm^3, and the lowest detected magnetic induction with signal – to – noise ratio equal to 1 at supply current of 3 mA is $B_{min} \approx 11$μT.**

Keywords - multidimensional magnetometry; 2D in-plane sensitive Hall device; Lorentz force action; three-contact Hall element; functional integration.

I. INTRODUCTION

The most advanced 2D and 3D vector microsensors are those using the Hall effect principle, since their action involves only one simple and well-defined physical phenomenon. Some of the major advantages are: the position of the multidimensional device with respect to the magnetic source is not as critical as in the case of a 1D sensor, the better orthogonality determined by the planar process, the perfect matching of the channel sensitivities and more. Irrespective of the pronounced progress, these integrated vector transducers feature some essential drawbacks. They have complicated design containing many contacts and numerous connections between them, which restrict fabrication technology and reduce spatial resolution. Another problem is the channel cross-talk and offsets, which impede metrological accuracy. All 2D and 3D Hall devices suffer from these drawbacks [1]–[15]. For example, the contact numbers are 8 – 10 and even more, while the average cross-talk and offsets without compensation reaches around 3.5 - 4 % at induction B = 1.0 T and 7-9 mV, respectively. The $\boldsymbol{B}_x$, $\boldsymbol{B}_y$ and $\boldsymbol{B}_z$ components of field $\boldsymbol{B}$ can be measured via functional integration of orthogonal and in-plane sensitive Bipolar Magneto Transistors (BMTs) located into a single substrate. Two in-plane differential BMTs with central emitter, a common active region and mutually perpendicular orientations of the other contacts (collectors and bases) are sufficient for the in-plane detection of components $\boldsymbol{B}_x$ and $\boldsymbol{B}_y$. Unfortunately, the main sensor problems remain, and these are: channel offsets, cross-talk, strong temperature dependence of sensitivities.

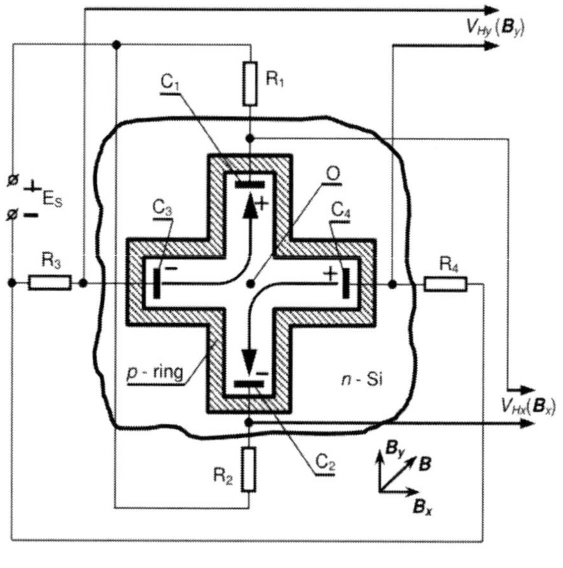

Figure 1. Schematic top-view of silicon 2D integrated Greek-cross Hall device.

The key reason for these drawbacks is the complicated transducer mechanisms acting in the magnetotransistor substrate. That is why the Hall principle of operation remains very frequently used for multidimensional magnetometry. In this paper, we present a novel single-chip sensing device for measurement of two orthogonal in-plane magnetic field components using one and the same transducer region, featuring simple design, high spatial resolution and improved characteristics.

The rest of the paper is structured as follows. In Section II, we present the concept and fabrication of 2D device. In Section III, we show the operating principle, and in Section

IV, we describe the experimental results. We conclude the work in Section V.

II. CONCEPT AND FABRICATION OF THE 2D HALL DEVICE

The new multidimensional device consists of an *n*-Si Greek-cross surrounded by a deep *p*-zone. In each end of the cross, symmetrically to its centre O, there is one ohmic n^+-n contact C_1, C_2, C_3 and C_4, which is connected to one load resistor R_1 ...R_4. Resistors R_1 and R_2, which are located opposite to contacts C_1 and C_2, are fed into one terminal of supply E_S, while resistors R_3 and R_4 are connected to the other ends, as shown in Figure 1. The pairs of contacts C_1-C_2 and C_3-C_4 are the differential outputs $V_{Hx}(\boldsymbol{B}_x)$ and $V_{Hy}(\boldsymbol{B}_y)$ for the two in-plane components $\boldsymbol{B}_x$ and $\boldsymbol{B}_y$ of the magnetic-field vector $\boldsymbol{B}$.

Notwithstanding the lack of a central supply electrode as with conventional 2D and 3D Hall magnetometers [6]-[9] [11]-[15], through the original design and circuitry, mutually perpendicular current couples I_{C3O} and I_{OC1}, and I_{C4O} and I_{OC2} respectively, are formed, as shown in Figure 1.

The experimental prototype has been implemented using part of the processing steps applied in bipolar Integrated Circuits (IC) technology. The low-doped *n*-Si plates are 300 µm thick, with resistivity $\rho \approx 7.5$ Ω.cm. The carrier's concentration is $n \sim 4.3 \times 10^{15}$ cm^{-3}. Similar to [17] [18], four masks are employed in the fabrication process. Mask 1 determines the n^+-implanted zones for ohmic electrical contacts C_1...C_4 with the substrate, as the depth of the ohmic n^+-n junctions is about 1 µm. Mask 2 forms areas for the deep Greek-cross *p*-ring. The *p*-ring constricts the effective volume of the sensor and prevents the surface current spreading. All this increases the transducer efficiency of the novel 2D device. Mask 3 defines the metallization layer and bonding pads. Mask 4 is intended for the contact opening in the surface layer SiO_2 for the electrical contact between the metal and the n^+ zones. The width of the deep surrounding *p*-ring at the surface is about 20 µm (on the mask). The dopant donor concentration of the n^+-n junctions is $n \approx 10^{20}$ cm^{-3}. The size of the ohmic contacts C_1...C_4 is 20 x 5µm^2; the length and the width of the Greek-cross are 70 µm and 30 µm. The thickness of the effective area is defined in first approximation by the trajectory of currents $I_{C3,C1}$ and $I_{C4,C2}$ penetrating in the *n*-Si substrate with depth of 30 – 40 µm [15]. As a result, the effective operational volume of the cross is about 70 x 30 x 40µm^3, which provides high spatial resolution of the new device. The sensor has the following internal resistances: $R_{C1,2} \approx R_{C3,4} \approx 860$ Ω. Resistors R_1... R_4 are at least by one order of magnitude greater than the effective resistance between ohmic contacts C_1 ...C_4, their value being equal to 10 kΩ. At this stage, the 2D in-plane sensitive Hall device is in hybrid realization (resistor elements R_1...R_4 are discrete).

III. OPERATING PRINCIPLE

The current paths in the device from Figure 1 start and end on the heavy-doped n^+ contacts C_1 ...C_4. The planar ohmic electrodes C_1 ...C_4 represent equipotential planes to which, in the absence of external magnetic field $\boldsymbol{B}$, $B = 0$, current paths I_{C1}, I_{C2}, and I_{C3}, I_{C4} respectively, flow perpendicularly to the upper surfaces of the *n*-Si slab, deeply penetrating into the bulk of 30 – 40 µm [15]. The current lines $I_{C1,2}$ and $I_{C3,4}$ in the other parts of the substrate in first approximation are parallel to the upper surface. Therefore, the two trajectories $I_{C1,2}$ and $I_{C4,3}$ are curvilinear. As a result of the uniformity of the structure, as well as of contacts C_1 ...C_4, the two currents components $I_{C1,2}$ and - $I_{C3,4}$ are equal in value and opposite in sign. As a result of technological imperfections, mechanical strain and stress during chip metallization and capsulation, temperature gradients and the like [1] [2] [4] [12] [15] [16], at outputs $V_{Hx}(\boldsymbol{B}_x = 0)$ and $V_{Hy}(\boldsymbol{B}_y = 0)$ of the device, at field $B = 0$, offset $V_H(B = 0) \neq 0$ appears, notwithstanding the fact that load resistors R_1... R_4 are equal. Full compensation of the offset at the differential channel outputs is carried out by connecting to the load resistors of low-ohmic trimmers. By varying the trimmer values, the offsets vanishes, $V_{Hx}(\boldsymbol{B}_x = 0) = V_{Hy}(\boldsymbol{B}_y = 0) = 0$. The original structure from Figure 1 forms, irrespective of the absence of supply electrode in centre O, two identical 3-contact (3C) mutually perpendicular in-plane sensitive Hall devices, possessing two end contacts each, C_1–C_2 and C_3-C_4, [1] [2] [19] [20]. This unexpected solution results from the fact that, with respect to centre O of the cross, current components I_{OC1} and - I_{OC2}, and I_{OC3} and - I_{OC4}, respectively, feature equal values and opposite directions. The topology of these current paths is the same as in the case where, in centre O, there is a third supply contact. Such innovative structure of the 3C sensor is described for the first time.

In magnetic field $\boldsymbol{B}$, $\boldsymbol{B}_x > 0$ and $\boldsymbol{B}_y > 0$, the well-known Lorentz force $\boldsymbol{F}_L = qv_{dr} \times \boldsymbol{B}_x$ and $\boldsymbol{F}_L = qv_{dr} \times \boldsymbol{B}_y$ controls the lateral and vertical components of the drift velocity v_{dr} [1] [2] [19] [20]. In the trajectory parts O – C_1 and O – C_2, as well as O – C_3 and O – C_4, respectively, the force $\boldsymbol{F}_L$ acts in opposite directions. Therefore, the force $\boldsymbol{F}_L$ shrinks or expands the trajectories towards the surface of the substrate, or towards the bulk. As a result, Hall potential appears on the boundary near to electrodes C_1 and C_2, and C_3 and C_4, respectively, and additional (e.g. negative) non-steady-state charges proportional to fields $\boldsymbol{B}_x$ and $\boldsymbol{B}_y$, and current $I_{C1,2}$ arise. Thus, opposite-sign Hall potentials are generated on the respective contacts C_1–C_2 and C_3-C_4. This operation is as in three-contact in-plane sensitive Hall element [19] [20]. Through the circuitry connections, the opposite-sign potentials along the two axes *x* an *y* form the respective Hall voltages on the two differential outputs $V_{Hx}(\boldsymbol{B}_x)$ and $V_{Hy}(\boldsymbol{B}_y)$ for fields $\boldsymbol{B}_x$ and $\boldsymbol{B}_y$, as shown in Figure 1. Thus, magnetic field $\boldsymbol{B}$ generates in the *x*-*y* plane simultaneously linear and odd output voltages in the channels.

IV. EXPERIMENTAL RESULTS

The output characteristics $V_{Hx}(\boldsymbol{B}_x)$ and $V_{Hy}(\boldsymbol{B}_y)$ of the new Greek-cross Hall configuration are presented in Figure 2. The channel sensitivities are equal to $S_{RI} \approx 110$V/AT. The non-linearity is small and does not exceed 0.5 % within the range + 0.6 T ÷ - 0.6 T. The effective spatial resolution is high, constituting about 70 x 30 x 40 µm^3, which allows to detect more detailed magnetic-field topology.

We realized the measurement of the cross-talk of the 2D device at fixed values of the supply current, I_s = const, after

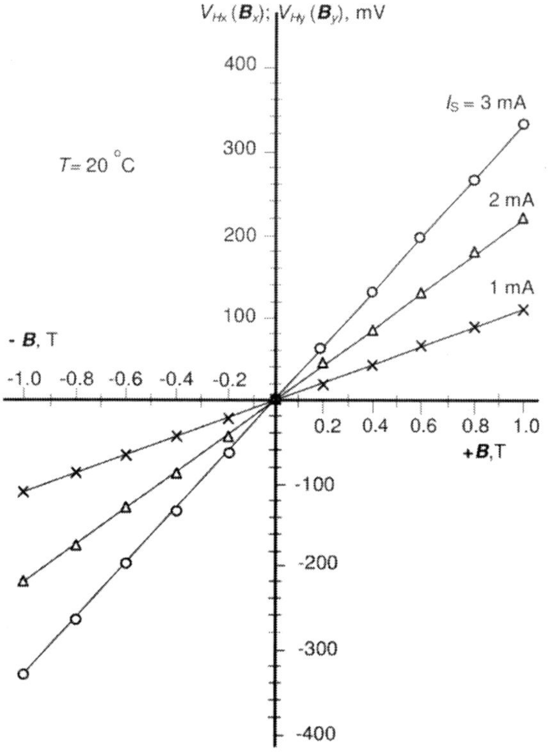

Figure 2. The channel characteristics $V_{Hx}(\boldsymbol{B}_x)$ and $V_{Hy}(\boldsymbol{B}_y)$, offsets are compensated in advance, the current I_s is as a parameter.

the nullification of the two output offsets, using the following approach.

The first step is experimental determination of the channel characteristics of the two outputs – the sensitivity by Hall voltages $V_{Hx}(\boldsymbol{B}_x)$ and $V_{Hy}(\boldsymbol{B}_y)$. The next step is applying homogeneous variable magnetic induction B parallel to one of the axes x or z. The other output (parasitic) the signal from the y-channel is measured.

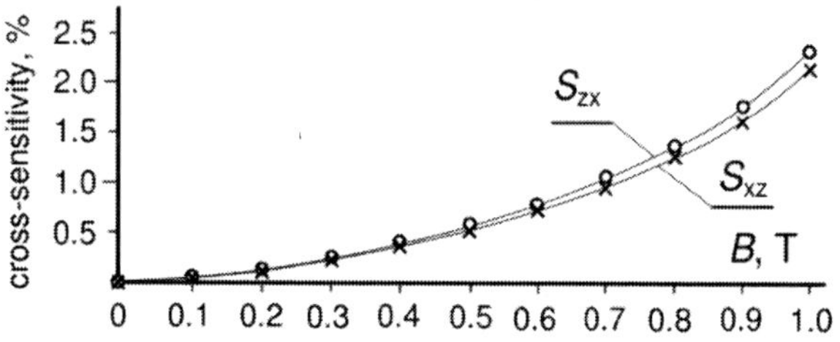

Figure 3. Cross-sensitivity C.S. (cross-talk) of the two-axis device from Figure 1 as a function of induction B, T = 20 °C. The cross-talk at induction B = 1 T reach no more than 2.3 %

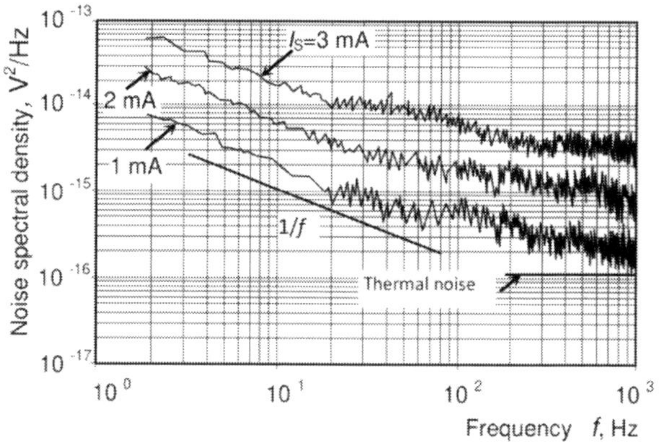

Figure 4. The measured power spectral density of noise of one channel $V_{Hy}(\boldsymbol{B}_y = 0)$ without magnetic field, the supply current I_s is as a parameter. T = 20°C. The noise density for channel $V_{Hx}(\boldsymbol{B}_x = 0)$ is the same.

The procedure described is repeated for the other orthogonal direction x. The cross-sensitivity in our case is mainly due to the geometrical magnetoresistance MR ~ B^2, reaching no more than 2.3 % at induction $B \leq 1.0$ T, as shown in Figure 3. This is a very promising result.

The internal noise of the 2D Hall device without interface circuitry within the range 10 Hz $< f \leq$ 1 kHz is of the $1/f$ type, as shown in Figure 4. With the increase of bias current I_s, the noise increases, too. The mean lowest detected magnetic induction B_{min} over a Δf = [5Hz ÷ 500 Hz] bandwidth with signal-to-noise ratio S/N = 1 at supply current of 3 mA is $B_{min} \approx 10 - 11$ μT, where $S_A = \Delta V_H/\Delta B$ is the absolute magnetosensitivity, and $S_{NV}(f)$ is the voltage noise spectral density across the respective output contacts of the new configuration. The induction B_{min} is determined at fully compensated offset in an appropriate magnetic shielded box.

The measured power spectral density of the internal noise in channels $V_{Hx}(\boldsymbol{B}_x)$ and $V_{Hy}(\boldsymbol{B}_y)$ is shown in Figure 4, where the supply current I_s is a parameter at T = 20 °C.

The temperature coefficient of the magnetosensitivity reaches about 0.1 %/ °C. The established temperature coefficient of the device resistance is $TC_R \approx 0.1$ %.

The thermal behaviour of the fully compensated outputs $V_{Hx}(\boldsymbol{B}_x) = V_{Hy}(\boldsymbol{B}_y) = 0$ at a given temperature T_0 originates from the same active transducer region. In our case, the offset compensation is carried out at T_0 = 20 °C. The obtained output voltage-to-residual offset ratio, for example at T = 40 °C, reaches about 6 x 10^3 at induction B = 1 T. This is a optimal result, as shown in Figure 5. With the increase of supply current I_s, as typical for Hall sensors [1] [2], the temperature drift at the output increases. For this reason, a trade-off between drift and sensitivity should be sought. In our case, this situation is achieved at current $I_s \approx 2$ mA. According to the results, the value of the temperature drift is low. The temperature coefficient of the offset drift reaches no more than 0.1 %/°C.

All measurements of the characteristics of the new 2D device were performed in full compliance with the methodology explained in detail in [1] [2].

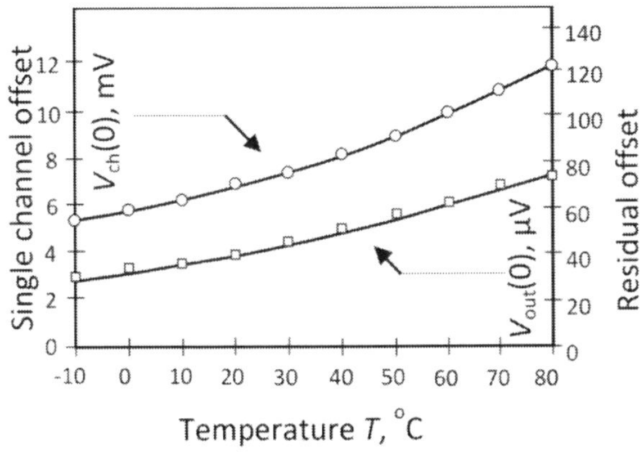

Figure 5. Temperature dependences of the single-channel offset $V_{ch}(0)$ and residual offset $V_{out}(0)$ of the arrangement in Fig. 1, at a supply I_s = 3 mA.

V. Conclusion

The novel 2D silicon magnetometer for simultaneous measure of two orthogonal components of the magnetic field using a common sensor zone provides good prospects for many applications. Comparing the obtained results with the state-of-the-art shows that the novel 2D Hall sensor possesses at least 15 % better cross-talk, the channel offsets are fully compensated easily by trimming, and the contact numbers are only four. A detailed study of temperature influence on the 2D microsensor characteristics behavior is forthcoming. These results will be used in low-field magnetometry. The fabrication of a fully integrated version of the new 2D sensor is underway. The repeatability of magnetosensitivity and temperature coefficient of sensitivity, in our case, are defined as the maximum variation in the channel output readings when induction B is constant, B = const. At least two calibration cycles are needed [1]. The repeatability of the new device will be determined in the future. The obtained performance is appropriate for contactless applications, such as in robotics and industrial control, tactile systems, space orientation, measurement of angular and linear displacements, speed sensors, end-of-travel transducers, compass, unmanned flight vehicles, navigation, automobiles – ignition timing, Anti-lock Braking System (ABS) systems and more.

Acknowledgment

This work was supported by the National Science Fund at the Ministry of Education and Science of Bulgaria under Project No. DN 07/18-15.12.2016.

References

[1] C. Roumenin, Solid State Magnetic Sensors, Elsevier, 1994.

[2] C. Roumenin, "Microsensors for magnetic field", in MEMS – a practical guide to design, analysis and application, J.G. Korvink and O. Paul, Eds, Norwich, NY: W. Andrew Publ., pp. 453-521, 2006.

[3] E. Ramsden, Hall effect sensors – Theory and application, 2nd ed., Elsevier, 2006.

[4] T. Kaufmann, On the offset and sensitivity of CMOS-based five-contact vertical Hall devices, Der Andere Verlag, Uelvesbull: MEMS Techn. and Engin., v. 21, 2013.

[5] M. Demierre, E. Schurig, C. Schott, P. -A. Besse and R. Popovic, "Contactless 360° absolute angular CMOS microsystem based on vertical Hall sensors", Sens. Actuators, v. A 116, pp. 39-44 2004.

[6] M. Paranjape, L. M. Landsberger and M. Kahrizi, "A CMOS-compatible 2-D vertical Hall magnetic-field sensor using active carrier confinement and post-process micromachining", Sens. Actuators, v. A 53, pp. 278-283, 1996.

[7] J. Pascal, L. Hebrard, V. Frick and J. P. Blonde, "3D Hall probe integrated in 0.35 um CMOS technology for magnetic field pulses measurements", The Proc. 6th Int. IEEE Northeast Workshop on Circuits and Systems and TAISA Conf., pp. 97-100, 2008.

[8] L. Franquelo et al. "Three-dimensional space-vector modulation algorithm for four-legmultilevel converters using abc coordinates", IEEE Trans. Ind. Electron. v. 53(2), pp. 458-466, 2006.

[9] C. -P. Yu, The study and application of a 2D folded Hall sensor chip, Nat. Taipe Univ. of Techn. Publ., p. 88, 2012.

[10] C. -P. Yu and G. -M. Sung, "Two-dimensional folded CMOS Hall device with interacting lateral magnetotransistor and magnetoresistor", Sens. Actuators, v. A 182, pp. 6-15, 2012.

[11] C. Wouters et al. "Design and fabrication of an innovative three-axis Hall sensor", Sens. Actuators, v. A 237, pp. 62-71, 2016.

[12] Ch. S. Roumenin, D. Nikolov and A. Ivanov, "A novel parallel-field Hall sensor with low offset and temperature drift based 2D integrated magnetometer", Sens. Actuators, v. A 115, 303-pp. 307, 2004.

[13] S. Lozanova, S. Noykov, A. Ivanov, G. Velichkov and C. Roumenin, "3-D silicon Hall device with subsequent magnetic-field components measurement", Procedia Engineering, v. 87, pp. 1107-1110, 2014.

[14] S. Lozanova, S. Noykov and C. Roumenin, "Three-dimensional magnetometer based on subsequent measurement principle", Sens. Actuators, v. A 248, pp. 281-289, 2016.

[15] C. Sander, C. Leube and O. Paul, "Three-dimensional magnetometer based on subsequent measurement principle", Sens. Actuators, v. A 222, pp. 329-334, 2015.

[16] F. Burger, P. -A. Besse and R. S. Popovic, "New fully integrated 3-D silicon Hall sensor for precise angular-position measurements", Sensors and Actuators, v. A 67, pp. 72-76, 1998.

[17] C. Schott and R. Popovic, "Integrated 3-D Hall magnetic field sensor", The Proc. of Transducers '99, Sendai, Japan, v. 1, pp. 168-171, 1999.

[18] D. Tanase, Magnetic-based navigation system for endovascular intervention, Grafische Commun. Publ.: Rotterdam, 2003.

[19] C. Roumenin and P. Kostov, "Planar Hall-effect device", Bulg. patent № BG 37208 B1/26.12.1983.

[20] S. V. Lozanova and C. S. Roumenin, "Parallel-field silicon Hall effect microsensors with minimal design complexity", IEEE Sensors Journal, v. 9(7), pp. 761-766, 2009.